THE POLITICS OF POSSIBILITY

THE POLITICS OF POSSIBILITY

Risk and Security Beyond Probability

LOUISE AMOORE

Duke University Press   Durham and London   2013

© 2013 Duke University Press
All rights reserved
Printed in the United States of America on acid-free paper ∞
Designed by Courtney Leigh Baker. Typeset in Whitman by Copperline Book Services, Inc.

Library of Congress Cataloging-in-Publication Data
Amoore, Louise.
The politics of possibility : risk and security beyond probability / Louise Amoore.
pages cm
Includes bibliographical references and index.
ISBN 978-0-8223-5545-8 (cloth : alk. paper)—ISBN 978-0-8223-5560-1 (pbk. : alk. paper)
1. International relations—Risk assessment.   2. National security—Technological innovations.
3. Terrorism—Prevention—Technological innovations.   I. Title.
JZ6368.A46 2013
355.'033—dc23
2013024843

Sections of chapter 1 appeared previously in "Algorithmic War: Everyday Geographies of the War on Terror," *Antipode* 41, no. 1 (2009).

A version of chapter 2 appeared previously as "Data Derivatives: On the Emergence of a Security Risk Calculus for Our Times," Theory, Culture & Society 28, no. 6 (2011): 24–43.

For Gracie and Tom

Contents

Acknowledgments

To reflect on the gestation of a book is to confront the impossibility of ever telling a complete story. One imagines always a process with a distinct beginning, a series of key moments along the way, and a defined point when the work is done. If this were the truth of the experience of exploring an idea, pushing at its edges, talking and writing about it over a period of years, then expressing thanks to all those who have played their part would be easy—for they would simply assemble along the route. Instead, of course, identifying the many moments when something new emerges, or when some idea long held dissipates and disappears from view, is profoundly difficult. I know only that I am fortunate beyond words to work with friends, colleagues, and interlocutors whose lively thinking and generous support are the very conditions of possibility of this book.

I am especially grateful to work with such wonderful colleagues in the Department of Geography at Durham University. Perhaps because some of my colleagues work in laboratories, model sea level changes, examine the dynamics of landslide or ice sheet, there is an atmosphere of experimentation and a support for pursuing a hunch! My profound thanks to colleagues past and present: Ash Amin, Ben Anderson, Mike Bentley, David Campbell, Angharad Closs-Stephens, Nick Cox, Mike Crang, Stuart Elden, Steve Graham, Alex Hall, Francisco Klauser, Paul Langley, Anthony Long, Colin McFarlane, Joe Painter, and Dave Petley. I thank them for their unwavering support, their generous contributions to many workshops and seminars, their capacity to ask difficult questions gently, and for all the times I found clippings from the London Review of Books or obscure computer modeling articles in my mail tray! I have also been extremely lucky to have such brilliant students—PhD students Emily Jackson, Diana Martin, Patrick Murphy, and Nat O'Grady; a quite extraordinary master's Risk and Security seminar class of 2011–12; and undergraduates in Politics/Space and Political Geography who challenge me every time.

The course of the research and writing of this book has been inter-disciplinary—I owe debts to theorist friends and colleagues in sociology, law, geography, international relations, and the arts, all of whom criticized and shaped my thinking and writing: Claudia Aradau, Jane Bennett, Roy Boyne, Roger Burrows, Martin Coward, Deborah Cowen, Dana Cuff, Matt Davies, Mick Dillon, Jenny Edkins, Kevin Haggerty, Kim Hutchings, Debbie Lisle, Luis Lobo-Guerrero, David Lyon, Adrian MacKenzie, Valsamis Mitsilegas, Veronique Pin-Fat, Michael Pryke, Evelyn Ruppert, Mike Savage, Mike Shapiro, Andrew Webster, Cindy Weber, and Maja Zehfuss. Thanks to Judit Carrera and colleagues at the Centre for Contemporary Culture Barcelona for hosting two inspirational conferences—Architectures of Fear and Tar-geted Publics—of interdisciplinary conversation and critique. This book has also benefitted enormously from debates hosted by Richard Tutton and colleagues at Lancaster University's Centre for the Social and Economic Aspects of Genomics (CESAGEN) and particularly from the events hosted by the Wellcome Trust. Marieke de Goede and her colleagues at the Uni-versity of Amsterdam have hosted a series of workshops and research vis-its that have influenced the ideas in this book beyond measure. The audi-ences at conferences and workshops over past years are too numerous to mention here, but they should know that their generous comments are deeply appreciated.

In the United Kingdom we are now perennially reminded that our re-search must have "demonstrable" impact beyond the academy. What is often forgotten, though, is that our work benefits immeasurably from the careful thought and insight of those who engage with the world through their practice. I have been extraordinarily fortunate to be able to debate the ideas in this book with a group of exceptional lawyers and advocates whose job it is to defend those targeted by the security techniques of the merely possible. I would like to thank, in particular, Frances Webber, Queen's Council, and Haroun Atallah of Islamic Relief, whose generosity in sharing their experiences has had a lasting impact on my sense of the effects of the politics of possibility. Thanks also to Gavin Sullivan and his colleagues at the European Center for Constitutional and Human Rights, particularly for their hosting, with Amnesty International, of the inspirational Berlin conference Ten Years After 9/11. In a quite different way the critical practice of the artists Marcos Ramirez and Meghan Trainor has opened up for me a new sense of potentiality.

Some of the research for this book was funded by the Economic and Social Research Council (ERSC) and the Netherlands Organisation for Scientific Research (NWO) bilateral grant Data Wars (RES062230592), which I was awarded along with my friend and collaborator Marieke de Goede. I am fortunate to have been able to speak with policy makers, software designers, borders agencies, mathematicians, and computer scientists, and I thank them profoundly for their assistance. Marieke and I were joined by an outstanding team of researchers, including Mara Wesseling, Jon Mendel, and Alex Hall. Alex was my research assistant at Durham University for four years—her lively interventions, measured critique, and indomitable persistence with fieldwork have been quite incredible. Other elements of the research were funded by the ESRC grant Contested Borders (RES250087), which I was awarded along with my colleague and collaborator Steve Graham. Steve's work on the technologies of security that penetrate urban architecture—as well as his encouragement to complete this book—has been inspiring. The final stages of manuscript preparation were funded by the Research Councils United Kingdom (RCUK) Global Uncertainties Fellowship award "Securing Against Future Events" (ES/K0002761).

Marking the end of a book is perhaps more difficult even than describing its between times. I am immensely grateful to Courtney Berger of Duke University Press for her wise counsel—all of the superlatives her authors use about her are true. Two readers of the manuscript, Mick Dillon and Michael Shapiro, have offered critical and supportive comments in equal measure, and the book is the better for their interventions; thank you both. Without my best friend Marieke de Goede this book would certainly not have found its end point. When she said "Lou, I do think it is done now, let it go," she may have been the only person who could have said it. It is a blessing indeed to have such a friend—for glasses of wine and novels, for shopping, and for philosophy on the train to Amsterdam, thank you. Thank you Gunther, Anna, and Caspar for making me feel at home in your home.

Finally, as always, thank you, Paul, for patience and support beyond words. It is always more than a room of one's own that is required. I know that I am extremely lucky to have found you, the man who quietly reads the draft, leaves the margins full of wisdom, and then takes our children, Grace and Tom, to the beach. Thank you, my lovely three, so much.

INTRODUCTION
On the Politics of Possibility

She'll scrutinize hundreds of visitors a day to keep us safe. Our solutions let her know what to look for. —Raytheon Systems' advertising campaign, appearing in UK newspapers in 2006

In the spring of 2008, the UK government announced the award of its substantial "e-Borders" contract to the self-styled Trusted Borders consortium led by the American weapons manufacturer Raytheon Company. Charged with the five-year roll out of what was to be the world's most ambitious data-driven border controls system, Raytheon's advertising campaign depicts a watchful border guard, ever attentive to the biometrically verified and risk-scored travelers whom she "scrutinizes to keep us safe." The data that are mined, integrated, and analyzed within e-Borders are of a specific type—they are designed to look for not only the settled probabilities of future risk (such as names on watch lists or no-fly lists) but also for the possible risks amid an array of future uncertainties. Such is the distinctive orientation of the politics of the contemporary sovereign state. In a world after the events of September 11, 2001, the imagination of "low probability, high consequence" events has become an overwhelming feature. From terrorist attacks and cybercrime, to flood risk and the crisis of inadequately risk-priced finance, the idea that uncertain futures—however probabilistically unlikely—be mapped and acted upon *as possibilities* has captured the Zeitgeist.

If the border guard is to scrutinize people at the borderline, the very site of the edge of territorial sovereignty, then this is made possible by an amalgam of commercial, private, military, and technological techniques. "Our solutions," as Raytheon proposes, "let her know what to look for." How are we to understand such a form of sovereign power, as it assembles together the software systems and risk models of commercial worlds with the watchful vigilance of state security? For, as the border guard assesses the border crosser in relation to a single risk-based score displayed on a screen, sovereign decisions abound—to detain, to refer to customs or policing authorities, to subject to further questions on identity and verifiability. And yet there is no definitive relation between the state's border agency (we decide) and the knowledge practices of private commercial consultants (we let her know what to decide). For the very technology of the screen that directs and delimits her attentiveness itself reaches back into multiple decisions and designations about past patterns of behavior, travel histories, financial transactions, and associations between people. The contemporary moment witnesses a complex and iterative form of sovereignty, one that breaches the comfortable delineations of public from private, political from economic, security from economy.

The question of what the contemporary sovereign state does, how it acts, with whom and by what means, has preoccupied philosophical and political debates.[1] The sovereign decision, Brian Massumi writes, is a "lightning strike" of power in which "to admit to discussing, studying, consulting, analyzing" is also to "admit to having been in a state of indecision."[2] Though sovereign decisions of many kinds (to go to war, to deport an asylum seeker, to reject a visa application, to restrict mobility) may appear as sudden flashes, their apparent immediacy conceals a complex of calculation, consulting, analysis, algorithmic modeling, and risk management that is the condition of possibility of contemporary security. Thus, when the philosopher Giorgio Agamben proposes that the Schmittian state of exception be understood as empty, "kenomatic," or an "anomic space," what is elided is precisely the lively, unpredictable, and complex life that thrives within that space.[3] Of course, for Agamben's critics it is this emptiness of the sovereign strike that represents the hole at the heart of his work, with the appeal that "political places never become merely void, the void is always filled by somebody or something else."[4] The sovereign strike is always already something more, something in excess of a single flash of decision.

In the chapters that follow I propose that, far from being an emptied out space or a space without politics, the apparent void of the sovereign decision is, in fact, teeming with life, technique, art, technology, violence, resistance, and potentiality. Heeding Michel Foucault's sense of power as productive, active in creating subjects and things, in making things happen,[5] the appearance of emptiness in the sovereign decision is itself productive. Indeed, as Raytheon's governmental "solutions" are derived from that which is absent, the missing unknown element sought via algorithmic and preemptive data mining, so contemporary security practice works on and through the emptiness and the void of that which is missing: inferring across elements, embracing uncertain futures, seeking out the excess. It is precisely across the gaps of what can be known that new subjects and things are called into being. Thus the commercial retailer's dream of an unknown consumer meets the state's nightmare of an unknown terrorist; the iris-scanned, trusted traveler becomes a condition of possibility for attention to the risky traveler "of national security interest," the designer of risk algorithms for casino and insurance fraud becomes a resource to homeland security.

In this book I offer a different way of thinking about the practices of sovereign power and the making of security decisions. It is a way of thinking about contemporary security practices that necessarily confronts the idea of economy and how we have come to think about economic life. Consider, by way of example, the founding of the Chertoff Group in 2009 by Michael Chertoff, the former secretary of the Department of Homeland Security (DHS), and his former chief of staff Chad Sweet. Addressing the European Parliament in 2007, Chertoff demanded that Europe accept the "benefits of this analytics technique" for border security, sharing Passenger Name Record data with U.S. authorities in order to "keep out dangerous people."[6] Following the election of Barack Obama, Chertoff and Sweet departed government to provide risk consultancy in the deployment of data and analytics for security, recruiting John Reid, the former UK Home Office secretary, along the way.[7] The emerging indistinction between public executive powers and an apparatus of administrative, commercial, and private expertise has become particularly evident in the delivery of homeland security. In 2005 Tom Ridge, the then U.S. secretary of the DHS, and the under secretary Asa Hutchinson resigned their government positions and became business consultants in the private sector. Former secretary Ridge, having taken a directorship of Savi Technology, a radio-frequency identification (RFID) technology company, founded the eponymous Ridge Global LLC, a consulting firm specializing in domestic security and crisis risk management. Asa Hutchinson, resigning from the DHS and running for governor of Arkansas in 2006, declared his presidency of the Hutchinson Group, a security consulting firm, though he did not initially declare his stocks in Fortress America Acquisition Corporation, a company for whom he is also a consultant.[8] Key figures in administrations that authorized technology companies and management consultants to help fight the war on terror, including Chertoff, Sweet, Reid, Ridge, and Hutchinson, among many others, are now key players in the burgeoning global homeland security market.

The vignette of Blair and Bush administration officials moving into the commercial complex of homeland security measures illustrates the problem of sustained distinctions between the public and the private, reasons of state and practices of economy, and sovereign power and commercial authority. During their time in office, they led the defining of emergency measures for exceptional times—declaring a post-9/11 "shift to a new normalcy" in which "the same benefits enjoyed by peaceful-living, freedom-loving people across the world are available now to terrorists as well."[9] In this context of a guarded globalization, with the United States Visitor and Immigrant Status Indicator Technology (US-VISIT) program's poster proclaiming "America's doors open and our nation secure" visible on the walls of every U.S. airport, the U.S. and UK governments authorized business knowledge with renewed vigor, "harnessing the power of the best minds in the private sector to enhance the security of our country while increasing efficiency."[10] Signaling a more visible turn to the state consulting science and technology industries, which had actually been long in evidence, the pursuit of simultaneous economic openness and border security has witnessed awards of multibillion dollar contracts to technology and management consultants, IT specialists, and RFID, data, and biometrics corporations.

Yet it is not the case that the new forms of alliance between economic and security expertise represent merely a privatization of security or even a strict securitization move within economy. Following Deleuze and Guattari, the "common central point" of an apparatus is "not where all the other points melt together," but rather it serves as "a point of resonance on the horizon."[11] The worlds of economy and security do not so much "melt together" as they become elements across which the imagination of future possibilities resonates, vibrates, and intensifies. William Connolly develops Deleuze and Guattari's use of the resonance machine in his work on how the elements of Christianity and capitalism "fold, blend, emulsify, and resolve incompletely into each other." For Connolly, the analytic of resonance displaces causal understandings of the mutual dependence among factors, making visible the multiple ways in which "in politics, these diverse elements *infiltrate* each other, metabolizing into a moving complex."[12] Indeed, in an earlier work Connolly has sketched out some of the elements of a security resonance machine whose whole far exceed the sum of the individual parts: "Airport surveillance, internet filters, passport tracking devices, legal detention without criminal charges, security internment camps, secret trials, 'free speech zones,' DNA profiles, border walls and fences, erosion of the line between internal security and external military action—these security activities resonate together, engendering a national security machine that pushes numerous issues outside the range of legitimate dissent and mobilizes the populace to support new security and surveillance practices against underspecified enemies."[13]

Thus it is that there is an intensifying resonance across spheres of economy and security, an infiltration of each one into the other, such that a moving complex emerges—a complex of the governing of emergent, uncertain, *possible* futures. The point of resonance on the horizon, I propose, is precisely a horizon of possible futures, arrayed in such a way as to govern, to decide, or to act in the present. Economy, one might say, is always and inescapably concerned with the unfolding of future possibilities. "Economic rationality," Foucault reminds us, "is founded on the unknowability of the totality of the process," representing an "essential incompatibility" with the "totalizing unity of the juridical sovereign."[14] The necessary unknowability of the future—so central to profit, speculation, Adam Smith's invisible hand, the figure of *Homo economicus*—appears as anathema to the sovereign founder of law, right, and the monopoly of legitimate violence. And yet at the level of knowledge and technique, as Foucault has it, "the principle of the necessary freedom of economic agents can coincide with a sovereign." There can be "perfect correspondence between the sovereign and the economic processes," such that economy offers to sovereignty a form of analysis of "what is taking place" in a world of free transactions and movements.[15] At the level of ontology, forms of economy offer forms of sovereignty a means to harness the productivity of possible futures and the capacity to reconcile openness, freedom, and mobility with the pursuit of security. Understood in this way, the alliances between sovereign power and private risk consultants appear impossible—"there is no economic sovereign"—if we explain them strictly in terms of causal processes of privatization or securitization.[16] Such alliances become possible only in the moments when the resonances of a world of possibility generate sovereign heat around economy as a means of securing uncertain futures and when economy seeks out security precisely as a source of profit from uncertain futures. In short, sovereignty and economy become newly and intimately correlated on the horizon of possible futures.

In what follows, my interest does not lie in a tale of economic powers or private authorities in world politics but rather in the distinctive practices of authorization that enable private consulting, risk management, and software and biometrics engineering to flourish as expert knowledges, to act as though they were sovereign, as proxy forms of sovereignty.[17] "Petty sovereigns abound," writes Judith Butler, "reigning in the midst of bureaucratic institutions mobilized by aims and tactics of power they do not inaugurate or fully control."[18] In Butler's terms the diffuse and dispersed forms of petty sovereignty do not stand at the heart or center, they do not inaugurate or control. One can perhaps still say with Foucault that there are no economic sovereigns, but read via Butler one can also say that there is no definitive political sovereignty.[19] If we are to speak not of definitive sovereign agents but only of novel modalities of sovereignty with plural sites and loci, then a different problem emerges. What are the specific arts, tactics, and technologies of governing possible futures? What forms of subjectivity, what types of population, are brought into being and made amenable to governing within the politics of possibility?

If the desire to govern possible futures has witnessed states embracing the capacity of economy to imagine and array possibilities, to forecast, to scan the horizon, to speculate, then this has been arguably most visible in the proliferation of consulting. The practice of governing by consulting—dispersing sovereign authority into a highly mobile apparatus of public, commercial, and military knowledges—is to be distinguished strictly from a focus on the actions, acts, and authorship of consultants per se. Though in the chapters that follow I do use the histories, programs, and knowledges of McKinsey & Company, PricewaterhouseCoopers, Accenture, IBM, and others as points of entry into my questions and argue that understanding their roles as expert authorities is critical to contemporary social science, the practices of consulting as a governmental strategy exceed the limits of these particular authorities. What is important here is that we are seeing the proliferation of *consulting*—a way of thinking, ordering, calculating, and acting on the world—rather than primarily the actions of *consultants* as identifiable agents. Thus it is not the case that the private economic sciences of management theory are uniquely placed at the service of the state, nor is it the case that state sovereignty is somehow ceded to private authority, but rather it is that the governing of and through life itself implicates novel, plural, and challenging arrangements of sovereign power. The practices of consulting are a key element in the contemporary mode of sovereign power that plays out on multiple sites and draws mobile lines between inside and outside, self and other, us and them, norm and exception.[20]

Risk, Uncertainty, Possibility

The principal technology emerging across the contemporary domains of security and economy is one of risk. The politics of possibility sees a seemingly limitless series of bodies, populations, spaces, buildings, financial transactions, tickets, movements, shapes, and forms divided and fractionated according to degrees of risk. This is not to say, however, that we live in a "world risk society" in which potentially catastrophic and uninsurable risks proliferate.[21] Instead, following a critical body of scholarship on the discourses and practices of risk, risk is a construction, a "way in which we govern and are governed."[22] As these critical risk studies remind us, risk cannot be isolated as a tangible entity or event, for it is performative—it produces the effects that it names.[23] Despite national security strategies that claim "we are entering an age of uncertainty," it is not the case that observable new risks have come into being; what has occurred is that society has come to understand itself and its problems in terms of risk management.[24] What matters is not so much a question of whether or how the world is more dangerous, more uncertain, or less safe but how specific representations of risk, uncertainty, danger, and security are distinctively writing the contours of that world. To consider risk as a means of arraying and acting upon possible futures is to engage with the practices that are enacted in the name of managing risk and uncertainty.[25]

Risk technologies have, at their heart, a particular relationship to the future. They hold out the promise of managing uncertainty and making an unknowable and indeterminate future knowable and calculable. For Ulrich Beck, the limits of risk society are reached when threats and dangers run out of control and actuarial calculations can no longer be made.[26] If we were to follow Beck's reading, both the so-called subprime crisis of 2008, which saw the disastrous effects of complex financial risk management techniques, and the catastrophic events of 9/11 together signal the limits of insurability and, therefore, the limits of modern forms of risk calculation. There is an implication for science and expertise here also. According to Beck's analysis, the exceptional events of what he considers to be a catastrophic second modernity render the scientific calculation of risk probabilities impossible. Indeed, for Beck what is exceptional about the advent of catastrophe risk is not only that scientific knowledge is unable to deal with the danger but also that scientific knowledge creates threats that it is unable to respond to.[27]

Contra Beck, however, the politics of possibility pushes back the limits of risk calculation beyond probability, differentiating ever more finite categories of risk, defining new and mobile exceptions, exclusions, and special zones, and radically redefining the relationship to science and expertise. As Mariana Valverde and Michael Mopas argue, practices of "targeted governance" shift the arts of government from discipline to risk, where "discipline governs individuals individually, risk management, by contrast, breaks the individual up into a set of measurable risk factors." This means of governing by risk permits the drawing of exceptions within and between individuals, with knowledge data giving the impression of a "smart, specific, side-effects-free, information-driven utopia of governance."[28] In contrast to insurantial risk modes, which calculate individual probabilities amid statistical knowledge of populations, novel emerging modes of risk act on and through what Gilles Deleuze termed the "dividual," a fractionated subject whose risk elements divide her even within herself.[29] Far from reaching the limits of insurability and calculation, the possibilistic risk mode exceeds those limits by allowing for differential degrees of inclusion and exclusion. Here the empty space of exceptional politics is particularly alive and thriving: for example, the financially excluded are partially (and lucratively) reincorporated and then subsequently expelled via their designation as "subprime borrowers"; the refugee is permitted to cross the border through the submission of biometric data, other elements of their life's potentiality in effect risk targeted and left behind; the migrant worker is afforded differential access to the circuits of global finance, making remittance payments via targeted and risk-managed channels.[30] Not strictly "included by means of their own exclusion," as Agamben frames the exception, they are more accurately included by means of a dividuated and mobile drawing of risk fault lines.

Through ever more complex sets of exclusions, exemptions, and exceptions, as Richard Ericson and Aaron Doyle explain in relation to the post-9/11 insurance industry, "many of the fields imagined by Beck to be uninsurable are insured."[31] Indeed, Ericson and Doyle argue that risk expertise is built on the back of "authoritative certainty in [the] face of limited knowledge, allowing definitive courses of action to be pursued."[32] Risk expertise is not, as Beck would have it, confounded by disaster and catastrophe, but its authority is derived precisely from the capacity to decide the exceptions that make it possible to act even in the face of radical uncertainty. Even where the limits of statistical risk knowledges of probability are breached by the exceptional case—a terrorist attack, flood event, hurricane, pandemic, or financial crisis—the more speculative knowledges of scenario planning, social network analysis, and predictive analytics reorient risk to action on the very basis of the imagination of those possibilities.

The specific modality of risk that I address in the chapters that follow has an anticipatory logic: it acts not strictly to *prevent* the playing out of a particular course of events on the basis of past data tracked forward into probable futures but to *preempt* an unfolding and emergent event in relation to an array of possible projected futures. It seeks not to forestall the future via calculation but to incorporate the very unknowability and profound uncertainty of the future into imminent decision. As François Ewald writes in his discussion of the precautionary principle, "decisions are made not in a context of certainty, nor even of available knowledge, but of doubt, premonition, foreboding, challenge, mistrust, fear, and anxiety."[33] The precautionary principle authorizes decision in anticipation of the uncertain future. By way of illustration, the "new normalcy," which is claimed in foreign policy and homeland security decisions, seeks "the better management of risks ahead of time."[34] Thus scenario planning, risk profiling, algorithmic modelling, information integration, and data analysis become the authoritative knowledges of choice. To manage risks ahead of time is to enroll modes of calculation that can live with emergence itself, embrace and reincorporate the capacity for error, false positive, mistake, and anomaly.[35]

With the possibilistic approach to risk, it is not the case, as Ulrich Beck would have it, that there is a crisis of scientific expertise, nor even strictly, as Ericson and Doyle say, that where "scientific data on risk is absent" there is a turn to "non-scientific forms of knowledge that are intuitive, emotional, aesthetic, moral, and speculative."[36] Rather, the relationships between science, expertise, and decision are radically rearticulated so that distinctions between "science" and "non-science" become more malleable. On the one hand, scientific data begin to incorporate the emotional, affective, and speculative domains, while, on the other hand, knowledges considered to be "non-scientific" are authorized as science. For example, data-led algorithms that model the movement of bodies or things across space coalesce with intuitive and speculative knowledges that imagine future scenarios. Within the data analytics used in new border control systems, for example, conventional probabilistic knowledges of actuarial risk calculation are allied with "threat print" techniques that allow for the "imagineering of future risks."[37] It is not that probabilistic risk models are eclipsed by new forms that work with emergent possibilities but that the degrees of doubt always already present within mathematical probability multiply and take flight as imaginable, if not strictly calculable, possibilities. "The precautionary principle," writes Ewald, "presupposes a new relationship with science and with knowledge," one that "invites one to anticipate what one does not yet know, to take into account doubtful hypotheses and simple suspicions."[38] Risk in the mode of possibility rather than strict probability, does not govern by the deductive proving or disproving of scientific and statistical data but by the inductive incorporation of suspicion, imagination, and preemption.

In many ways there is nothing particularly novel about the appearance of anticipatory approaches to risk within the politics of possibility. It has long been an assumption of liberal theories of risk and capital that profitable business decisions are taken in face of uncertainty. In Frank Knight's classic text published in 1921, for example, making decisions in the context of an unknowable future is of the essence of entrepreneurial activity: "profit arises out of the inherent, absolute unpredictability of things, out of the sheer, brute fact that the results of human activity cannot be anticipated and then only in so far as even a probability calculation in regard to them is impossible and meaningless."[39] The unpredictable and incalculable elements that can never be amenable to sovereign power are the very source of economic profitability. Knight's private entrepreneur or "adventurer" makes decisions in a context where "all instances of economic uncertainty are cases of choice between a smaller reward more confidently and a larger one less confidently anticipated."[40] In the context of the adventuring spirit of the entrepreneur, the unknowable environment is to be embraced, positively invited, for its intrinsic possibilities. In a dramatic reversal of Beck's assumption that there is a retreat from the commercial incorporation of certain risks at the edge of probability, what Tom Baker and Jonathan Simon call "embracing risk" suggests that the possibilistic mode encourages the drive for new areas of profit and the authorization of new actions and decisions.[41] In the immediate aftermath of the events of September 11, 2001, for example, companies such as London's Risk Management Solutions offered counterterrorism risk models that were derived from the natural disaster modeling in which they had specialized commercially for some time.[42] Far from reaching a limit point in the exceptional catastrophic event, risk techniques act at the edge of possibility, seeking out that which can profitably be attended to beyond the limit.

In this book I provide an account of the emerging alliances between the commercial economic embracing of risk and the preemptive mode of risk in state security. In the absence of a definable central agency or overseer, or vertical hierarchy of actors, there is a horizontal resonance between the rhetoric of risk as opportunity flourishing in the commercial world of consultancy and the anticipatory decisions of the post-9/11 security state. Consider, by way of example, the management consultants McKinsey & Company's advice to their corporate clients on "making the most of uncertainty": "At the heart of the traditional approach to strategy lies the assumption that executives, by applying a set of powerful analytic tools, can predict the future. . . . When the future is truly uncertain, this approach is at best marginally helpful and at worst downright dangerous."[43] Signaling a disavowal of conventional strategic thinking on tools for *predicting* the future, the McKinsey risk model advocates "running with risk" to preempt the future via scenario planning, live simulation, and modeling. In its allying of prediction with the dangers of missing the improbable but possible event, it resonates with the "low probability, high consequence" ethos of the "one-percent doctrine" documented by Ron Suskind in the Bush administration's approach to the war on terror: "even if there is just a one percent chance of the unimaginable coming due, act as if it is a certainty."[44] In order to act on the basis of future possibilities, one must eschew probabilistic conventions of strategic prediction wherein the 1 percent possibility would be filtered out.

Indeed, we might see McKinsey as one of the "invisibles" Suskind describes working away on the modeling, profiling, and data interfacing of the war on terror. In 2002, for example, the mayor of New York commissioned McKinsey & Company to report on the New York Fire Department's (FDNY) and New York Police Department's (NYPD) responses on and after September 11.[45] "The services the McKinsey consultants have rendered," stated Mayor

Michael Bloomberg, "should not be described as investigations, they have produced a forward looking analysis."[46] Again, disavowing the conventions of strategy and investigation, the reports do, indeed, look to anticipate the future in very specific ways. The exceptional circumstances of 9/11, they find, create "a new urgency for preparedness."[47] Among the recommendations, the FDNY is advised to "conduct a citywide assessment of potential risks," to create an "all hazards playbook" based on scenario thinking and "live simulations," and to "do more to anticipate future events."[48] To seek to predict the future on the basis of past events—"downright dangerous" as McKinsey suggests—would be a failure of imagination comparable with those identified as failings in *The 9/11 Commission Report*. As James Der Derian has argued in relation to forms of war that merge video game and movie entertainment with military technology, the authorization of McKinsey's analyses brings into play bodies of knowledge on living with emergent uncertainty that have become accepted norms in other spheres.[49] So, for example, McKinsey's advice to the NYPD to procure wireless electronics, tracking and identification technologies, and handheld mobile devices for future emergency collapses any meaningful distinction between private and public spheres of risk management. The emphasis on information sharing, data integration, and communications technologies in the FDNY and NYPD reports resonates across McKinsey's advice to private business on how to embrace risk and live with uncertainty.

To summarize my claims here: First, the principal point of resonance across the contemporary domains of security and economy is the idea of risk itself. As a means of arraying and acting upon uncertain futures, risk enables the fractionation of ever-more finite categories of life—*degrees of safe and dangerous, vulnerable and durable, mobile and restricted, identifiable and unidentified, verifiable and unverified*, and so on. If we take exceptionality to be the ever-present drawing and redrawing of lines to include by exclusion, then, in the contemporary manifestation of exception, risk models are the key means of drawing those lines.[50] Second, the mode of risk that is flourishing across the horizons of contemporary economy and security operates according to a possibilistic logic. It does not deploy statistical probabilistic calculation in order to avert future risks but rather flourishes in conditions of declared constant emergency because decisions are taken on the basis of future possibilities, however improbable or unlikely. Finally, the possibilistic mode of risk in the security sphere resonates strongly with the embracing risk rhetoric dominating the insurance, consulting, and information technology industries. The risk techniques that flourish on the horizon of possibilities, though, as I will show in the chapters that follow, are not those of auditing, accounting, statistics, actuarial science, and probability but instead are those of consulting, screening, remote tracking, biometric identifying, and algorithmic profiling.

Exception, Economy, Sovereignty

Engaging with the writings of Carl Schmitt, Giorgio Agamben locates the originary act of sovereign power in the capacity to declare exception. For Agamben, sovereign power operates through the categorization of forms of life, the drawing of lines between civil or political life (*bios*), and the stripped down vulnerability of unqualified bare life (*zoĐ*). In its contemporary form, Agamben proposes, the state of exception appears as a "permanent state of emergency," transforming provisional measures into an enduring "technique of government" that allows the sorting of safe and liveable lives from risky and unliveable lives.[51] It is not the case that the sovereign authority strictly excludes bare life in the declaration of exception but rather that the state of exception allows the inclusion of bare life via its very exclusion. As life itself becomes the primary object of sovereign power, so the bare life "originally situated at the margins of the political order" is "taken outside" so that it may be included within the juridical order.[52] The question of the designation of categories of citizen, alien, asylum seeker, refugee, legal or illegal migrant worker, for example, is not a matter of excluding what is supposedly alien, illegal, illegitimate per se but of taking them outside, rendering them as other so that their lives and bodies can be included within governable space.

Undoubtedly, Agamben's work on the figure of *homo sacer* and the space of the camp have seen his ideas taken up in the philosophy of contemporary life, perhaps most powerfully for his insight that sovereign authority and biopower act together, are copresent. For Agamben, the sovereign power "who can decide on the state of exception" produces a paradox: it enacts the suspension of law while simultaneously "guaranteeing its anchorage to the juridical order."[53] Put simply, sovereign power functions by authorizing acts that have the force of law even when they do not adhere to the rule of law. At a time of emergency or crisis, the state's designation of special powers may annul the usual rule of law but enable acts carried out by nominated authorities to have the force of law by virtue of their sovereign authorization. The ultimate expression of such an authorization is Agamben's "camp": a "kenomatic state, an emptiness and a standstill of the law."[54] The figure of the camp has been deployed to capture the biopolitics of contemporary security strategies, emphasising the zones of indistinction represented by spaces such as Guantanamo Bay and Abu Ghraib prison.[55] Others have seen the exception becoming the rule in the sorting and risk profiling of people at international borders and in the financial system.[56] Agamben's state of exception has come to define something of the nature of contemporary sovereign power in what Bülent Diken and Carsten Bagge Laustsen have called a "society of exceptions."[57]

For all that, Agamben's writings have gained purchase on thought about the shape of our contemporary world, the critical reception of *Homo Sacer* and *State of Exception* has paralleled a certain "forgetting" of his work on politics and political potentiality.[58] As Jenny Edkins writes, the "space left for politics" is "eclipsed for readers . . . in the context of the spread of the zone of indistinction and the reduction of politics to biopolitics."[59] There is an open question that hovers over the space of politics, over the exception as political space in and of itself. There is a pressing need to confront what appears as an emptied out space and to look seriously at what is at work in the contemporary politics of exceptionalism. As William Connolly suggests in his reading of Agamben, "the sovereign is not simply (as Agamben and Schmitt tend to say) *he* (or *she*) who first decides that there is an exception and then decides how to resolve it. Sovereign is *that* which decides an exception exists and how to decide it, with *that* composed of a plurality of forces circulating through and under the positional sovereignty of the official arbitrating body."[60]

Connolly opens the possibility to begin to challenge sovereign authority as the definitive originary author of the exception and to see the interplay between the positional sovereignty of the authorities "that decide the exception" and the "plural forces that insert themselves irresistibly into the outcome."[61] He envisages, within the idea of exception, an oscillation that flows between "juridically established authority" that appears to decide exception and "sanctioned authorities" who "express and shape the ethos."[62] Returning to the example with which I opened this introduction, Connolly's rereading of the exception allows us to see that the positional sovereignty of the official arbitrating body of the state effectively covers up the noise of other authorized bodies, part of a continual back-and-forth flow between plural forces of authorization.

It is precisely the plural authorization of exceptional measures that affords scope for action on the basis of possibilities. The positional sovereign power that invokes exception with the suspension of the strictly applied rule of law opens the space for proxy sovereigns that are designated to act with the force of law. As Judith Butler describes it, a "contemporary version of sovereignty" is produced within the exception, at the "moment of withdrawal."[63] How does this contemporary version of sovereignty manifest itself? How is it authorized to act and to decide? Noting that Agamben seems to want to "escape from the problem of sovereignty as fast as possible," Rob Walker suggests that much work needs to be done thinking through the capacity to decide exceptions and exemptions.[64] This work might start, he suggests, with an examination of the multiple forms of exceptionalism delineating the state, the individual, and the system of states. The practices of sovereign exception Walker identifies, though, have become particularly dependent on private and commercial expertise that acts by proxy, as though with the force of law—many of them technology multinationals, private consultants, and risk analysts. Their roles in the circulating declaration of exception, however, is much less well understood at this point than even the states, individuals, and systems of states that Walker proposes.

One way to think through the plurality of contemporary forms of the exception is to bring security measures into juxtaposition with the idea of economy itself. In part this is motivated by a frustration with the neglect of matters of economy by otherwise critical studies of security and geopolitics and the apparent refusal of otherwise critical studies of the economy to consider questions of security and sovereignty. A superficial reading might say that the practices of management consulting, risk analysis, and software design I single out for critical attention in this book are "economic" or "of the economy." However, in common with others who have sought to work with economy "beyond economism"—that is, beyond *the* economy as a prediscursive, pre-political, and self-evident material reality—economy is used here in its broadest sense, as a means of rendering mobile and circulating things, people, money, and objects calculable, knowable, and, therefore, governable.[65]

The significance of economy is not what it is, what is its essence, but instead how it has come to be a field of intervention and a means of governing.[66] "The art of government," writes Foucault, "is essentially concerned with answering the question of how to introduce economy—that is to say, the correct manner of managing individuals, goods and wealth within the family—how to introduce this . . . into the management of the state."[67] Foucault locates in economy a problematic of the art of governing the state, such that the "very essence of government" has come to mean "the art of exercising power in the form of economy."[68] The governmentalized state, for Foucault, "will not be someone who possesses an absolute decision-making power," but rather it will be one who governs the population as the head of a household governs home and family.[69] Understood in this way, the sovereign decision can never be an absolute and instantaneous flash of sovereign power, for it is necessarily acting on a terrain of economy and economic subjects. In answer to the question "how to govern in a space of sovereignty inhabited by economic subjects," Foucault identifies the physiocrats—the administrators, consuls, scientists of policy—as those who act as the "geometers of the economic domain forming part of the field of sovereignty."[70]

In late modern capitalism Foucault identifies a realigning of the economic away from the family and toward population as the target. The crucial point here is that, via population, "the problem of government" can be "thought, reflected and calculated outside of the juridical framework of sovereignty."[71] Put simply, economy becomes one of the ways in which sovereign power oscillates in and out of a strictly juridical mode of authority, coalescing the governing of the population with the management of the state. How is the population to be identified, enumerated, and accounted for? What are to be the thresholds of normal and deviant behavior? How is the nation to be protected? These are the questions that pertain to what Foucault calls a governmentalized state: a state that increasingly sustains sovereign authority and takes a slippery hold on economic subjects via economic knowledges that govern the code of conduct. If the practices of designating exception have, as Agamben suggests, become the norm in contemporary sovereign logics, then, following Foucault, these will, at least in part, seek to engage economy with political practice.

In this book I propose three central points of intersection between a Connolly-inspired politics that is plural and teeming with life and economy as an art of government. The first is that the declaration of exceptional times, emergency powers, and necessary measures authorizes new modes of economic savoir faire and makes it possible to target and enumerate population in new ways. To draw a genealogy of the designation of crisis or emergency is to reveal a rearticulation of the authorization of authority, particularly of science and law. During the Second World War in Britain, for example, techniques of enumerating the population via state-administered census and survey began to be called into question, with accounting and consulting practices engaged by the state to render national registers for the management of rations and prices. Essentially, as a science of enumerating the population, accounting sought for itself a publicly authorized authority on a par with medicine and law. In contemporary invocations of emergency and exception, where, as Nigel Thrift describes it, a "constant state of emergency" becomes a resource to global capital, a different relationship to expertise is envisaged, one in which a complex of public and private commercially derived data are deployed.[72] As in my opening examples, it becomes possible for a secretary of the DHS to declare that "science and technology are key to winning this new kind of war," authorizing all kinds of private authorities in the process, and then to promptly embody that authority as a homeland security consultant. Technologies such as RFID, biometrics, and body scanners, nurtured by economic knowledges that said it was possible to thrive on uncertainty and embrace risk, are technologies that now sell the same dream to the state in their promise to make manageable the risky mobile bodies of the global economy.

Second, the designations and conditions of the exception do not simply *become the norm* (or constitute a new normalcy), as so many contemporary social theorists would claim, but instead they operate through the norm itself or, more precisely, via the movements of a mobile norm. Slavoj Žižek identifies what he calls the depoliticized realm of expert knowledge in which "the unconditional demand" is made "that things should return to normal."[73] In the context of what he has elsewhere referred to as the "universal exception," though, the experts' demand for normality takes on a different dynamic.[74] As Foucault writes, by appealing to techniques of normalization, "expert opinion" is able "to show how the individual already resembles his crime before he has committed it."[75] Patterns of normalities are in this sense anticipatory—they identify future events before they take place. Security techniques, algorithmic technologies, and knowledges—in the workplace, at border crossings, in the financial system, and so on— embody and decide exception not simply *as* the norm but *via* processes of normalization. Indeed, in the case of my opening example of Raytheon's border control systems, the norm is hyper-mobile. What is considered a normal pattern of movement on this day, at this time, at that moment, in these circumstances, is normal only under those conditions. In association with other criteria, the norm itself may be flagged as risk, as abnormal. Far from simply "becoming the norm," the rapid and fleeting decision on exception is a norm that is always in the process of becoming; the norm "is an interplay of differential normalities."[76]

Finally, where the declaration of exception acts on and through life itself, it must also produce a particular economy of decision. How are the exceptions decided and on what basis are decisions made within the exception? For Jacques Derrida, a decision is not a decision if it simply redeploys calculative practices in order to decide. A decision cannot, in Derrida's reading, be determined by the acquisition of knowledge, for then it is not a decision but "simply the application of a body of knowledge of, at the very least, a rule or norm."[77] Many contemporary exceptions appear to be decided precisely on the grounds of an appeal to expertise, to a body of knowledge that can make the decision informed or scientific. Recall the opening epigraph, "our solutions let her know what to look for," where the border guard's decisions are deferred into an already calculated set of risk scores. In Derrida's terms such decisions are not decisions at all but merely appeals to an already calculated judgment. "The decision, if there is to be one," he writes, "must advance towards a future which is not known, which cannot be anticipated."[78] In this sense, behind the scene of screen and risk score, there are multiple decisions made that are hidden from view. From the writing of algorithmic code to the "stress testing" of security techniques in selected "pilot" spaces, plural decisions fill the void of exception. Though the desire to act on the basis of possible futures may appear to annul and close off political decision, in fact decisions are made everywhere and all of the time. To retrieve those decisions and pry open their acute difficulties is to relocate the politics of an otherwise gleaming and technoscientific set of solutions.

Consulting, Authority, Expertise

What we have come to know as consulting, consultancy, and consultants find their etymological roots in the Latin *consulto*, meaning to ask the advice of, and *consultum*, meaning to decree. It has become almost commonplace to acknowledge the participation of consulting professionals and consulting knowledge in the shaping of the contemporary global political economy.[79] Moreover, the rise of the technocrat and the advent of government by expertise is alluded to in many contemporary discussions of the transformation of sovereign power.[80] Yet the proximity of commercial consultants to state decrees at times of emergency and security measures remains significantly unexamined. Claims are made that "sovereign power" has come to be "shared with large private interests" or that "private professionals have the advantage of exercising authority."[81] The authorities that matter, according to such analyses, are "most prominent in the defense sector" and in the "specific habitus of the security professional." In this way the spheres of economy and security persist as identifiable and distinct spheres whose relation is one of causality. Yet is the specific appearance of mapping data in military reconnaissance a matter of economy or security? Does the mining of data on airline passenger name records act through economy or security? If we take seriously the implications of Foucault's Clausewitzian inversion, that "politics is the continuation of war by other means," then we should consider not only those authorities associated with the technologies of war but also the authorities whose knowledges pursue war by other means.[82] When commercial consultants McKinsey & Company and IBM give testimony to the 9/11 Commission and the U.S. Joint Congressional Inquiry, they do not simply advise on the data and communications necessary in times of emergency but rather authorize security decrees that will live on to have effects on the lives of people.

In his search for a paradigmatic model of the state of exception, Giorgio Agamben offers an institution of Roman law: the *iustitium* or the suspension of the law. What is interesting for my introductory discussion is the processes of authorization that are produced within the iustitium when an emergency situation is decreed. In the Roman republic the consuls acted as something akin to chief magistrates who convened the Senate, served as generals in military campaigns, and appointed leaders or acted as dictator in exceptional circumstances when the constitution was suspended. As Agamben explains, a "senatus consultum ultimum" (final decree of the Senate) would be enacted to declare an emergency situation, calling upon "the consuls, the tribunes of the people, and even, in extreme cases, all citizens, to take whatever measures they considered necessary for the salvation of the state."[83] In this sense the state of exception is not a space in which the authorities of war, defense, or security prevail but rather where public and private authorities coalesce and all citizens may be authorized to act and to decide.

Within Agamben's archetypal state of exception, the advice of the consuls is pivotal to the act of declaring an emergency, and, at the same time, the authority to take necessary measures is conferred upon the consuls and the citizens. Citizens acquire the right to decide and to act by command of the consuls and are called upon to act with proxy responsibility for the self-defense of the state. Indeed, in his later work Agamben has identified a move to locate sovereign authority via *oikonomia* (from the greek *oikos*, the administration of the household), in the social body of the people.[84] Thus, in the state of exception there is no creation of a singular new locus of authority—a private expert "author" of decisions—but instead "every citizen seems to be invested with a floating and anomalous *imperium* that resists definition within the terms of the normal order."[85] As sovereignty and economy become juxtaposed in new ways, as citizens are enrolled in programs of counterterrorist vigilance, as even the most improbable suspicions and judgments become the basis for action, the decision on the exception itself is multiplied.

I do not suggest that commercial consultants, risk managers, or software designers represent the contemporary manifestation of the consuls in our present day iustitium. However, as sovereign power is compelled to find new ways to authorize itself, the appeal to particular forms of expertise becomes an important means of authorization. The politics of possibility ushers in what Michael Dillon has called a "knowledge-obsessed" form of sovereignty, actively deferring its decisions to risk analysts, biometrics corporations, crisis consultants, and information technology experts.[86] Though there is no linear shift from state-based knowledges (for example, state scientific facilities or centralized public data collection) to commercial consulting, it is the case that Agamben's declaration "videant consules" (let the consuls see to it) affords sovereign status to a vast array of knowledges of emergency, risk, and crisis.[87] As Didier Bigo suggests in his analysis of the exceptional politics of immigration, the permanent sense of crisis, as well as the promise of its resolution by technology, is "driven by the creation of a transnational field of professionals in the management of unease."[88] These experts in unease are uniquely implicated in not only *designating* the exceptional circumstances and telling us what is to be feared—be it global recession, financial crisis, terrorist attack, immigration crisis—but also in *declaring* and *supplying* the technologies that come to be the necessary response to emergency.

What are the specific conditions in which new bodies of expertise come to be authorized? In the chapters that follow, I will show how the events of September 11, 2001, and the period that became fashioned after the war on terror cleared the ground for many techniques that were already ubiquitous in commercial applications to make the crossover into security applications. The RFID technologies that are being heralded as the future for securing identification objects (passports, visas, biometric identity cards) on the move, for example, are commonplace in supply chain management applications. It is their use in homeland security techniques, though, that sees them emerge as the smart and technology-led solution to identity management. As a note of caution, this is not to overstate either the novelty or the coherence of what appear to us as new forms of alliance of economic knowledge and sovereign authority. Only five months after 9/11, a panel of IT and management consultants testified to U.S. Congress that "had information coordination technology been properly in place before September 11, there may have been a different outcome."[89] The testimony to the 9/11 Commission of companies such as IBM and Deloitte reveals how the information coordination techniques used by global firms could be deployed by the state in order to preempt security threats. It is the exceptional circumstances declared after 9/11 that open up the possibility for the experts in the unease of global markets to become the experts in the unease of state security. It is not the techniques themselves that are novel, then, but their authorization in new spheres and their seeping into the seams of new areas of life.

It is not only the events of September 11, 2001, but also the events of November 2001 that contribute to the specific conditions for the emergence of a politics of possibility. The accounting scandal that led to the bankruptcy of U.S. energy and service giant Enron precipitated the collapse of accounting multinational Arthur Anderson, discrediting auditing practices more broadly and ushering in imperatives for business service providers to seek new income streams. Crucially, Arthur Anderson's lucrative non-audit consulting contracts with Enron were widely perceived to have impeded their ability to provide independent, impartial, and transparent accounting and auditing disclosure. The post-Enron Sarbanes-Oxley (SOX) Act of 2002 sought to salvage confidence in accounting and auditing by, in effect, enforcing the divorce of accounting from consulting services. The SOX Act created the Public Company Accounting Oversight Board (PCAOB) to regulate public accounting firms and enforce audit standards and, importantly, prohibited the accounting firms from providing a range of other consulting services for their audit clients. The post-Enron environment has seen a dramatic splitting of consulting from accounting and auditing, an ongoing series of mergers and acquisitions, and a proliferation of new consulting services, including, of course, reputational risk management services for the Sarbanes-Oxley era.

The political implications of the splitting of what are assumed to be the imaginative and futures-oriented practices of consulting from the perceived rational and objective practices of accounting and auditing are considerable. Consider, for example, the IBM contract between 2005 and 2007 for the UK Home Office's pilot for the e-Borders program. Projects Semaphore and Iris were designed to integrate databases on airline passengers entering and leaving the UK and, ultimately, to link the data to biometric identifiers. In the post-Enron period, IBM has become the largest global consulting multinational, acquiring information technology consulting and management consulting services from CapGemini Ernst & Young, PricewaterhouseCoopers, and Ascential. Indeed, their acquisition of the data integration multinational Ascential in 2005 was a deal simultaneously sought by Oracle and SAP, all of whom, like IBM, now have designated homeland security practices.

The post-Enron divorce of accounting from consulting authority has been critical to the changing landscape of the authorization of expertise. In many ways the SOX Act has freed up consulting services from the regulatory frameworks of accounting, enabling the proliferation of risk consulting, software and IT services, and other services that transgress the limits of public and private spheres. Such is the extent of the opening up of these spaces of expertise that, in 2004, global management consultants Accenture were awarded a $10 billion contract to manage the security of all U.S. air, land, and sea ports of entry. Heading up the Smart Borders consortium that included Oracle and Deloitte, Accenture's homeland security contract was awarded just three years after its change of name from Anderson Consulting in 2001 and, critically, only four years after its independence from Arthur Anderson in 2000. There can be little doubt that the authorization of private consultants such as Accenture to decide on exceptions and make preemptive decisions via biometrics, RFID, algorithmic modeling, and so on has required a specific representation of these knowledges as beyond accounting and auditing. Even when selecting a new name, Anderson Consulting derived Accenture from "accent on the future." In this sense, though the politics of possibility I depict in this book perhaps could not be envisaged without what Michael Power described as the "audit explosion" in which accounting practices emerge as "a powerful institution of risk profiling," they also mark a distinctive departure in the authorization of expertise.[90] While we might see the risk models of accounting and auditing as authorizing preventative knowledges, acting through expert *oversight*, the risk models of consulting authorize preemptive knowledges that act through anticipatory *foresight*.

In the next two chapters, which comprise part 1 of this book, I focus on the *techniques* that characterize the contemporary politics of possibility. Chapter 1 is interested in how the politics of possibility have become authorized as a means of governing amid uncertainty. I approach the problem of how specific proxy sovereigns become authorized to act and to decide by juxtaposing two examples of the state's turn to expertise in times of war. The deployment of commercial accounting technologies of Price Waterhouse in programs of rationing, price controls, and the restructuring of wartime manufacturing in Britain during World War II authorized new modes of expertise via the declaration of exceptional times. Yet in these wartime examples of sovereign power appealing to commercial expertise in the governing of population, the methods and techniques of accounting and statistical business calculation were strictly brought to bear *on* war. By contrast, the contemporary appeal to war as exceptional grounds for the turn to science, data analytics, and risk algorithms extends the practices of economy *via* war into life itself. The enumeration of population in mid-twentieth-century war, though it exceeded nineteenth-century techniques of survey and census, acted to prevent shortages on the basis of probabilities drawn from past data. The contemporary politics of possibility marks a change in emphasis from the statistical calculation of probability to the algorithmic arraying of possibilities such that they can be acted upon. Redeploying the data analytics first devised for retail and consumer profiles, the "association rules" of new security software establish possible projected futures of guilt by association.

Chapter 2 is concerned with the novel modality of risk that characterizes the politics of possibility. When the former UK prime minister Tony Blair gave his testimony to the Iraq Inquiry in 2010, he explained his decision to go to war on the basis that "the crucial thing after September 11 was that the calculus of risk changed."[91] In his evidence he is clear that the material and observable threats posed by Iraq were not at issue per se—there had always been "leaks" in the policy of containment, he said, and these leaks remained—the intrinsic threat remained much the same. Yet a world of containment, sanctions, monitoring, and international conventions somehow could not be reconciled with a post-9/11 sensibility. Put simply, it was not that the risk had changed but that the very calculus of risk had changed: it was no longer a matter of containing leaks or assessing the probability of future leaks (perhaps even the search for weapons of mass destruction is it-self obsolete) but instead the imperative of action on the basis of the future catastrophe of those leaks—action when there is low probability but high consequence. As Blair testified, "they killed 3,000 people, but if they could have killed 30,000 they would have"—it is necessary to act to preempt what they *would* do, if they *could*. In this chapter I map out the contours of this changed risk calculus, explaining how commercial bodies of knowledge on "embracing risk" and "thriving on uncertainty" are coalescing with contem-porary forms of security risk. Decisions on the threshold of war are thus made not strictly on the balance of probability, nor even to prevent some event from happening, but rather through the imagination of possibilities, in order to act upon an event in its unfolding.

Having mapped the contours of the particular kind of apparatus at work in the politics of possibility, part 2 turns to consider the specific *spaces* through which the politics of possibility materializes. Chapter 3 explores perhaps the most significant spatial and political manifestation of the con-temporary politics of possibility—borders and new forms of border control. In March 2010, 250 newly appointed "match analysts" began their work at the UK's National Border Targeting Centre (NBTC). Attending to the screened data on border crossings in and out of the UK, they "judge[d] the strength of computer generated alerts" and passed risk-flagged data on to border control, law enforcement, or intelligence agencies. In a world in which the events of 9/11 have been rendered a problem of border security for which the solution is a "joining of the dots" of data, it is precisely such risk-based judgments that rewrite the geography of the borderline. In the border writing for our times—ever present but entering the visible register in programs such as the UK's NBTC and e-Borders projects and the U.S. Automated Targeting System (ATS)—what the border is, where the border begins and ends, and what crossing a border means are old questions that confront us anew. In chapter 3 I am concerned with the mosaic spatial form of emerging border techniques, a mosaic comprising what I call, following the forensic geneticists, their "life signatures"—signatures that exceed an identifiable human subject, gathering together multiple other subjects and things. Focusing on the writing of the borderline through automated target-ing, DNA profiling, biometrics, and whole-body scanning, I propose that the contemporary border is written in and through the mobile life signatures of dividuated people.

Chapter 4 is concerned with the locations and locative capacities of security devices. In an empty industrial facility on a bright March morning in 2004, a team of three Accenture consultants demonstrated a new concept in border security to a U.S. government delegation. Scanning the fingerprints of the government officials, taking their digital photographs, and inserting an RFID tag into their passports, the Accenture "mock" border used a vehicle speeding past the security scanner to prove their concept: the scanner "read the digital information contained on the RFID chips of all four government officials in the vehicle, displaying their pictures on an electronic billboard as they passed by."[92] Most often depicted as a locative device that "animates" otherwise inert objects, RFID appears to hold out the possibility of locating and securing things on the move, securing in and through mobility itself. In this chapter I show that technologies of mobile identification are, in fact, merely geographical systems of address (Thrift 2004) to be understood in the context of other historical codes of address, from Morse code to barcode.[93] Heeding Jane Bennett's compelling reminder that we consider the vibrancy and active capacities of all things, and not only as animated by or instrumental to human design, I attend to the liveliness and life of security devices.[94] Thus it is that the small coiled tags, now present in many national passports, do not merely echo the traces of the movements left behind by security's subjects but instead dwell within the very transactions of people, objects, places, and things.

In chapter 5, the opening of part 3, I turn to the question of the aesthetics of a politics of possibility. From the screens of software designers looking for the ultimate visual array of data connections to the everyday visualities of suspicion in public vigilance programs such as "if you see something, say something," the politics of possibility invites attentiveness to the affective judgments of something that "feels right" or "looks out of place." Focusing on the development of techniques to visualize risk in crowded public places, I take as my illustrative route into this problem the curious juxtaposition of eighteenth-century English artist William Hogarth's *The Analysis of Beauty* and twentieth-century theoretical quantum mechanics. How does a person or form of interest come to be singled out and acted upon? What are the distinctive forms of profiling at work, and how do they act on the outline profile of a person? Do such techniques represent novel and slippery forms of racial prejudice that judge on the basis of what the DHS terms "behavior and not background"?

In each of the chapters of this book I am concerned with not only drawing out the nature of the contemporary politics of possibility but also suggesting its contingency and fragility, its necessary incompleteness and inherent contestability. If the task of mapping the contours of the politics of possibility is one that involves a careful and detailed probing of complex relations of power, then it is also one that must necessarily engage with the always copresent relations of dissent and resistance. As Gilles Deleuze has put the problem, "life becomes resistance to power when power takes life as its object . . . the two operations belong to the same horizon."[95] Understood in this way, the exercise of power at a threshold of what is possible must always and at the same time implicate relations of resistance at that same threshold, the two knotted together unless and if only power itself ceases to be. In chapter 6 I make a distinction, following Deleuze, between the politics of possibility and a politics of potentiality. Arguably critique is made extraordinarily difficult when the very terrain of criticism—that which escapes, the excess, the return, the mistake and error—becomes incorporated within the security technique itself. Though acting on human potentialities and proclivities is itself becoming a ubiquitous mode of governing contemporary life, this is a form of governing that can only act on a potentiality that is already actualized as a possibility—a plane that would have been boarded, a border that would have been crossed, a future violence that would have been fully realized. There are other forms of potentiality flourishing in the interstices of this way of governing life itself, forms of potentiality that are incipient, never fully grasped or realized. Drawing on examples of art installations and novels that are intrigued by the lively engagements of security technologies in the contemporary city, I explore the plural and fleeting interruptions in the politics of possibility.

Part I.
TECHNIQUES

1. ON AUTHORITY
Probabilities for a World of Possibility

> Weather energy goes round in circles, runs down corridors, cascades down stairways. It diffuses, regathers, reforms, diffuses again. It moves in jets and trickles, is divided by layers thick and thin. It's always moving through one system to another, taking different shapes over time. That's why there'll always be the unexpected. The number will not help you solve that problem directly. But if you want help with your war . . . the extent of the unexpectedness can be modified, increasing the probability of prediction. Don't think of the date for your invasion, or you will make a prison for yourself. Think of your data instead. How does it fit into the surrounding context? —Giles Foden, *Turbulence*, 190

In 1944 in a remote Scottish village, Henry Meadows, a young mathematician working for the UK's Meteorological Office, seeks the secret Ryman number that will make possible the crucial five-day advance forecasting of the weather for the D-Day landings. In Giles Foden's novel *Turbulence*, a depiction of the relationships between prediction, probability, weather, and war, the strategic decision on the date of invasion is but the visible surface of a series of frenetic backroom calculations and disputes between forecasters. As Foden's protagonist Meadows complains, acknowledging something of the performative force of his forecasts, "it was as if we were now expected not just to predict the weather but *make* it, in order that the vast ensemble of men and machines could at last be unleashed upon the enemy."[1] His mentor, and the author of the much sought after equation,

Wallace Ryman has warned him not to focus on the analogue reading of patterns of past weather events, or the "prison" that is the date of the invasion itself, but to observe the differential layers of the weather system, to allow for movement, circulation, and the unexpected. Yet Meadows's colleagues are uneasy at what they see as the inferential "approximation" being invited into their statistical calculations of future weather. "The Americans' analogue models," objects his superior, "use historical data statistically to extrapolate how current weather will develop." "With the greatest respect to our allies," replies Meadows, "I don't think that is what Ryman was talking about. He would say you could have hundreds of years of data and still get it wrong. You might pick up some quasi-periodic phenomena but the singularities could be completely against the grain."[2] Statistical extrapolation from a series of past weather events, Foden's character tells us, could in itself represent a danger to sovereign judgment, missing, as it might, the singularities against the grain, the outliers that elude the series.

In Foden's novel the authorization of a sovereign decision—on the basis of which the lives of two and a half million men, and perhaps a war, could be secured or lost—is displayed in its vivid complexity. Behind the visible decision to authorize the invasion are multiple layers of numbers, calculations, science, laws, disputes, errors, guesswork, gut-feelings, and instincts. The dispersal of authority into this complex network, we might say with Ian Hacking, is one specific means by which the sovereign is lent objectivity via number.[3] In the sovereign decisions on the exception, it is precisely the declaration of emergency and special measures that clears space for the dispersal of decision into multiple authorities, plural enumerations. If William Connolly's sense of an exception as the *that* which decides, the that "comprised of a plurality of forces," is to be brought into conversation with the rich histories of science and statistics of Hacking or Lorraine Daston, then what is needed is an analysis of how authorizations multiply under the positional sovereignty of the state.[4] How, in short, do multiple layers of number and calculation authorize, and become authorized by, the sovereign decision on exception?

In this chapter I focus on specific instances of the designation of exceptional times, the institution of necessary measures, and the authorization of particular forms of number. As in Foden's world of forecasting to "modify the extent of the unexpected," I am interested in how specific forms of probability have been contested or adopted as credible for use in apparently objective sovereign decisions. On the one hand, the "approximate" speculative knowledge of commerce and economy—otherwise thought to be a poor basis for a security judgment—appears to be invited into government techniques during times of war. On the other, it is precisely by means of sovereign enrollment in the strategies of war that economic knowledges of circulation and laissez-faire are afforded the kind of credibility otherwise reserved for science, medicine, and law. The question of whether Ryman's number could be credibly deployed in a sovereign decision is a question of the allowable extent of the incorporation of possible elements within probabilistic statistical models. Forecasting the weather five days in advance in the 1940s, and even today, demands more than statistical extrapolation—there are gaps, and these gaps are filled with computer models, subjective probabilities, equations, disagreement, intuition, and expectation. Likewise, the absence of long-term historical "threat" data on events such as terrorism has encouraged more speculative and imaginative forms of calculation. Where data on past events are incomplete or absent, probabilistic knowledge is loosened to incorporate assumptions about that which is merely possible. I illustrate my point in this chapter with reference to two such instances when forms of probability and statistical knowledge were enrolled within the complex of sovereignty: the accounting practices placed at the service of the state in the governing of population in World War II, and the computer science and consulting practices enlisted within the so-called war on terror of the twenty-first century.

The histories that I discuss here, though, should not be interpreted as a linear course from what Stephen Collier calls the "archival-statistical" model, exhibited by the move from Price Waterhouse in Britain during the 1940s to the data-led consulting of IBM and others in the twenty-first century.[5] In 2002 IBM acquired the consulting arm of Pricewaterhouse-Coopers, making it possible for them to promise the "integrated business solutions" of information technology coupled with systems consulting. In a limited sense, there is a common thread linking the wartime accounting of Price Waterhouse to the contemporary homeland security solutions of IBM—effectively they became the same organization. It is a thread that I hope will dispel some of the myths of a post-9/11 radical break with the past and turn to science and technology. My concern, though, is not with the telling of a single linear story of authorizations at times of war but rather with the distinctive practices of enumeration and statistical analysis that make the authorization of exception possible. In Britain during the 1940s, the state's deferral to "expert" systems of identification and classification was strictly a "preventative" measure, designed to prevent future shortages of vital commodities.[6] Such prevention, as Giorgio Agamben understands it, "prescribes and produces order," in contrast to preemptive measures that "intervene and guide disorder."[7] In the contemporary authorization of possibilistic knowledge, like Foden's modification of the unexpected, the apparent order (of the weather, economy, security, and so on) is merely one statistical representation among many others. "We have to alter our data gathering," urges Foden's Ryman, "make sure we realize what we are looking at, and be prepared to approximate where we cannot measure."[8] It is precisely this altering of data gathering, to approximate beyond the limit point of measurement, the very modification of the unexpected future, that characterizes the contemporary enrollment of systems of numbers into security.

Necessary Measures: Counting, Accounting, and War

In his discussion of the relationship of the state of exception to war, civil war, and insurrection, Giorgio Agamben describes the "transformation of a provisional and exceptional measure" designed for circumstances of emergency into a "technique of government."[9] The contemporary state of exception, via the emergency measures of two world wars has, he argues, witnessed the expansion of executive powers and the gradual erosion of their boundary with juridical and legislative powers. For the exception to, as Walter Benjamin predicted, "become the rule" and enter the domain of governing daily life, the institution of temporary necessary measures itself needs to become routinized, even ordinary.[10] The world wars served an important function in this regard, providing "a laboratory for the testing and honing" of emergency measures so that they may be deployed as more permanent practices of governmental control.[11] Understood thus, war is the visible face of the authorization of exceptional measures, while the laboratory it affords to techniques of governing provides a more durable space in which exceptional measures may be lent greater permanence. Agamben devotes much of his work to the exposition of how emergency and necessity emerge as a means of authorizing a perennial exception. The question of *measures*, though, or the means of counting and accounting for emergency that are developed in the laboratory of war, has received much less critical attention. Consider, for example, Agamben's citation of Franklin D.

Roosevelt's emergency powers for fighting economic crisis during the Great Depression:

> I assume unhesitatingly the leadership of this great army of our people dedicated to a disciplined attack upon our common problems. . . . I am prepared under my constitutional duty to recommend the *measures* that a stricken Nation in the midst of a stricken world may require. . . . But in the event that the Congress shall fail to take the *necessary measures* . . . I shall ask for the one remaining instrument to meet the crisis—broad Executive power to *wage war against the emergency*, as great as the power that would be given to me if we were in fact invaded by a foreign foe.[12]

Agamben's focus on how war is used to declare an exception is not limited to the special circumstances of military war itself but extends to the strategic imagination of all governmental problems as problems of war. To wage war against the emergency is to govern the population as one would govern a stricken and impoverished household—to manage scarcity, to allocate finite resource in ways that differentiate between competing claims. Thus the exceptional granting of extended executive powers extends to the "unlimited power to regulate and control every aspect of the economic life of the country."[13] The necessary measures are not merely the military means to wage war but are precisely of the economy itself, dwelling within the capacity to govern what circulates, to decide what moves and what or who should have movement circumscribed. And yet the economic life Agamben alludes to here is not simply, as he seems to suggest, one distinct domain for the use of warlike exceptional powers. It is, rather, one of the most significant conduits for the authorization of new authorities and the very defining of new powers. The governing of economic life becomes an element within the field of sovereign power, such that the measures of economy define what is possible for the sovereign decision. In short, when considering questions of necessary, provisional, or emergency measures, it may be as important to think about what is meant by "measures" as it is to reflect on the nature of emergency.

If one interrogates the measures that are instituted as necessary measures amid war—the systems of enumeration, accounting, and measurement— the idea of exceptional measures that become the norm begins to look quite different. For the measures, derived as they are from economy, are always already normal or of the norm as such. What are the prosaic and ordinary measures of necessary measures? What is the system of accounting in the designation of emergency powers and how is this accounting made possible? To declare a "war against the emergency" and instigate "necessary measures" for a "stricken Nation," it is necessary to have a means of knowing the population. The "making up" of a people, a population, a national economy, is made possible, as Ian Hacking has put it, via "the enumeration of people and their habits."[14] The sovereign authority to declare exception and institute necessary measures is not meaningful without a measure that makes population classifiable, countable, and, in a sense, accountable for their norms, habits, and behaviors. As Jacques Derrida proposes in relation to how the full force of law is authorized, there is a "mystical foundation of authority," a credibility that is ascribed to the actions of police who are not the police, "faceless figures" who are not content only to enforce the law but "to intervene whenever the legal situation isn't clear, to guarantee security."[15] The institution of necessary measures produces new authorities who intervene to promise to guarantee security—statisticians, accountants, and actuaries whose economic savoir becomes part of the field of sovereignty. As temporary, necessary measures appear to become permanent ways of governing, the laboratory of war authorizes plural "faceless figures" to refine the exceptions and exemptions.

Authorizing by Numbers: The Accountants in World War II

Throughout the first eighteen months of the Second World War, the British government did not institute emergency measures in the domestic economy. In terms of the rationing of food and the regulation of wartime food supply and commodities pricing, the government was "limited both in knowledge and preparations."[16] In part, the absence of a set of emergency measures for the management of possible future shortages is explainable in terms of the absence of a defined problem of scarcity. In the known past event of the First World War, the prices and supply of non-food consumer goods were not subject to controls. "The problems of the Second World War existed in the First World War," documents the official civil history of wartime measures, "but the controls did not."[17] It is this process of the identification of a problem, a set of deficiencies in past practices, that is integral to the authorization of new techniques of enumeration. Economic problems, in the strict sense of problems of circulation, supply, and exchange, do not simply appear as defects to be remedied, they must instead be represented as problems, made recognizable so that, as Peter Miller has put it, "another way of calculating can be made available."[18] In Britain during the 1940s, the identification of the problem hinged on the question of number—on the perceived inadequacy of data, the paucity of information, and the inability to deal with future risks. Faced with the problems of how to administer civilian production and consumption under wartime conditions of restricted foreign exchange, shipping, transportation and fuel, raw materials and labor, the British Board of Trade defined a problem of accounting: how to account for, and thereby control and limit, the civilian consumption of goods.[19] The collection of accurate statistical data on the population was, in effect, thought to be the condition of possibility for making wartime decisions in the face of an unknown future.

When, in the early 1940s, the British Board of Trade began to devise an accounting system for the emergency rationing of commodities, they identified their problem in terms of statistical knowledge of the population. The board's "deficient statistics" on past household consumption, it was held, made it all but impossible for the government to adopt "a forward-looking mind" capable of the foresight for "advance appreciation of wartime problems."[20] In the absence of reliable statistical data on past patterns of consumption—so went the argument—decisions on rationing could take no meaningful account of likely future effects. How, for example, could decisions be made about the regulation of clothing manufacture for the armed forces and for utility civilian use in the absence of meaningful archives of past data on textiles manufacture? How could standardized rationing levels be established without statistical knowledge of how much flour or butter or how many yards of fabric a household normally consumes? What was government to make of the "apparent variations in need" among a civilian population whose "production effort" underpinned "the power of the fighting services"?[21] If rationing was to mark an exception from the norms of consumption in daily life, then how could the exception be decided without knowledge about "what is normal" or "what is happening"? Such a deviation from the norm could not be achieved, it was argued, without "up-to-date statistical information," "sample surveys," and "census data."[22] In short, the sovereign capacity to decide on the exception relied in large part upon a knowledge of economy and household that would otherwise be impenetrable to the state.

The sovereign power of a state, of course, is substantially defined by its enumeration of population, it's "*Statistik*" or the body count on which it founds its authority.[23] The "imagined community" of the nation-state has had particular recourse to numbers in order that it might "know itself and its power."[24] At the outbreak of war in 1939, the British government's traditional means of enumeration—the census, last conducted in 1935—was already four years old. The Board of Trade found itself unable to exercise its emergency powers in the economy without the objective knowledge that it assumed to reside in statistical data on the population. Such was the "magnitude of sacrifices" required from the public, that it was held to be "crucial to achieve a more accurate count than the census alone can supply."[25] Of course, the practice of conducting a census has historically been central to the authorization of sovereign power. The censor—from the Latin *censere*, meaning to appraise or judge—was the Roman magistrate with authority to take a census of adult male citizens and their property in order to calculate taxation and military obligations and to assess political status. In the absence of a census or political body count, the censor's ability to censure, exclude, prohibit, or ban is circumscribed.[26] Described by Ian Hacking as "an affair more of colonies than of homelands," the census afforded the colonial state a means of classifying, counting, and categorizing their subjects.[27] The historical emergence of body counts to enumerate and account for colonial subjects, as Arjun Appadurai suggests in his discussion of systems of classification in colonial India, disciplines the "unruly body," bringing it back into a zone of manageability, recuperating it and accounting for it within "normal" ranges of acceptability.[28]

In many ways, the wartime Board of Trade sought precisely to redeploy colonial forms of body counting within the homeland on the grounds of exceptional times. In the absence of accurate census data, the board authorized accountants from the firm Price Waterhouse to devise techniques for accounting for the population and to administer new restrictions on supply: "The need to control and monitor the workings of an economy at war necessitated the recruitment of accountants as administrators and advisers, many being granted considerable *executive authority*."[29]

Indeed, the Price Waterhouse accountants who were to be seconded to the Board of Trade from 1940 had, in the 1920s, devised the accounting systems of the Indian railway companies. The government turned to accounting practices for a system of numbers that could both reveal information about the habits and behaviors of the population and devise techniques to govern production and consumption. Accountants were to become the "body of men who played an invaluable part in all the Board of Trade's essays in control."[30] Though today it would scarcely surprise us to think of accountants within government, in the 1940s this remained an extraordinary break with the prevailing political suspicion of accountancy. The board's accounting staff grew from 2,000 in 1939 to 6,500 by 1942, with accountants seconded from commercial industry and expatriate British accountants practising in the European offices of firms returning to work in Whitehall. Accountants had, from the beginning of the Second World War, been designated a reserved profession and exempted from military service so that their expertise in auditing, pricing, and costing might be deployed in essential military industries. As the British government faced the pressing questions of how to manage economies of civil industry and rationing, though, accountants found themselves called back from other duties and seconded to government. W. E. Parker, a Price Waterhouse accountant, recounts how he was summoned from military exercise in Northumberland to report to Whitehall:

> How could I desert my battalion, leaving them to go off and fight and probably be killed while I sat in Whitehall? . . . On the other hand I had no doubt that I was a much more competent accountant than I should ever be a soldier. . . . I was very heavily occupied indeed . . . how to prevent traders from concentrating on the higher priced goods when they had only a limited quality to sell; how to release whole factories for war production; how to make certain there would be enough supplies to meet the clothing ration, unexpectedly strained as it was.[31]

On his redeployment from the military to Whitehall. Parker noted the similarities between "the strategies of troop deployment" and the techniques for managing "wartime production." In both spheres the accountant confronted a common problem: how to govern the circulation of complex and mobile people and things. Michel Foucault differentiates the strict juridical system of governing scarcity, one that "prevents food shortage, ensures that it does not take place, price control, the prohibition of hoarding," from what he calls the "physiocratic doctrine" that makes the "freedom of commerce and the circulation of grain" the fundamental "principle of economic government."[32] When the accounting experts in the governing of economic circulation were invited into emergency planning, we see an extraordinary fusion of the strict prevention of shortage ("prohibition of private food wastage") with the governing of rates of usage ("the statistical position of foodstuff").[33] With the physiocratic doctrine, the world of economy that Foucault suggests "must be obscure to the sovereign" begins to resemble a form of Statistik, a useable form of numbers that "gives the sovereign the possibility of exact knowledge of everything taking place within his country," a form of numbers that is integral to the sovereign capacity to decide exception itself.[34] Thus even the wartime management of scarcity ceases to be strictly a matter of preventing in advance or prohibiting and harnesses instead the economic knowledge of circulation precisely to govern the effects, to govern the reality of fluctuations. The circulations, systems of exchange, flows of money, fluctuations that can have "no economic sovereign," as Foucault has it, can nonetheless supply forms of knowledge of life itself, a life of norms and practices "taking place" that would be otherwise unavailable to the sovereign decision.

The secondment of professional accountants to government in World War II not only signaled a reconfigured relationship between sovereignty and economy, between state and commercial authority. Importantly, the engagement of accountants in the techniques and technologies of war also authorized the expertise of the enumerators in new ways. During the First World War, when the deployment of data and statistics was almost entirely absent from the emergency governing of civilian spheres, the accounting profession did not have reserved status. The pages of the profession's journal the *Accountant* records a public debate as to whether "a duly qualified professional accountant could serve his country better in the present crisis than by enlisting."[35] By 1916 the *Accountant* was "pleased to note" that the "professional knowledge and training of accountants" was beginning to be "recognised as of more value to the state employed on technical work than when used in the firing line."[36] The First World War saw only a limited public acceptance of the authority of accounting expertise, though, and there was extensive public criticism of the eventual inclusion of accountants among the certified occupations.[37]

The turn to statistical data as a means of managing the home-front war efforts of the Second World War not only provided the calculative basis of an economy of exception but also was an important moment in the authorization of accounting techniques. Though the apparent executive powers of accountants in wartime were temporary in the strict sense of a designated exception, they were more durable with regard to the state's lasting enrollment of techniques of enumeration that exceeded the cataloging of censuses and surveys. "The printing of numbers," writes Ian Hacking, was "a surface effect," beneath which lay new techniques and technologies of enumeration and "new bureaucracies with the authority and continuity to deploy the technology."[38] The scientific expertise that the accountants aspired to when they looked to the professional credibility of medicine and law was afforded through the exceptional measures of war. The legitimacy granted to accounting authority called up a science of mechanical objectivity and probability that promised the state actionable data to deal with an uncertain future.[39] Through the deployment of data, costings, and justifications for the controversial clothing rationing programs, the accountants standardized models of counting that endured beyond the limits of the designated state of emergency. As Theodore Porter has argued, the statistical knowledge of accounting creates new calculative spaces where "widely scattered people are induced to count, measure, and calculate in the same way."[40] In this way the residue of special measures persists beyond the emergency itself and into more permanent practices of governing. A system of accounting, taking a measure, is not simply a way of costing and apportioning the world, it is also a representation of the world, of what we think we can know about the world. A changed system of accounting does not simply change the measure but also the world and how we see it, how we apportion it, how we differentiate and divide it.

Deciding by Data: Technology Consulting and the "War on Terror"

In 1941 Price Waterhouse accountants introduced a utility scheme for controlling the quality, price, and materials of wartime clothing, deciding upon their estimates by "multiplying up the output of Marks & Spencer."[41] In the absence of reliable statistical data on past rates of production and consumption, the accountants turned to already existing commercial knowledge. Fifty years later, it was to be the commercial data of the British clothing retailer Marks & Spencer (M&S) that would again decisively shape the most pervasive and influential contemporary sovereign adoption of expert enumeration: data mining. In 1992 the IBM research fellow Rakesh Agrawal, widely considered to have pioneered the techniques of identifying useable patterns in large volumes of data—data mining—met for lunch with a senior executive of M&S. Working on the IBM Almaden Research Center's Quest program, Agrawal was interested in "the ability to find patterns in accumulated data."[42] The M&S executive with whom Agrawal had lunch, meanwhile, explained his frustration that vast quantities of point-of-sale data were collected on the daily transactions in their stores but that they "did not know what to do with that data." The research paper that resulted from the meeting between Agrawal and M&S, published in 1993, outlined the principles of data mining to the world, illustrating the utility of consumer algorithms with experiments using M&S data. It has become the world's most widely cited research on the techniques of data mining and, arguably, the most significant contemporary economic knowledge of transaction and circulation made available to the field of sovereign power.

Though the techniques of data mining may have their origins in the most banal and ordinary aspects of everyday life, it is here in the minutiae of prosaic transactions that the contemporary logic of data and decision becomes possible. "Consider a supermarket with a large collection of items," writes Agrawal. "Typical business decisions might include what to put on sale, how to design coupons, how to place merchandise on shelves in order to maximise profit, etc."[43] Conventionally, the analysis of past data, Agrawal argues, has been used to make statistically informed decisions about future business. At the point of his intervention, however, computer databases made available only global data about cumulative sales over a given period of time. In effect, this historical data could only be used to identify broad trends and to track forward from past patterns. The relationship between past, present, and future was such that data on past purchase events were extrapolated into the future in order to make commercial decisions in the present. However, "progress in bar-code technology," Agrawal finds, has spatially relocated data from store level to item level, making it "possible to store *basket* data on items purchased on a per-transaction basis."[44] The overwhelming significance of data on a basket of items—a transaction—is that for the first time inferences can be made about the probable relationships between those items, patterns identified within and between transactions. In contrast with strict statistical extrapolation from historical data—for example, on Saturdays 60 percent of sales are foodstuffs, or in June the sale of swimwear increased to y—the data miners screen transactions "for association rules between sets of items" and "present an efficient algorithm for that purpose."[45] Agrawal's examples of commercial questions that the algorithm could model include such prosaic queries as: What pattern of purchases is associated with Diet Coke? What pattern of items has to be sold with sausages in order for it to be likely that mustard will also be sold?

What proportion of transactions that include bread and butter also include milk? The deployment of algorithmic calculations in this context signals an important move from the effort to predict future trends on the basis of statistical extrapolation of historical data to a means of preempting the future, drawing probable futures into imminent and immediate commercial decision.

From the IBM Almaden team's initial experiments with M&S data, the use of customer relationship management (CRM) data techniques have become ubiquitous to the governing of large commercial enterprises.[46] The extension of databases from point-of-sale transactions to loyalty cards, store cards, and credit cards has witnessed the data-mining elements of a business become as profitable as the commercial sales. How, though, did Agrawal's promise to his client—of "improved functionality in taking advantage of this information"—migrate from economic techniques of data collection and analysis to the domain of the sovereign decision? To understand the "improved functionality" that data mining is now promising to sovereign decisions, it is useful to consider how the commercial experts in mathematics and computing brought their systems to bear on problems of security.

At a U.S. House subcommittee hearing in February 2002, a panel of commercial software engineers, mathematicians, and consultants, including IBM and Accenture, gave testimony on how their existing data-mining techniques could be put to use in the war on terror. Notably, their reflections on the events of 9/11 signalled the already present residue of a future threat available in existing databases. "Our enemies are hiding in open and available information," they reported, "but currently this is stovepiped in separate databases." Had algorithmic search capacities been in place, they proposed, "9/11 could have been predicted and averted."[47] Like the commercial enterprise seeking the unexpected habits of a consumer yet to come, the experts testified to government, national security would require knowledge of the unanticipated threat yet to come. In their final report, the subcommittee concluded that "had information coordination technology been properly in place before September 11, the preattack activities of the hijackers could have been identified and prevented. There may have been a different outcome."[48] To be clear, it is not that the advent of a war on terror ushered in a raft of novel and unprecedented security technologies. In fact, quite the reverse is true—the events of 9/11, and the exceptional measures that were so quickly declared, actually cleared space for the sovereign enrollment of mundane, ordinary techniques that had been used in the gathering of everyday transactions of bread and sausages for some eight years.

The authorization of the mathematics of algorithms in the aftermath of 9/11, as we will see in chapter 2, has fundamentally reoriented the sovereign decisions made on the lives of people. The primary allure of Agrawal's data mining for the state, was that, just as his techniques offered M&S and Walmart the capacity to use transactions data in order to act on the basis of future unknown consumers, they promise the state the possibility of deploying transactions data preemptively, in advance of a possible event. In 2002, when the United States' leading mathematicians met at the National Research Council to discuss "the mathematical sciences' role in homeland security," Rakesh Agrawal reflected on the "qualitative similarities" of commercial and security applications of his particular system of data mining:

> What is current state-of-the-art in data mining? Well, commercial applications which you can characterize as behavior recognition using transactional data—examples are fraud detection, credit card usage, tax evaders, or churn analysis, where you look for customers who are likely to quit your services in the future. Now, homeland security problems are very similar qualitatively to many of the commercial applications. But they are much harder, the stakes are higher. If your data mining algorithm on a consumer database doesn't quite get all of the customers who might be attracted to your product, well, your client is going to realize slightly less profit and probably won't even know it. Here, if we make a mistake it is highly visible and can lead to catastrophes.[49]

In his discussion of the potential and the limits of his data mining for security applications, Agrawal notes that "we cannot always rely on data from the past," suggesting that "the profile of a suicide bomber has completely changed from what it once was."[50] In the absence of data on past events, Agrawal's techniques draw together the relations across pieces of data from otherwise unrelated databases. Thus, existing commercial data on transactions are assembled together with, for example, images from websites or text from Internet chat rooms. Presenting the possibilities afforded to homeland security by data mining, Agrawal displays an exemplar of a "text reveal" technique used on a social network analysis of a possible terrorist network:

Can we do it? Number of items is extremely large, number of transactions is extremely large. You are talking all of the possible names
that could become items. You are trying to find out relations that
might exist. So, here combining text data and images. This is a site in
Pakistan and what is happening here is these sort of different characteristics we are interested in, they are written into the rules. It has
things like financial support, Islamic leaders and so on . . . so we can
get a profile for the site, and a series of leads to other second level
associated sites.[51]

The emphasis is on the breaking down of data into component elements
that can be recombined and written into the algorithmic rules, such that
one might "find out relations that might exist." There can be little doubt
that Agrawal's work at IBM Almaden has decisively shaped contemporary
security, quite fundamentally changing the "backroom" calculations of the
exception and the capacity of the state to decide on the basis of the merely
possible. In 2010 IBM was the leading contractor in U.S. homeland security markets, exceeding the value of the contracts of more conventional
defense companies such as Lockheed Martin and Raytheon; IBM's Intelligent Miner software is deployed across the U.S. Transportation Security
Administration's networks and is the key platform for border security data
mining; and IBM software designers and consultants led on the £15 million
pilot projects Semaphore and Iris to biometrically secure UK borders. The
logic of the mathematics of algorithms, it's seductive promise to be able to
identify the relations of AB in association with XY, where W is also present,
has been authorized rapidly in the context of the war on terror. As Agrawal
himself asserts, "history does not repeat, it changes abruptly. This is exactly
what happened on September 11."[52] Put simply, where the state has relied
upon the tracking forward of past patterns, the sudden changes and erup-
tive events will always be missed—strict mechanical probability fails. What
was wanted was a system that could identify the incipient, the potential,
the merely possible. As the U.S. Department of Justice reported in 2002
on the use of data mining in identifying possible links between suspicious
transactions and behaviors: "Through what has come to be called 'data
mining' and predictive technology, we seek to identify potential terrorists.
In a search for terrorists and terrorist cells, we are employing technology
that was previously utilized primarily by the business community."[53]

Since 9/11 data mining, and its associated technologies of software design and risk consulting, has become the mathematical mainstay in the war on terror. Yet precisely how has the specific turn to private commercial data systems become authorized to act as though sovereign? Certainly, this is not adequately explained by accounts of the "privatization of security" or by the simple outsourcing of state security to commercial providers. Executive decisions made on the basis of data mining—detention at international borders, stopping or seizing financial transactions and shipping containers, refusing asylum and immigration applications—authorize a mode of calculation as though it had juridical authority. What needs to be thought about, as Derrida reminds us, is what it is that "permits judgment," what it is that "judgment itself authorizes."[54] How is it that the knowledge gained via data mining becomes authorized to act and permitted to judge?

Let us return to Giles Foden's novel *Turbulence* by way of opening up this problem of authorizing novel forms of enumeration and calculation. Foden's protagonist Henry Meadows contrasts the conventional statistics of analog weather forecasting with the capacities of subjective inference: "The analogue method involved selecting weather types from past periods that most closely matched the current weather and seeing what happened before. It was a bit like case law. The future is extrapolated from the past, with the forecast extending to as long as six days ahead. . . . But his system was different, he didn't apply past situations religiously. He allowed a kind of jiggle, a wrinkle, into his system, a space for his own intuition."[55] In Foden's novel, and in order for the sovereign decision to invade to be authorized on the basis of a forecast, the strict extrapolation of past events could not be applied. For the tracking forward of past weather patterns into the future afforded insufficient information about the twists, turns, and surprises within the necessary five-day period. The strict probability of future incidences of past events is loosened—a kind of "wrinkle" allowed for, a space of intuition opened up.

It is precisely this invitation of the intuitive and the speculative within the calculation of probability that characterises the contemporary authorization of algorithmic judgments. For each of Agrawal's rules, for example, he stresses the importance of a Bayesian numeric "confidence" score, an indicator of what he refers to as "conditional probability" that two or more elements are indeed correlated. In her seminal works on the histories of probability, Lorraine Daston characterises twentieth-century developments in inference statistics as "harking back to the reasonable calculus of the eighteenth century," inviting inductive inference back into calculation.[56] In this sense a probability of statistically objective numbers is a distinctively nineteenth-century phenomenon, with both eighteenth-century rules of chance and contemporary forms of inference more open to the incorporation of what Foden calls "a space for intuition." In the use of Bayesian inference models, for example, some of the concerns that were driven out by the nineteenth-century drive for objective numbers are reincorporated, such that "a new generation of probabilists seek to translate expert judgments into numbers and rules."[57] With the data-mining probabilists seeking to, as Agrawal has it, "make patterns actionable," we see a form of probability that embraces the subjective, allows for discretion and choices on the part of the observer, opens up to let change happen. As the historians of probability remind us: "Subjective and objective probabilities coexist peacefully in applications like weather forecasting, where both past frequency of precipitation and the individual forecaster's personal conviction about tomorrow's possible downpour come into play."[58]

In sum, it is not the case that possibilistic and inferential forms of numbers drive out or displace probability in contemporary security. Rather, multiple forms of probability coexist within a complex of authorized forms of possibilistic knowledge, past frequencies, and personal convictions, which all come into play together.

The Force of Law: Norm and Deviation

For Giorgio Agamben, the specific technology of the state of exception is not "the confusion of powers," executive and juridical, which he says has been "all too strongly insisted upon," but rather the "separation of 'force of law' from the law."[59] At the root of the distinction between rule of law and force of law, at least as Agamben sees it, is the opposition between the norms of law, or the norms that are enshrined in law, and "the norms of the realization of law." Authorities may act, then with the force of law if "it pleased the sovereign," and, though they may not adhere to legal norms, they actively deploy the norm in order to realize law, to enforce or to control. Put simply, it is exactly the suspension of the rule of law that allows for the full force of law to be exercised—that force itself always already lawful because it is underwritten by the sovereign power to decide law. "In the decision on the state of exception," writes Agamben, "the norm is suspended or even annulled, but what is at issue in this suspension is, once again, the creation of a situation that makes the application of the norm possible."[60]

In order for a state of emergency to become normalized, the normal rule of law is suspended so that the radical norm—the norm that divides, excepts, exempts, or excludes—can be instituted.

If it is the case that Agamben's exception is more teeming with decision, judgment, calculation, and data than we have heretofore acknowledged, then an important element of this lively exception will be the capacity to decide on the norm and, significantly, on deviation from the norm. "The moment of truth in Agamben's account," observes William Connolly, lies in his signaling of the thriving array of late modern technologies of the expert: "corporate advisers, physicians, biologists and geneticists," enlisted and authorized to apply the norm.[61] Yet, of these experts in the application of the norm, we know very little, particularly when it comes to how ideas about the norm and deviation from the norm become a means of enforcing law. If, as Rob Walker suggests, we find ourselves caught up in "radically novel forms of norm, normativity and normalization," then how are these novel forms of the norm made possible?[62] In what ways are *measures* of the norm and deviation from the norm becoming the authorized basis for decision?

Nikolas Rose and Mariana Valverde have argued compellingly that what we are witnessing is categorically not some form of periodization from the institutions of law to governance via norms. It is not a strict change from the rule of law to the administrative governing by the norm, underwritten by the full force of law. In their careful genealogy of the relations between law and norms, they see "the authority of authority" being consistently "established and defended through alliances between the different legitimacies conferred by law and expertise."[63] There is a kind of iterative complex or assemblage of authorities that produces a hybridization of law and the norm in contemporary society. In the sections that follow I return to my two examples of "wartime" alliances between state and commercial knowledges in order to better understand how expertise is authorized—via new forms of the norm—to act with the force of law. In each instance I am interested in how proxy sovereigns emerge that can decide on thresholds of normality and deviance, limits of admissibility to citizenship and personhood. As we will see in later chapters, it is these lines, written in new ways, designating normal and abnormal, safe and risky, inside and outside, that characterize the contemporary politics of possibility.

Price Waterhouse accountants, authorized to act with the sovereign-backed force of law in Britain during the Second World War, did not simply apply their economic systems to problems of public order and administration. Their systems of accounting became the basis for exceptional rationing measures, with the effect that techniques of calculation became law, enacted with the force of law. As one accountant seconded to government recalls, "the accountants provided answers to the state's questions and the lawyers embodied the answers in legal orders."[64] The relationship to law did not, however, end with their advice to legal authority; it extended into investigation and enforcement: "the accountants worked in teams under the guidance of an ex-police officer, making test purchases without coupons or with loose coupons, providing ocular evidence to traders that they were being watched."[65] In a conventional sense, the accountants were authorized to engage in the surveillance of the population and, importantly, to provide incontrovertible and objective "ocular evidence" of infraction. The idea of expertise as dwelling within the neutrality of an external observer— expert "eyes"—is particularly powerful here. Indeed, the history of modern objectivity is itself bound up with "the sciences of the eye"—the ability to observe and visualize a problem through distanciated and objective eyes.[66] Faced with both the impossibility of total surveillance of the wartime economy and the improbability of closing all black market loopholes in the system, the authorization of the measures relied upon the credibility of claims to enumerative expertise. Public disquiet at the "uneven sacrifices" of an "unfair" rationing system, which placed "disproportionate burdens" on the poor, was met with a greater emphasis on the publication of the accountants' investigations into fraud in the system.[67] Numerical and pictorial evidence of the grounds of expert decisions became central to the claim to statistical credibility. The teams of investigative accountants designated "goods that had illegally reached the home market," "bogus quota holders," "wanted traders," and "faked auditors certificates," actively writing the lines between licit and illicit, legal and illegal, safe and dangerous.

The capacity to decide upon the norm, on the exemptions and exceptions from the norm, is a crucial element of the authorization of data systems. For Ian Hacking, as the "avalanche of printed numbers" pervades society in the nineteenth century, new forms of law come into being that are "analogous to the laws of nature" and the physical world but "pertain to people."[68] These new laws governing the conduct of people, expressed in terms of mathematical formulae, make their judgments on the basis of "normalcy and deviations from the norm."[69] Hacking's work documents the important nineteenth-century moves from the census-style collection of "large number" data on people, things, monies, or armies, for example, to the targeting of regularities and patterns in volumes of data. In effect, the norm comes to the fore in the governing of society when it is proposed that the "normal" distributions and deviations of aggregate data are replicated in representative samples and even in individual bodies.

The nineteenth-century Belgian statistician Adolphe Quetelet pioneered modern thinking on statistical norm and deviation. He was intrigued by the regularities and patterns present in apparently random data that were replicated across multiple social scales. The unpredictability of an event that disrupts the social fabric, such as a criminal act, contrasted with the apparent regularity and patterns of such events over space and time: "Why should something so lawless as murder, so disorderly and irrational as suicide, occur in almost uniform numbers from year to year? What form of fatality could drive people to do away with themselves according to so strict a budget?"[70] Quetelet's nineteenth-century questions of order and disorder in society were concerned with what he assumed to be underlying social tendencies or regularities "behind" the numbers. He observed the Gaussian distribution, or "bell-shaped curve," of the physical sciences—showing an assumed "normal" distribution that clusters around the mean—and applied it to human and social phenomena. As Lorraine Daston notes, "in every domain, Quetelet saw the archetype of the normal curve behind the great welter of data."[71] The behaviors, physical attributes, and habits of people in Quetelet's "social physics" adhered to his magical bell curve, with an identifiable norm which he called *l'homme moyen*, the "average man."[72] As Hacking describes it, Quetelet "gave us the mean and the bell-shaped curve as fundamental indices of the human condition."[73]

It is not only that the norm becomes a means of measuring or accounting for society and social behavior but also that it becomes a means of creating and ordering a future society. Quetelet's contemporary, Francis Galton— founder of the biometric school of statistical research—was interested not strictly in the norm as average or mean but in deviation as exception to the norm.[74] Galton's vision of a useful statistical science was one that could create measures capable of ordering society, "converting a mob into an orderly array."[75] In this sense Galton took a step that Quetelet did not: he offered the idea of the normal distribution—exhibited in photographic evidence and fingerprints, for example—as a means of policing society (see chapter 4). By the early twentieth century, according to Matt Metsuda, the measurement of bodies and their translation into numerical data that could be distributed by telegraph to multiple authorities had become a new mode of securing the state from the abnormal or deviant.[76]

Of course, the rise of the norm and deviation from the norm not only makes society and social data appear in new ways but also authorizes new authorities to calculate the norm and identify deviations. The moves made by Quetelet and his contemporaries marked the beginning of a process of authorization of judgments on conduct, habits, and traits contained within statistical data on society. In his Collège de France lectures of 1975, Foucault describes the emergence of what he calls "techniques of normalization" in which expert opinion acts with the force of, and in advance of, juridical decision.[77] In his comments on medico-legal expertise, Foucault suggests that inferential knowledge about the "normal" correlates of "poverty," "failure," or "instability" allows experts "to show how the individual already resembles his crime before he has committed it."[78] The appeal to expert witness is akin to Quetelet's observations of regularities in statistics on crime and suicide—it seeks out the normal laws of human conduct and identifies deviation from such norms. Citing expert psychiatric assessments presented in criminal trial, Foucault writes that "as experts we do not have to say whether he committed the crime he is accused of." It is the role of the expert to "assume he did commit it" and "explain how he would have committed it, if he had done so."[79]

The position of expert authority in assessing the norms and deviations of human conduct, then, is to judge the conduct in advance of juridical judgment. To a degree, this is how the expertise of the wartime accountants acted in relation to legal authority. The accountants, on the basis of statistical knowledges about "normal" distributions and "average" individuals and households, identified deviant practices ("underground" economies, "bogus" coupons, "fraudulent" claims for additional rations, and so on), and the lawmakers drafted new legislation to make these practices illegal. In this sense the authorization of accounting expertise made it possible for particular juridical decisions to be reached and for judgments to be made. However, it is not until the Quetelet-inspired statistical science of probability, with its bell-curve distributions and standard deviations, met the inferential and speculative logics of the late twentieth century that the norm became a new basis for judgment—what I describe in chapter 2 as the mobile norm. The contemporary turn to expert data in the defining of norms emphasizes not what can be strictly predicted by statistics but what is possible, what decisions can be taken on the basis of possibility and in the face of indeterminacy.

Judgment by Computation

No public decision, no risk analysis, no environmental impact, no military strategy can be conducted without decision couched in terms of probabilities. By covering opinion with a veneer of objectivity, *we replace judgement by computation.*
—Ian Hacking, *The Taming of Chance*, 4

There can be no sovereign decision—mundane or strategic—without probabilities, without judgment by computation, as Ian Hacking has put it. Though he is surely correct to emphasize the veneer of objectivity that is afforded to the sovereign by enumeration, it is not strictly the case that judgment is *replaced by computation* but that judgments are *made via computation*, by the imaginative calculation of the possibility, and not the strict probability, of a future event. The computational judgments that we are seeing emerge in the present day turn toward data-led security are predominantly judgments made on the basis of computer-mined data. As I have described, the leading exponents of data mining sought precisely to replace the ideas of "mechanical laws" between items in a set of data, or standard distributions along a bell curve, with "association rules" between transactions across databases.

Indeed, Rakesh Agrawal's early work made the case for data mining on the basis of the ability to "generate all significant association rules" between apparently disparate elements of data.[80] The association rule is not strictly a probabilistic measure of the relations among elements, but it is also possibilistic. That is to say, it supplies degrees of likelihood that do not adhere to the bell-shaped curve but can incorporate the "outliers" that would otherwise inhabit the forgotten tails of the bell curve. Algorithms are mathematical maps of associational relationships, what J. R. Quinlan calls "decision trees," in which each subsequent branch represents a possible connection.[81] The virtue of the decision tree for its proponents is that in large volumes of data it can "screen out" "noisy and incomplete information," in order to follow the specified branches, while sustaining the relations to apparently less significant items.[82] A simple commercial algorithm might find, for example, that where a value xyz is present (let us say when a cinema ticket x, for a specified film y, is purchased at a given time z), a second value p (let us say a meal bought in a foyer fast-food restaurant at another given time) is associated with a 40 percent likelihood. Significantly, the algorithm establishes the associations between x, y, z, and p, not as definitive norms but as contingent and mutable, modulating over space and time.

Of more interest to homeland security questions, of course, has been algorithmic decision trees based on, for example, the associations between specified behaviors across a range of fields. As Agrawal explains, "once you have the decision tree—and it will have to be designed for specific requirements—a new person comes in and we don't know whether this person is a high risk or a low risk, and we run the records through the decision tree, we are able to make a prediction."[83] Algorithmic decision trees built as software have become the technique of enumeration par excellence for the so-called war on terror. A "new person" can come in, as Agrawal describes it, but he or she will never be a stranger. For some element of their data will always already be in association with some other element gathered from other subjects and events. The veneer of expert objectivity that the computational judgment affords means that new authorities are continually being authorized to identify fast moving and distributed norms and deviations. Consider, for example, the identity management and technology consultants Oracle, who currently supply the U.S. Department of Justice and federal intelligence agencies with nonobvious relationship awareness (NORA) software. According to Oracle consultants, NORA enables their clients to identify "obscure relationships between customers, employees, vendors, and other internal and external data sources."[84] Using algorithms developed for the Las Vegas casinos, NORA looks for "behavior patterns or personal associations that hint at terrorist activity" and "turns data into actionable intelligence."[85] The norm, and the deviation from the norm, has departed the standard distributions of the bell curve in such systems, and attached itself to the relations between items. In practice, of course, the so-called decision trees always already embody assumptions about human behavior and characteristics—for example, racial profiles embedded within facial recognition algorithms, ethnic or religious practices flagged as anomalous, name algorithms accorded risk scores—though these are concealed within the mathematical logics. It is not difficult to find, for example, the proliferation of "associations" with Islamic faith mobilized as risk indicators within the writing of security algorithms. As we will see in the chapters that follow, though, the authorization of numbers as code conceals the difficulties and politics of sovereign decision beneath a technoscientific gleam. This is the overwhelming and politically troubling implication of the veneer of objectivity, alluded to in Hacking's history of statistics, as it plays out in the contemporary war on terror: special measures become perennial and appear as incontrovertible. The political decision to prevent someone from boarding a plane, to detain them at a border or a railway station, to deport them on suspicion of posing a threat, to freeze their assets is increasingly obscured in a computational judgment that is ever more possibilistic and difficult to challenge.

The War by Other Means

The sovereign designation of exception to the rule of law may appear, as Brian Massumi depicts it, as a "lightning strike" of sovereign power, an immanent decision that does not pause "to consult or to analyse."[86] Certainly, this is the visible surface of the exception, the appearance of a flash of executive power that gives us the U.S. Patriot Act, the UK Terrorism Act, circuits of extraordinary rendition, and administrative courts of secret evidence.[87] Yet the very moment of the decision on the exception is a moment teeming with activity—with the authorization of new forms of authority, novel techniques of accounting for people and population, rafts of dividing practice that travel across social domains, thriving forms of control that circulate within the exception itself. The sovereign decision on the exception is not a void then; it is a productive space where things happen, a space filled with people, practices, techniques, and judgments whose effects may be violent or prejudicial in ways that we had not previously imagined. To profess the emptiness of the exception is to miss the politics that demands examination and response. In this chapter I have focused on some of the historical continuities of the sovereign enrollment of enumerators and their systems of numbers, in part because it seems important to emphasize that contemporary sovereign decisions do not break with the past. The Second World War experiments with accounting for population through data on production and consumption have had durable effects. Not least, the coalescence of accounting measures with strategies of war has become far from exceptional.

There are significant distinctions to be drawn, though, in order to specify what, precisely, it is that is new or novel about the contemporary politics of possibility. Both of my examples discussed here clearly deployed variants of probabilistic thinking in the absence of a definitive archive of historical data—in 1939 the census data was simply useless, and in 2002 the very idea of past data on terrorism events is absurd. Heeding Lorraine Daston's warning that mechanical statistical probability and inferential probability have historically dwelled together in various ways, contemporary security measures have invited in intuitive and imaginative inference in unprecedented forms.

First, the specific designation of war as exception functions quite differently in the period that has come to be known as the war on terror. In the twentieth-century authorization of accounting for wartime civil planning, the methods and techniques of economy were brought to bear on war itself. In many ways the disciplinary governing of scarcity, through prohibitions, entitlements, and proscriptions, continued to loom on the horizon. Though the techniques applied were derived from knowledge of circulation, of supply and demand, of the nature of *Homo economicus*, they blended with juridical forms of sovereignty to produce government identifiable as wartime government. What was wanted from the system of numbers was knowledge of the probable effects on economy and society of particular state interventions made in the name of emergency. By contrast, the twenty-first century appeal to war as exceptional grounds for authorizing new security algorithms has extended the practices of war, via war, into life itself. That is to say, the contemporary system of numbers conducts and continues war "by other means."[88] Inverting Clausewitz's formulation that war is the continuation of politics by other means, Foucault extends the practices of war into politics, such that politics is, precisely, "the continuation of war by other means." The politics of possibility that authorizes algorithmic war governs in a warlike fashion, identifying enemies, echoing the architecture of friend and foe, while "beneath the surface" of technical calculation seethes "the noise and confusion of war."[89] As I explain in the chapters that follow, the authorization of mathematics and technoscience is presented as the clean, smart, objectively data-led alternative to other forms of security. But it is not without violence, not without victims, far from it.

Second, the twentieth century wartime techniques of accounting for rationing were engaged in enumerating the population in a *preventive* mode. The prevention of shortages and the securing of production for defense and armaments has a particular orientation to risk and the future. In the face of an uncertain future, the state sought to store, to plan, to maintain inventory, to ward off and forestall future risks. As we will see in chapter 2's mapping of a new risk calculus, the preventive mode is eschewed by contemporary preemptive techniques. Indeed, the vast proliferation of data mining and analytics for security is taking place against a backdrop of the impossibility of prediction. Seeking out precisely the unpredictable and the potentially catastrophic, algorithmic systems supply the sovereign with partial, incomplete knowledge of possibility. Thus, as Rakesh Agrawal reflects on the use of his algorithms for travel patterns across multiple databases, "you do partial computations within each database, and then combine the partial results."[90] It is through such partial fragments that the risk derivative I discuss in the next chapter emerges. The absence of past historical data scarcely matters to such systems of number—they deploy partial fragments in the search for that which is an incipient, potential future. Giles Foden's fictional mathematician Henry Meadows considers the success of his number in identifying a window in the weather for the D-Day landings: "Extrapolating from immediate connections, we have to keep an idea of all connections hovering before us. Because the whole cannot be reached, we can grasp it only by intuition—by chasing not the specifics but the beautiful ghost of an idea. . . . Incompleteness is what points to the idea of the whole. It shows the way to whatever is emergent at the limits of any system. I wanted to tell them how I had come to my decision by deliberately subduing the complete mathematics, and allowing in a simulation of randomness."[91] The specifics, the whole, the complete mathematics of probability, these are exactly "subdued" in the authorized calculations of the politics of possibility. On the surface of the sovereign decision there is an appeal to the objective and impartial logics of mathematics, computer science, and business consulting. Beneath that glossy surface there are layers upon layers of incompleteness, multiple moments of intuition and proxy judgemnt, whose political effects are scarcely seen.

2. ON RISK
Securing Uncertain Futures

The rockets *are* distributing about London just as the equation in the textbooks predicts. As the data keep coming in, he looks more and more like a prophet. It's not precognition, he wants to say, all I'm doing is plugging numbers into a well-known equation, you can look it up in the book and do it yourself. —Thomas Pynchon, *Gravity's Rainbow*, 63

In his novel *Gravity's Rainbow* Thomas Pynchon—the novelist himself a former technical writer for Boeing—depicts the coincidence of two sets of otherwise apparently random data. On a carefully drawn map, an "ink ghost of London," the statistician Roger Mexico has marked out 576 squares, the strikes of German V-2 rockets represented by red circles. "Can't you tell from your map here," demands his colleague Ned Pointsman, "which places would be safest to go into, safest from attack?" "No," replies Mexico, "every square is as likely to get hit again . . . the odds remain the same as they always were. Each hit is independent of all others."[1] In the rendering of his map of the risk of future rocket strikes, Mexico claims no predictive insight, no preemptive decision or precognition; "plugging numbers into a well-known equation," he simply follows a probabilistic formula; "you can do it yourself." Meanwhile, the American Lieutenant Tyrone Slothrop creates his own London map of his sexual encounters in the city—a "cluster near Tower Hill, a violet density about Covent Garden, a nebular streaming on into Mayfair, Soho," each paper star corresponding precisely with a v-2 rocket strike yet to come.[2] For the spies and the military strategists Slothrop's apparent preemptive instincts are "the perfect mechanism." "He's out there," reflects Pointsman, "he can feel them coming, days in advance. It's a reflex. A reflex to something that's in the air right now . . . a sensory cue we just aren't paying attention to, something we could be looking at but no one is."[3] While Roger Mexico's world of strict probability calculates risk on the basis of the "likelihood of being hit," Tyrone Slothrop's world of possibilities anticipates future risks on the sensory terrain of sexual opportunities.

In a quiet London office in 2009, Pynchon's character Pointsman's ambition—to make it possible to know how to be safe from attack, to render the calculable data of Mexico's map but to do it via the preemptive and affective logics of Slothrop's scattered data points—is apparently in process of realization. A group of mathematicians, software designers, and computer scientists "work out the best set of rules" governing the links between otherwise scattered items of data.[4] Their lines of code build the architecture of algorithmic association rules through which data will be "flushed" and future security risks will be anticipated. Supplying diverse domains, from border security and public space surveillance to fraud detection in insurance, the programs deploy data mining and analytics in order to derive indicators of differential risk: risk flags, maps, and scores that signal possible future risks. The individual elements of data may have low probabilities as risks in themselves, but once they are disaggregated, reaggregated, and assembled as associated elements, novel and possibility-based forms of risk calculus begin to emerge. It is precisely in this way that apparent low probability, high consequence events are made amenable to governing by risk. Though they may defy strict probabilistic and statistical forms of risk calculation, when arrayed as associated possibilities they open space for the inference of futures yet to come.

In the world after 9/11, the question "how do we thwart a terrorist who has not yet been identified?" comes to dominate the horizon of security, with the answer coming in the form of risk-based techniques that seek a "joining of dots that should have been connected before 9/11."[5] The forms of calculation that dominated nineteenth- and twentieth-century prudential risk management—the collection of data on population, statistical analysis, predicted futures, and preventative measures—thus become envisaged as risks themselves. In their tracking of past patterns forward into probable futures, they are thought to screen out precisely that improbable event whose impact could be catastrophic. So, for example, the 9/11 Commission found that the hijacker profiles in use at U.S. airports at the time of the attacks were based on past patterns of events that could never have imagined or anticipated the hijackers yet to come.[6] To return to Thomas Pynchon's novel, Roger Mexico's "plugging the numbers into a well-known equation" can be read as the prudential and statistical approach to risk. Such a statistical approach calculates each probability of a rocket strike in the singular, having no regard for the possible correlations among the targets. There may be clusters, patterns, and gatherings, but they are not subject to anything more than chance itself. It is only when Mexico's statistical map is coalesced with Slothrop's sensate, inferred, and anticipatory map that unforeseen events begin to come into view. In this chapter I propose that the emerging form of risk calculus is derivative in the sense that it infers a range of possible futures on the basis of multiple past data elements—elements from which it is derived but toward which it is largely indifferent. I am interested here particularly in four defining characteristics of the risk calculus in its contemporary derivative form: temporality and the orientation to uncertain futures; norm, normality, and deviation; spatiality and the arraying of possibilities; and the reconciling of security with mobility. I will begin, however, by elaborating on what I mean by derivative forms of risk.

Derivative Forms

In January 2010, when Tony Blair, the former UK prime minister, testified before the Iraq Inquiry, he explained his preemptive decision to go to war in Iraq, stating that "the crucial thing after September 11 was that *the calculus of risk changed.*"[7] Throughout his testimony, Blair held that the material and observable risks posed by Iraq to British security were not at issue per se—there had always been "leaks" in the policy of containment, he said, and these leaks remained—the intrinsic threat remained much the same. Yet a world of containment, sanctions, monitoring, and international conventions somehow could not be reconciled with a post-9/11 sensibility. Put simply, it was not that the risk had changed but that the very calculus of risk had changed. No longer strictly a matter of managing risk by containing leaks, monitoring threat, or assessing the probability of future leaks, the emphasis shifts to the capacity to act on the basis of what is not known.

What comes to matter is the capacity for action on the basis of possible future catastrophe involving those same leaks, action when there may be low probability but high consequence.

In Blair's abandonment of the strategy of containment and his decision to go to war, we see a shift of focus to the securing of the effects of what leaks out, a desire to act on and through their very unfolding. As François Ewald describes the "remarkable change in the risk schema," in anticipatory approaches "we are trying to anticipate risks whose existence has not yet been proven."[8] In contrast to risk management that seeks out knowledge in order to reduce uncertainty, Ewald depicts a mode of risk that "introduces uncertainty into both decision and sanctions," such that "the worst hypothesis" is imagined, and "one is judged not only by what one should know but also by what one should have suspected."[9] To seek out knowledge of the possession of weapons of mass destruction becomes less significant than the suspicion of some future consequence. In Ewald's terms we might understand Blair's decision to go to war precisely on the basis of his imagination of the worst hypothesis: "The point about this terrorist act was that over 3,000 people had been killed on the streets of New York, an absolutely horrific event, but this is what really changed my perception of risk, the calculus of risk for me: if those people could have killed 30,000 they would have."[10]

Understood in terms of a risk that is in excess of the event as such, for the Blair government to heed Hans Blix's balance of proof of weapons of mass destruction would be to miss the anticipation of risks not yet proven. Tony Blair's Iraq Inquiry musings on what "could have" or "would have" happened had the 9/11 attacks implicated chemical or biological weapons captures the imagination of worst case scenarios. The emphasis of risk assessment ceases to be one of the balance of probability of future threat and occupies instead the horizon of actionable decisions, making possible action on the basis of uncertainty. In assembling together and associating two otherwise isolated and unproven elements—Saddam Hussein's possible weapons program and the potential use of chemical and biological weapons by terrorists—Tony Blair's testimony embodies the heart of contemporary forms of risk calculus. Once multiple risk elements are drawn together in relations of association, enduring uncertainties can be rendered as distinct and actionable possibilities. "Even if Dr. Blix had continued," testified Blair, "Saddam retained the intent." Indeed, in the final analysis Blair asks to be judged not on the basis of what was known in 2003—"sometimes what is important is not to ask the March 2003 question but to ask the 2010 question, supposing we had backed off?"—but indeed on the basis of what would have happened had what he suspected come to pass. Overall, and perhaps inadvertently, Blair was correct to identify the emergence of a new risk calculus, though not because the world had become a more dangerous place after 9/11; instead, the "would have," "could have" atmosphere of a world after 9/11 makes possible the loosening of certainties about individual risk elements and the search for associated data capable of signaling future intent.

How, then, does the contemporary security risk calculus function on the basis of unknown elements, suspicions, and inferred intent? Importantly, just as Pynchon's rocket strikes and sexual encounters are associated, related but not causal—"all talk of cause and effect is secular history"—the contemporary risk calculus does not seek a causal relationship between items of data, but works instead on and through the *relation* itself.[11] Thus in the design of security algorithms, for example, there is an ontology of association with a mathematical means of calculating uncertainty, a risk equation: if *** and ***, in association with ***, then ***. The asterisks mark an unknown value that comes into view only through its association with other unknown values. In the decisions as to the association rules governing border security analytics, the equation may read: if past travel to Pakistan and duration of stay over three months, in association with flight paid by a third party, then risk flag, detain; if paid ticket in cash and this meal choice, in association with this flight route, then this risk score and secondary searches; if two tickets paid on one credit card and seated not together, then these questions at the border. Understood in this way, it is not strictly collected data on identifiable risks that become security interventions but a different kind of abstraction that is based precisely on an absence, on what is not known, on the very basis of uncertainty. Coalescing the imaginative mapping of Slothrop's preemptive sensory cues with the protocols of Mexico's numbers plugged into a "well-known equation," the risk calculus draws into association an amalgam of disaggregated data, inferring across the gaps to derive a lively and alert new form of derivative—a risk flag, map, or score that will go on to live and act in the world.[12]

Whether in the form of a calculus for deciding on preemptive war on the basis of future possible intent (as in Blair's Iraq testimony) or in the form of what Marieke de Goede and I have termed the "banal pre-emption" of security risk algorithms, contemporary risk techniques act upon and through people, populations, and objects in novel ways.[13] To be clear, the emerging security risk calculus is not a more advanced form of abstraction than one might find in statistical or prudential modes, but rather it is a specific form of abstraction that distinctively coalesces more conventional forms of probabilistic risk assessment with inferred and unfolding futures. Risk techniques in their derivative form mobilize a novel amalgam of disaggregated data—reaggregated via algorithm-based association rules and visualized in "real time" as a risk map, score, or color-coded flag. In this sense risk calculations on the basis of derivatives do not rely upon the conventional forms of collecting data and governing population that we see in modern disciplinary forms.[14] It is not that derivative forms supersede disciplinary modes, and indeed among the elements of the security risk equation are conventionally collected visa and passport data, but rather that the *relation between* the elements is itself changed. As Michel Foucault put the problem in his lectures in 1978, "mechanisms of security do not replace disciplinary mechanisms" as though a succession of techniques, but instead "what above all changes is the dominant characteristic, or more exactly, the system of correlation between juridico-legal mechanisms, disciplinary mechanisms, and mechanisms of security?"[15] It is precisely the emergence of novel forms of correlation that are distinctive to the contemporary risk calculus.

Of course the capacity to calculate risk via new forms of correlation, on the horizon of uncertain futures, is an entirely familiar idea in the realm of the financial derivative. Derivative instruments in finance are novel forms of risk management in which the relationship between the instrument and an assumed underlying value becomes fleeting, uncertain, and loose. "The central characteristic of derivatives," write Dick Bryan and Michael Rafferty, "is their capacity to dismantle or unbundle any asset into constituent attributes and trade those attributes without trading the asset itself."[16] By "slicing and dicing" and reaggregating underlying values, the financial instrument of the derivative thus sheds any encumbering causal relation to the underlying asset. Indeed, as Duncan Wigan suggests in his analysis of financial derivatives, the instruments "abstract from any linear relationship to underlying processes of real wealth creation," rendering them "indifferent" to the components of individual stocks or bonds, for example, on which they draw.[17] In this way the reward characteristics of the derivative are sustained in a way that is indifferent to the risks of individual underlying elements. Thus, for example, the so-called subprime crisis sliced and bundled together mortgage-backed securities into collateralized debt obligations, indifferent to underlying values such as house prices or capacities to repay mortgage debt.[18] In the derivative form, the risks of mortgage default, home repossessions, unemployment, and a whole range of life chances are not treated as threats in and of themselves but as sets of relations that can be unbundled, reattached to other elements, and repriced. One might intuitively suppose that the state of emergency precipitated by the subprime crisis has marked the limit point of managing risk by derivative, and yet the response to the financial crisis has itself ushered in the demand for ever more precise and finite degrees of risk disaggregation.

The derivative forms of risk calculation that are emerging in contemporary security practice share important affinities with the financial derivative. Loosening their commitment to what François Ewald describes as the "analyses of situations based on statistics and probabilities," derivative forms relax their relation to strict probability, inviting in other possibilities and associations.[19] They infer possible futures on the basis of underlying fragmented elements of data toward which they are for the most part indifferent. It is precisely this capacity to move, to be shared, divided, traded, or exchanged indifferent to, and in isolation from, underlying probabilities that is at the heart of derivative risk flags, maps, and scores. Indifferent to the contingent biographies that actually make up the underlying data, risk in its derivative form is not centred on who we are, nor even on what our data say about us, but on what can be imagined and inferred about who we might be—on our very proclivities and potentialities.

Temporalities: Making Present the Future Consequences

In contrast to forms of risk that seek out statistical knowledge of population in order to prevent the worst from happening, contemporary derivative forms imagine a population whose dynamics are as yet unknown, a population yet to come. It is not strictly the case that security risk systems of automated targeting, integrated databases, and software-coded calculations witness some form of acceleration in terms of temporality, though of course this has been a central theme in discussions of "netwars," "virtuous war," and so on.[20] Indeed, by contrast, risk in its derivative mode allows for a certain quality of suspended time—a stilling of the frenetic crossings of the global political economy in advance of arrival. The significance of the temporal register of risk lies not in a speeding up but in an algorithmic "framing of time and space" that has a distinctive orientation to the unknown future.[21] As Brian Massumi has put it, "pre-emption brings the future into the present. It makes present the future consequences of an eventuality that may or may not occur, *indifferent to its actual occurrence*."[22] The preemptive temporality of derivative forms of risk does not seek to predict or prevent a particular future, as in systems of pattern recognition that track forward from past data, for example, because it is precisely indifferent to whether a particular event occurs or not. What matters instead is the capacity to act in the face of uncertainty, to render the gaps in what can be collected or known actionably.

In contemporary security risk, the relation of past, present, and future is reconfigured such that future uncertainty can be acted upon in the present, even when there is little or no knowledge of past instances or probabilities. Significantly, derivative forms of risk signal the extraordinary fungibility of the risk calculus and the unique capacity to define new temporal arrangements for managing the uncertain future. Understood in this way, what Ulrich Beck has called the "world risk society" can never mark a temporal break or limit point, reached when science and law cease to respond to the proliferation of "potentially catastrophic and uninsurable events."[23] Likewise, Richard Ericson and Aaron Doyle trace a risk limit reached in a "terrorism that strikes at the heart of risk society," rendering past ways of taming chance and uncertainty impossible and presenting "a stark reminder of the limits to risk assessment and management."[24] Such assumptions, that risk calculation has reached its limits at the threshold of a world depicted in terms of catastrophe (whether terrorism, climate change, landslide, or flooding), forget that risk is precisely a technology of limits—a means of pushing at the limit of what is possible. Far from reaching its limit point in an era of potentially catastrophic futures, risk in its derivative form precisely mobilizes the possibility of catastrophe in order to calculate and decide even where there is doubt. Akin to the "one percent doctrine" with its call to make catastrophe risk the basis of security decisions—"if there is a one percent chance of an event coming due, act as though it were a certainty"—derivative techniques abstract the security instrument from the underlying components of that which is already known.[25] In short, uncertain futures do not bring about the temporal limit point of risk calculus; rather they become its modus operandi.

Of course the development of risk in modernity in many ways is concerned with a struggle with the problem of time. In wresting the laws of chance from the gods and placing them in the hands of science and mathematics, nineteenth- and early twentieth-century risk techniques adhered to a strictly linear time.[26] The collection of knowledge on the past—in the form of data analyzed for statistical patterns and calculated in the present—became the predominant risk tool for predicting and controlling the future. Thus, for example, survey and census data on population became a means not only of governing life but also of constituting and categorizing people.[27] As a form of abstraction, the orientation of these survey-based risk forms can be likened to that of a photograph or snapshot in terms of decisions about angle, framing, sampling, and replicability in the future. Risk in its derivative form, though it draws on some conventional elements of survey data, no longer visualizes population strictly via survey but rather through techniques of projection. Projections are produced from fragments of data, from isolated elements that are selected, differentiated, and reintegrated to give the appearance of a whole. The multiple decisions about what to select, how to isolate, and what should be joined to what fall away in the appearance of a projected whole—a complete risk indicator.

In her discussion of filmic projection, Anne Friedberg suggests that "for motion to be reconstituted, its virtual reach relies on a missing element, a perceptual darkness between the frames."[28] Like filmic projection, the gaps between underlying elements are precisely what makes the projected futures of derivative risk forms possible. As one major IT consulting company supplying European border security programs explained in an interview, "having different types of data sets allows you to do searches *across* those pieces of data, to be as certain as you can be that you understand who's coming into the country and why they're coming and whether or not you should take action."[29] For the suppliers of software and risk management solutions for national security, the emphasis is on what can be conducted "across" items of data, on and through their very relation, in order to uncover future intent and to act upon it. There can be no certainty about the association between data on a flight route, a method of payment, a ticket type, or a past "no show," for their relation is not causal but correlative. In isolation each data item offers little to the calculation of probable risks. Once associated together, though, what matters is the capacity to make inferences across the data, such that risk derivatives can be recognized, shared, and actionable. As Randy Martin has argued compellingly in relation to financial derivatives, "derivatives remove reference from the commodity."[30] The derivative, once freed of its direct relation to a commodity, becomes the referent point alone. Thus, to return to our example of border security risk, the U.S. inspector general concluded in his review of data analytics that "association does not imply a direct causal connection," rather it "uncovers, interprets, displays relationships between persons, places, and events."[31] What matters is that some form of correlation can be drawn in the relationships, a correlation that is nonetheless indifferent to the specificity of persons, places, and events. As Donald MacKenzie notes in the "base correlations" that make financial derivatives actionable as instruments, it is the very relation itself that renders a calculable risk score, a numeric signal on the trader's screen, a flag on a border guard's screen, an already encoded course of action.[32]

The derivative's ontology of association is overwhelmingly indifferent to the occurrence of specific events, on the condition that there remains the possibility for action: in the domain of finance, the derivative can be exchanged and traded for as long as the correlation is sustained; in the domain of security, the derivative circulates for as long as the association rules are sustained. In the process of making something actionable, of course, as Alain Badiou signals in his engagement with the mathematics of set theory, "the event is *decided* as such in the retroaction of an intervention."[33] The event is never merely a matter of "what happens," but on the contrary it can be thought only by "anticipating its abstract form" and revealed only "in the retroaction of an interventional practice."[34] Where the association rules of a piece of software code anticipate future arrivals in abstract form—inferring "who's coming into the country" or "why they're coming"—they release into the world a risk calculus that intervenes retroactively in order to decide the event.

Norm and Anomaly: "On This Particular Day, at This Particular Time, in This Moment"

The emergence of derivative forms of risk calculus demands something of a renewed critical thinking about how it is that life itself becomes a terrain of government. In Foucault's lectures in 1976, which comprise *Society Must Be Defended*, he delineates from "the power of sovereignty" to "take life and let live" his analytic of biopower: the "technology of power over the population" in a form that "consists in making live and letting die."[35] As Stephen Collier suggests, this stark annexation of biopolitics from sovereignty contrasts to a second later mood in Foucault's work on specific forms of biopower.[36] In Foucault's late reflections, the idea of governing as a government of population "makes the problem of the foundation of sovereignty even more acute and it makes the need to develop the disciplines even more acute."[37] In contrast to an epochal move from sovereignty to discipline to security, Foucault depicts their copresence as "a triangle: sovereignty, discipline and governmental management, which has population as its main target and apparatuses of security as its essential mechanism."[38] In the initial formulations population arose as a series of traits and behaviors that, once accurately categorized and calculated, can be acted upon as norm and anomaly. It is in this way that health data become vaccination program, education data render possible curriculum, assessment, and audit, knowledge of the urban citizen becomes a sanitation program, and so on.[39] Yet as the formulation of biopolitics moves to consider the sovereign as dealing with a complex and aleatory milieu of the human species, the relation to the norm itself appears altered: "This calculation of risk shows that risks are not the same for all individuals, all ages, or in every condition, place or milieu. There are therefore differential risks that reveal, as it were, zones of higher risk and, on the other hand, zones of less or lower risk."[40]

No longer pursing a clear delineation of norm from anomaly, risk in its derivative form functions through a *mobile norm*. Where, as Foucault proposes, "normalization posits a model and tries to get people, movements and actions to conform to this model [the norm]," in the security apparatus he observes "the plotting of differential curves of normality."[41] In contrast to a world in which biopolitics eclipses sovereign and disciplinary power, we see a security apparatus that mobilizes specific techniques for deploying the norm to govern uncertain and unfolding populations. The techniques of the disciplinary society and the exercise of sovereignty become correlated elements in a mobile and modulated approach to the norm. Neither the lightning strike norm established by the king, nor strictly the normalization of a self-governing disciplinary society, the differential curve of normality breaks subjects and objects into elemental degrees of risk such that the norm is always in a process of becoming.

It is precisely such differential normalities that circulate in the associative writing of derivative risk calculations. As the deputy director of the UK e-Borders program explained in an interview, the risk-flagged anomaly in a series of travel transactions "would never be self-evident. Only self-evident on this particular day, at this particular time, in this moment." When the software designers and mathematicians emphasize the importance of "setting the gauge"—the refining of the algorithm governing the rules between items of data, so that data can be "flushed" or "washed" through—this does not depict a filter that catches those mobile bodies, monies, or objects who deviate from a known norm. Rather, the derivative works with a mobile norm, a norm that is itself modulated and aleatory, governed not by normalcy and deviations but by differential curves of normality. The e-Borders official describes a customs officer who can visually scan pages of data on multitransit-point sea routes, identifying an apparently suspicious set of travel associations (multi-leg journey associated with particular sea ports, associated with cash paid) as normal in specific circumstances, where the behavior is linked to a contract seaman returning home. "That is what we are trying to do," he reports, "to automate that kind of intuition, encode it." The making of the association rules that automate such judgements is an iterative process described as a "rapid fire Q&A" between the software designers, immigration, customs and counterterror officers, policing authorities, and frontline border personnel in the "offline team"—for example, "what should the age range be for the drug mules route?," "should we associate seating patterns with this one way ticket?," "is the 50%+ risk score useful as an indicator at that time of day?"[42] Though the risk derivative is indifferent to the underlying data, it does, as Brian Massumi suggests "assert its own normality, of crisis: the anytime, anywhere emergence of the abnormal," living and circulating through multiple decisions about potential threats.[43]

Among the designers of border security software, much is made of the fact that the derivative does not live on in the conventional sense of being retained as a risk indicator attached to an individual. Understood as a referent point that is distinct from, and indifferent to, underlying values, however, the derivative persists in the building and refining of the mobile boundaries between normal and risky behaviors at a given moment. Commenting on the mining and analysis of travel data, a European commissioner reports that their "data serve two purposes, they serve the real-time risk assessment—do you fit the risk level? If not then they will serve a secondary purpose, which is they will give an indication of how normal people travel compared to other kinds of people."[44] In the iterative and oscillating setting of the risk gauge, the oft-cited "99.9 percent of people going about their business, journey, or holiday in a perfectly normal manner" is folded back into the ability to calculate risk against a modular norm. A "low-risk" derivative persists in the offline modeling of future rules, such that the fleeting encounter between frequent flier, iris scanner, and automated gate manifests at some future date in other forms of encounter with other subjects. Though some elements of mobile subjects may appear to move unencumbered through the mesh of the risk calculus, other elements become detached and circulate in new ways that attach to the possibilities of intervention on other future subjects.

Indeed, even the apparent "false positives" we might highlight as symptomatic of the excesses and slippages of the risk-based techniques are successes on the register of refining the mobile norm. The false hits of multiple security interventions that prove negative can never be errors in the terms of the derivative, for they too are folded back into association. In Europe, for example, the apparent risk flag produced by the association of a ticket paid by a third party, one way, less than five days before travel produced clusters of false positives around ski routes where insurance companies repatriating injured travelers replicate this pattern. The apparent cluster of errors does not pose a problem to the writers of the lines of code, though, for they simply write in new rules that ameliorate the associative risks of particular departure locations. The addition of an association with particular flight routes to reset the risk derivative in those circumstances illustrates the indifference to error in, or alternative reading of, the underlying data.

The risk derivative not only loosens the disciplinary relation of data to norm, it also embodies an indifference to conventional Galilean scientific notions of evidence and accuracy.[45] As Lorraine Daston has argued powerfully in relation to the histories of scientific experiments and instruments, the history of science reveals not strictly a desire for ever greater degrees of accuracy and objectivity but also in fact a quite distinct emphasis on precision, for an "intelligibility of concepts" that "by itself stipulates nothing about whether and how these concepts match the world."[46] To put the matter simply, it is of lesser consequence whether a risk assessment accurately captures a set of circumstances in the world, than whether the models can be refined for sufficient precision to engage action. If the governing by norm we associate with risk probabilities required the "large number" collection of data in order empirically to identify, validate, and calculate patterns—such as, for example, in the use of actuarial models and insurance calculation—then the mobile norms of derivatives are oriented not to the conventional archive and *collection* but to *discarding*. When it is risk *possibilities* and not *probabilities* that are sought, large quantities of data are simply screened out. What matters is not the accuracy gleaned from large volumes of data, analyzed and statistically assessed, but the intelligibility of the derivative as an instrument, its precision as a basis for decision. As one security software designer put the problem: "It's about throwing away an item of data if it doesn't help you make the right decision. . . . We want the right amount of data to make a good enough decision, to take the right action at the border, to stop that person, refer to the police. It's giving them enough information for them to take the right action, with the right type of risk, enough information to make a judgement."[47]

When what is sought is the precision of the derivative risk flag itself, and its capacity to enact a decision, there is no resort to archiving in the conventional sense; the underlying data items can be all but instantaneously discarded, leaving only the trace of their association. Arguably, when the controversies surrounding the extradition of European passenger name record (PNR) data to the United States resulted in the reduction of underlying data fields (from thirty-four to nineteen), or when the Canadian privacy commissioner ruled that in-flight Halal or Kosher meal choices as "cultural indicators" be filtered out of PNR fields, these actions failed to adequately apprehend the life of the derivative.[48] The derived risk flags and scores are not dependent on the fixed norms of collected or archived data— "it's not about collecting more data," argues the UK Border Agency, "that just makes the stack bigger. We are throwing the straw away." Because the derivative is produced via mobile norms that screen out much of the data, the political space of response that says "protect," "limit," "make private" is problematized. In a sense it no longer matters precisely what the authorities are permitted to collect or how it is stored or protected. Akin to the financial derivatives that allow for *exposure to* the risk-reward characteristic of underlying assets without having to *possess* them, the security derivative is exposed to the underlying data without collecting them, created across the gaps and absences, in the interstitial spaces of inference and expansion.

Spatialities: An Array of Possibilities

The very idea of the derivative has long been considered to have a "virtual quality," such that financial derivatives are said to have a "strangely imaginary or virtual character," even where the emphasis is placed on "how virtuality is produced," as it is in the social studies of finance.[49] In the encoded and digital systems that are the space of the derivative it is most often an abstracted and virtual world that is depicted. Yet, as Brian Massumi reminds us, the knotted and folded potentialities of the virtual are not to be understood on the same plane as the calculated rationality of possibility that we find in the digital world. "Nothing is more destructive for the thinking and imaging of the virtual," argues Massumi, "than equating it with the digital."[50] In the digital processes of programming and the writing of code Massumi locates a "numeric way of arraying alternatives so that they can be sequenced," a means of rendering calculable possible futures "step after ploddingly programmed step."[51] Understood in this way, the ontology of association does not aspire to virtuality at all but to actuality and the actualization of an array of possibilities. In this sense, returning to Pynchon's novel, the derivative coalesces more with Roger Mexico's statistically inferred map than with Tyrone Slothrop's affective world of preemptive sensation. When Ned Pointsman seeks to fold Slothrop's sensate map back into the capacity to foresee and intervene, or when the intuitions and inferences of software designers become an association rule, this does indeed become a numeric way of arraying alternatives, an already encoded systematization.

To be clear, the contemporary risk calculus functions through the arraying of possibilities such that they can be acted upon. The significance of the array is that it allows for multiple possible sequences of events to be held together horizontally within a single purview. In this sense the array, as a spatial calculus, begins to occlude the series or seriality of prudential risk techniques. Where the series requires a linear chain of causal links between elements, such that an overall risk probability can be calculated, the array works with the emergent unfolding of events as possibilities in themselves. In asking "what holds things together?," as Deleuze and Guattari remind us, the "easiest answer seems to be provided by a linear model," a "coded linkage" of causes and effects.[52] The array of possibilities is held together not by chains of causality but by associative relays that are, in Deleuze and Guattari's terms, "distributed across the network." Thus in the algorithmic decision trees of security software we see multiple possible courses of events held open simultaneously. Indeed the techniques for visualizing differential risks on screens and across databases precisely distribute risk variance across an array of possible futures.

Perhaps the seductiveness of the idea of the virtual as the dwelling place of the derivative lies in part in the apparent dominance of the visual in its representation. Whether it is the screenic domain of the derivatives trader, the vigilant visualities of border security, or the scopic regimes of the flood-risk map writer, the color-coded flags, screened scores, and red-and-blue maps appear acutely visual.[53] Yet the appeal to the "sovereign sense" of the visual further establishes the derivative as an already encoded array of possibilities, this apparently "most reliable" of senses underwriting the rationality of the association.[54] "Let's say I have one thousand border staff," explains one security software consultant, "the offline analysis is complex, but it must be fed back in a decisive format—that is what the system is about, displaying it on their screen."[55] What appears as the virtual realm of algorithm and screen is more precisely understood as a visual economy—a means of dividing, separating, and acting upon arrays of possible futures. As the art historian Jonathan Crary has argued, echoing Massumi's sense of the digital as the systematization of the possible, the visual is "not primarily concerned with looking at images but rather with the construction of conditions that individuate, immobilize and separate subjects, even in a world in which mobility and circulation are ubiquitous."[56] At the point that the risk derivative becomes visualized on the border guard's screen, "technology," as Barbara Maria Stafford has argued, "screens out what supposedly does not matter," directing and delimiting attention.[57] The virtual knots and slippages that were present in the room where a mathematician's intuition met a software designer's aesthetic sensibility fall away in the appearance of an already decided course of events. In the desire for precision over accuracy, the visualization "automates the response," as the designers explain.

Understood not strictly as a world of abstracted virtualities or screenic vision but more precisely as a domain of the arraying of possibilities by association, risk in its derivative form cannot be seen as it is so often portrayed—as the irrefutable electronic footprint of the data subject, left behind in the residue of a digital world. Rather, the derivative has become a means of dividing, separating, and particularizing subjects, literally bringing them to attention and making them subjects of interest. Thus, for example, when the bombings in London in July 2005 coincided with IBM's trial of the UK's e-Borders program—Project Semaphore—Tony Blair requested that Semaphore be extended to the Pakistan–London flight routes, and a new person of interest was written into the risk calculus and brought to attention: "the British citizen of Pakistani origin." The risk screening of PNR data visualizes subjects of interest through the surface data but also, as Kaja Silverman has observed of the screen, "through the illusion of depth, a deep reach into databases and analytics."[58] As commercial players have reported, it is not the surface items that provide the "complete picture of a person" that is sought—"that only tells us who someone is, we want to know why they are here." My surface data may say that I am a British citizen, but the analytics will ask why I am here.

What are the implications of visualizing subjects in this way? Alexandra Hall

and I have elsewhere considered this to be a form of "digitized dissection"—
an anatomical disaggregation of a person into degrees of risk.[59] How does a
person of interest come to be seen? How are they targeted? How can they
respond? Could they ever reply "no, that is not me" or "it is me but that
is not why I am here, that is not my intention"? When the writers of risk
algorithms for the U.S. Automated Targeting System (ATS) account in an
interview for their disinterest in the underlying personal data, in a sense
this is the case—for it is the capacity to abstract and intervene that counts:
"When you're doing analysis to refine rules, that's completely anonymous.
You may know everything else about them except their name—they're unknown. Except, well they're not, we know lots about them, we know there
is a person who has been doing this and this and this. We just don't know
their name yet and we can stop them before we know it."

Such is the extent of the indifference to the singularity of underlying
data or evidence in the making of the derivative, that the slippages and excesses of the systems center precisely upon those underlying elements that
perhaps ought not to be missed. For example, as the derivatives of the sub-
prime market continued to proliferate in 2006, the underlying foreclosure
rates on mortgages (foreclosure itself a disciplinary technique of punishing
the debtor) arguably should have signaled an increasing problem.[60] Similarly, the failed apparent transatlantic bombing attempt on December 25
was said to have evaded security because of the "failure to join up the dots"
in PNR analytics and notably not, as the *New York Times* highlighted, because of the failure to simply identify a name that already existed on a
watch list.[61] So overwhelming is the pursuit of the as yet unknown future
risk that the sounding alert of the watch list—a disciplinary form of security
risk management, buried deep below the visible surface of contemporary
emergency governing—is rarely heard.

Securabilities: Thriving on Uncertainty

On the walls of Chicago O'Hare Airport, risk consultants Protiviti display
their business services in risk management, their trademarked "Know Risk,
Know Reward" logo casting its glow as passengers proceed to the U.S. border. To know risk, to find a capacity to calculate uncertainty, in these terms
is not at all the same as knowing dangers, recognizing threats, or averting
uncertain futures. Quite the contrary, in the world illuminated by Protiviti's
lightbox advertising, the greatest risk is to take no risks at all. To achieve

complete security, absolute knowledge of the future and all it holds, would be to fail to capitalize on the potential rewards. Understood in this way, the parameters of the contemporary risk calculus are not defined strictly in terms of achieving *security* or "finding a safer place," as for Thomas Pynchon's wartime characters, but more accurately as affording sufficient *securability* for rewards to be realized. To know risk is not to secure against the future (as in earlier preventative and prudential risk forms) but to find a means to harness its energies and effects. The contemporary risk calculus emerges amid a landscape of globalization, a world of mobilities, of people, objects, money, and ideas on the move. Both *The 9/11 Commission Report* and the review of the London bombings of 2005, for example, foreground the question of securing mobility itself, "keeping our borders open" and "our vibrant city moving."[62] To render the uncertain future securable (as opposed to secure) is to "embrace risk," to open up to the future, to keep things in movement even in the face of possible threat.[63]

When Michel Foucault mapped the tentative contours of a security apparatus, for him it was oriented not to the concern to prevent events from happening, to "allow nothing to escape," but rather to "let things happen."[64] Associating disciplinary techniques of governing with the will to prevent and stop things from happening, "to prevent it and ensure it does not take place," for him the "space of security" refers to "possible events," a "different sort of problem" that must "allow circulations to take place."[65] While disciplinary techniques position mobility and security in a fraught relation, one in which prevention is achieved precisely by stopping, halting, and prohibiting, the security apparatus seeks out the affinities of mobility and security. "Discipline does not deal with detail in the same way as apparatuses of security," proposes Foucault, because discipline's function is "to prevent everything, even and above all the detail," whereas apparatuses of security "rely on details that are not valued as good or evil in themselves."[66] What Foucault calls details we might think of as our data elements whose value as such is only ascribed through their relations to other elements. Disciplinary techniques need have no regard for the things that emerge in the detail, for they intervene to prevent and prohibit irrespective of singularities—to stop movement is to annul detail.

Yet a world characterized by the mobilities of globalization is a world replete with small details, details that are amplified at the intersection of security and mobility. Once in movement, the management of bodies, objects, financial flows, diseases, and so on becomes precisely a matter of detail, a matter of "sifting the good and the bad, ensuring that things are always in movement, continually going from one point to another."[67] In effect the raison d'être of the contemporary risk calculus is to differentiate the good and the bad in movement, to deploy the details of differential norms and qualities of mobility in order to make a security decision possible.[68] A world of mobility is thus rendered a world of possibility on all fronts—offering as it does an enhanced set of patterns, traces, and transactions of lives and things on the move. In the world of the financial derivative, mobility at the service of security is writ large—what matters is not whether a particular underlying value rises or falls but only that this volatility or "implied volatility" has itself been rendered tradeable.[69] In effect, movement in any direction can be made securable so long as it is possible to correlate the mobility to some future amalgam of possible outcomes.[70]

The derivative risk calculus places mobility at the service of security by trading on and through the thriving and teeming details of circulation. Unlike the prudentialism of settled out categories in risk modes that rely upon statistical probabilities—for example, this profession, that salary, this neighborhood, that health history—risk in its derivative form modulates via mobility itself. Like its commercial genealogy in retail data mining and consumer algorithms that I discussed in chapter 1, the risk derivative does not seek out the settled categories of "this customer," "this traveler," "this migrant" or "that visa applicant," but instead it wants to recognize bodies and objects in movement, in and through their very transaction. To give an example, one group of software designers, who have in the past supplied the U.S. government with social network analysis tools for security applications, locate the origins of their codes in commercial "customer intelligence." The writing of association rules for customer intelligence raises questions of the movements across and relations between people and places—"do these customers influence each other?" and "is this link significant?" The data residue left in daily transactions and mined for risk criteria is not strictly a body of evidence of what a mobile subject did or did not do but a set of relations, for example, between products, from which the derivative can be written.

The business knowledge that dominated early twenty-first century models for embracing risk and thriving on uncertainty has thus become a resource to a sovereignty that similarly seeks securability in place of security. In the year that they changed their name to Accenture, Anderson Consulting declared that "in today's economy you have to embrace risk in order to master it and thrive."[71] Their clients, they suggested, had abandoned former "safe" strategies of risk assessment "under the pressures of globalization," "embracing change" and accepting that "there is no reward without risk." The adaptability of an organization that could act on events, from financial crises to new investment opportunities, as they emerge and unfold would, the consultants argued, prove a vital resource in a world of mobile people and capital. Six years later, and following the U.S. government's multi-billion dollar award of the United States Visitor and Immigrant Status Indicator Technology (US-VISIT) border security contract to Accenture (see chapter 3), the global consultants brought the embodiment of reconciled security and mobility to the heart of Europe. Opening their "automated gate" simulator in Brussels in 2008, Accenture invited politicians, aviation authorities, and security officials to test out their "pre-screening, biometrically identifying" mobile border that could, as its designers see it, adapt and change in real time. In effect, the automated gate replaces the border guard at an airport security checkpoint or on an international rail terminal plaza—the derivative risk flag or score automating the decision as to the opening and closing of the gate. It does indeed appear to, in our terms, open up to let things happen, embracing the uncertain movements of the world economy precisely in order to use the detail to calibrate the risk calculus. The risk-based rules and algorithms that govern the automated gate, in order to learn, to change daily and evolve, require precisely the circulations and mobilities that pass through.

An Equation for Angels

Why is your equation only for angels, Roger? Why can't *we* do something, down here? Couldn't there be an equation for us too, something to help us find a safer place? —Thomas Pynchon, *Gravity's Rainbow*, 63

The opening epigraph in this chapter signaled the dilemmas and difficulties of deploying a derivative risk calculus in order to find a safer place, to achieve a world of security. Pynchon's statistician Roger Mexico has "tried to explain" to his lover Jessica that the V-bomb data cannot project the risks of future rocket strikes, there being a "difference between distribution, in angel's eye view, over the map of England" and the contingent uncertainty "of their own chances, as seen from down here."[72] There is a gap, he reminds us, between the Poisson distributions on his map and the anticipation of an event that is radically and unalterably uncertain. For Mexico, the contingent chances of their lives in the bombarded city are not amenable to calculation; they are beyond the limit point of a risk calculus. The two worlds—of statistical probabilities and emergent possibilities—are difficult to hold together, and Jessica "couldn't keep them both in sight."[73]

As I have proposed in this chapter, though, the poverty of probability in anticipating possible futures definitively does not signal the limit point of the risk calculus. Because strict probability occludes the black swan event— the improbable, high-impact occurrence—the statistical calculations that were for so long at the heart of modern approaches to risk are rendered insufficient.[74] In order for the low probability, high consequence event to be anticipated, the risk equation incorporates the horizon of possibility itself, inviting speculation and inference into calculation. What can be inferred on the basis of this element in association with this, where this third element is also present? What are the possible relations of these past behaviors, and how should they be scored? Such are the algorithmic equations of the derivative risk calculus.

The contemporary form of risk calculus works hard to keep both in view—the insufficient probabilities that continue to supply elements of the underlying risk data, and their inferential counterparts of associated possibilities. It is precisely this work that is the work of the derivative. As I have described in this chapter, the risk derivative breaks up the linear time of past, present, and future of the modern risk equation, eschewing the serial causality of past data patterns, present risk assessment, and future prevention. In its derivative form, the risk calculus folds future possibilities into present decisions, making present the future consequences of events that may or may not come to pass. Thus, as in Tony Blair's testimony before the Iraq Inquiry, the past event of 9/11 serves to make present a vast number of possible futures. As we have seen, the calculus deploys a norm that is quite distinct from statistical norms and their standard deviations: a mobile norm that adapts to its environment, fleeting in its risk application but enduring in its capacity to travel to other places and have effects on other people and objects. The derivative disrupts the spatial calculus of the risk series, supplementing it with the space of the array, holding together multiple possible futures such that action can be taken as they unfold. The security software analysts call this the "actionable decision," the one that is taken not on the basis of certainty but in fact under conditions of doubt as to the trajectories of the many arrayed paths. Finally, I have proposed that the derivative risk form is concerned not with the pursuit of security per se, nor with finding a safer place, but rather with the capacity to keep things moving, to guarantee the securability of circulations of people, money, things, and ideas.

In the chapters that follow in part 2, I turn my attention to the spaces where this calculus is mobilized, to the zones, borders, and landscapes where it enacts its sovereign decisions. From the use of biometric identifiers and body scanners at international borders to the commercial tracking of objects with sensor technologies, the calculation of possible risks dwells among an extraordinary multiplicity of people and objects. It is to these people and objects that I will return in part 3, where the effects of the derivative risk form come more fully into view. The security calculation is written, as Pynchon's Jessica realizes and as Friedrich Kittler suggests in his analysis of data and technoscience, by "scanning lines and dots of a situation that forgets us."[75] The derivative risk form acts through us and the prosaic, intimate, banal traces of our lives, but yet it forgets us. As necessarily incomplete, complex people and as vital, lively things in the world, the calculus must necessarily forget. What is it that is forgotten by the risk techniques of the politics of possibility? It is the potentialities of a life that is lived amid myriad uncertainties. There are, of course, threats and dangers that could not be anticipated, but to live in association, to have relations, to be a life, as Gilles Deleuze puts it, a "life indefinite," a life of potentiality, this is also the promise of that which is never amenable to calculation.[76] As we shall see, the capacity to array possible futures in a risk calculus does not exhaust the full range of possibilities, the potentiality of the future.

Part II

SPACES

3. ON THE LINE
Life Signatures and the Writing of the Border

Ancestral DNA testing will not be used alone but will combine with language analysis, investigative interviewing techniques and other recognized forensic disciplines. The results of the combination of these procedures may indicate a person's *possible* origin and enable the UKBA [UK Border Agency] to make further enquiries leading to the return of those *intenting* on abusing the UK's asylum system.
—John Travis, "Scientists Decry 'Flawed' and 'Horrifying' Nationality Tests," 14

"The thing about raster graphics," Tariq was saying, "is that you can precisely manipulate an image by altering a single dot at a time. . . . What they'd like to do with real people if they could. I work on bitmaps to make better pictures." . . .
   She remembered what Tariq had said to her—how it was what they would like to do with real people if they could. . . . They were morphing her pixel by pixel into what she was not, the unknown terrorist. —Richard Flanagan, *The Unknown Terrorist*, 76, 207

On March 11, 2004, 191 people were killed in the bombing of four commuter trains in the Spanish capital of Madrid. In a police raid one month after the attacks took place, the suspects detonated a bomb that tore through their apartment, killing them and a police officer at the scene. For the Spanish authorities, the problem of identifying the unknown suspected terrorists whose remains were found inside the building quickly became translated as a forensic problem of identifying national origins. Could the analysis of DNA from the scene provide evidence of the involvement of either the Basque separatist group Euskadi Ta Askatasuna (ETA) or a group affiliated with Al-Qaeda? The forensic geneticist Christopher Phillips was asked to establish the ancestry of the suspected bombers from DNA drawn from the remains in the bombed out apartment. On the basis of the assumption that the Basque separatist group ETA would be broadly distinguishable from groups affiliated with Al-Qaeda along European and North African lines, Phillips pointed to the effects of centuries of migration on the Y chromosome, such that "in genetic terms" Europeans and North Africans "can be thought of as the same population."[1] In terms of establishing clear borderlines between national populations, the scientist suggested, conventional forensic genetics would not be up to the task—the Y chromosome is an insufficiently finite indicator of geographical origins. Phillips's team pursued a more finitely targeted technique, genotyping thirty-four single DNA variants known as single nucleotide polymorphisms (SNPS or "snips") on other chromosomes found to be linked to the bombings. They concluded that the DNA found on a toothbrush at the apartment almost certainly belonged to someone of North African origin, possibly an Algerian.

Despite conventional DNA *sequencing* techniques failing to reveal a probabilistic national origin, the micro-*array* of SNP analysis allowed for action to be taken on the basis of possibility. As the genetics team put the issue, "DNA should be used to suggest what a suspect might look like" and not only to "match individuals already in the database."[2] When the possibilities of "what the suspect might look like" as signaled by the SNP analysis were later cross-matched with crime databases, the "unknown terrorist" was matched to a relative in an existing database, an Algerian named Daoud Ohunane, who was suspected of planning the Madrid attacks. In a move from forensic evidence in the strict sense of one-to-one matches to inference from subtle SNP variations, the borderline is written not between assumed national populations, or people "already in a database," but instead on the basis of finite markers on the chromosome itself. Put simply, advances in genetic techniques appeared to hold out the possibility of inscribing the borderline in a more finite way that anticipates an unknown subject yet to come fully into view.

When, two years later, the Madrid genetic scientists were approached by the UK Home Office for the pilot of their Human Provenance Project (HPP), the preemptive possibilities of SNP arrays became mobilized to infer the national origins of detained persons seeking asylum. The HPP is designed to assess the likelihood that persons claiming asylum in the

UK might "abuse the system," specifically in the case of the pilot to infer whether those claiming origins in Somalia could be from other countries such as Kenya. Among many other leading scientists questioning the validity of the program, the Madrid team sought to differentiate their work on the bombings of 2004—*the forensic gathering of evidence after the event*— from the HPP's "wild inferences" of future infractions yet to take place. "I thought it was for forensic purposes," complained Phillips, "not for border controls."[3] What the forensic geneticists have overlooked, though, is precisely the extent to which contemporary border controls mobilize correlations between fragments of a human subject, incomplete but, once assembled, used to define the borderline itself and who may cross it. Thus it is that the gathering of evidence of terrorist activities after the fact seeps into the preemptive search for indicators of intent capable of anticipating future possible infraction, collapsing meaningful distinctions between counterterrorism and border control measures. In this sense border controls are increasingly described as *forensic* in approach, appearing to make ever more finite distinctions within and between categories of population and life itself.

As in the opening epigraph of this chapter, the sovereign capacity to write the borderline in and through the lives of people gathers together multiple elements of what is thought to be known about a person—each element, in the singular, a mere possibility, as we saw in chapter 2—in order to give the appearance of an emergent subject. Despite substantial scientific opposition to the deployment of DNA's "life signatures" for security decisions,[4] the techniques are defended via an appeal to the possibilities of their being assembled together. Thus, in a meeting with the Human Genetics Commission, the UK Border Agency (UKBA) emphasized that "the genetic tests are not used in isolation" but would instead "act as a filter" combined with other data elements to "prioritise which asylum seekers should be searched against the Kenyan fingerprint databases" and "make the mesh on the sieve a lot finer."[5] The appeal to a multielement mosaic of (equally contingent and disputable) elements that we might also call life signatures—from biometrics and language analysis to financial transactions and travel patterns monitoring—becomes the basis of a so-called forensic border control. Like the Monte Carlo fallacy, in which a series of values does not change the probability of a future outcome (a run of even numbers in a series of throws of the dice does not make an odd more likely on the next throw, for example), the assembly of improbable, imprecise, or chance elements does not render the overall inference more certain. And yet, while improbable in the singular, arrays of life signatures become actionable as border security devices, as though their gathering together reduced the residual doubt.

It is precisely this gathering of life signatures that characterizes contemporary sovereign decisions on the borderline. What I have elsewhere termed the "biometric border" not only signals a turn to digital technologies, molecular techniques, and data analytics in the politics of the border and its management.[6] It simultaneously dissects bodies into granular degrees of risk, such that mobile subjects are inscribed with, and carry with them, plural encoded borderlines. By contrast with Melinda Cooper's proposal that the "biopolitical relations" of late capitalism definitively displace the territorial lines of "geopolitics," the biometric border exhibits the capacity to write the lines of geopolitics biopolitically, finding novel ways to map and divide the cartographies of our world.[7] From the Greek *geo* (earth) and *graphein* (writing), as Matthew Sparke reminds us, the geo-graph of the borderline is written in ways that defy the strict geometry of a line at the edge of territory.[8] The earth writing of our times reflects the *dispositif* envisaged by Michel Foucault when he noted that "apparatuses of security have the constant tendency to expand, new elements are constantly being integrated."[9] The integration of new elements takes place through the mobile writing of borderlines delineating safe or dangerous, of risk or at risk, eligible or ineligible, an "optimization of systems of difference, in which the field is left open to fluctuating processes."[10] The life signature optimizes the system of difference in such a way that the sovereign decision on the border can remain open to the fluctuating processes of capital flows and labor migration. As one border security program, the United States Visitor and Immigrant Status Indicator Technology (US-VISIT)—itself replete with life signatures of many kinds—displays on the walls of all U.S. land, air, and sea border crossings: "Our Borders Open, Our Nation Secure." It is the life signature's capacity to optimize the finite systems of difference and differentiation that underwrite a border whose geo-graphy is perennially open *and* secure.

Understood in this way, the writing of the borderline becomes a practice of discrimination and division that works by a curious connecting of elements, a "connecting of the dots," that seeks out lines of association, correlation, and inference. As Michael Dillon has put the problem, there are "differentiating and dividing practices" that not only write definitive "inclusions and exclusions," but also "modulate eligibilities, liabilities and legibilities."[11] And so, as the finite 'snips' on the Y chromosome of the person seeking asylum is cross-matched to a Kenyan fingerprint database, the dissecting lines define the very limits of what can be seen or recognized of this person and their claims. As Richard Flanigan notes in his startlingly observant novel, *The Unknown Terrorist*, "pictures" of the unknown terrorist emerge "by altering a single dot at a time, pixel by pixel." His protagonist, the "Doll," finds the petty fragments of her life—the cash she has saved from her job as a lap dancer, her encounters with strangers who become "associates," the mundane transactions of her daily life—expanded and aligned together in ways that defy their singular innocence and point toward a dangerous threat. Tariq only "changed images, dot by dot," Flanigan's protagonist recalls, while the security authorities "were doing something far bolder, morphing her pixel by pixel," turning her from a woman into "cartoons, headlines, opinions, fears, fate," until she resembled what she was not "the Black Widow, the dancer of death, the unknown terrorist."[12] The Doll is not merely excluded, taken outside and divided from the rest of society. Rather she is divided within herself, included by means of the exclusion of elements of herself, she "becomes what she was not."

If the border increasingly dwells in a series of life signature points and lines from which a picture of a person is inferred, then the sovereign decision on the borderline can be invoked anywhere, anytime, for anyone. Flanigan's Doll is an Australian citizen, her claim to belonging effaced by the other person who emerges in the writing of the lines of safe/dangerous, us/them by the Australian authorities. Similarly, the Somalian arriving in Europe, makes an asylum claim that cannot be heard amid the assembling of fragments of language tests and DNA that might infer a possible Kenyan origin. When Giorgio Agamben invokes the "iustitium" of Roman law—a standstill or suspension of the rule of law in the state of emergency—he identifies a "floating and anonymous imperium" that enlists all authorities and citizens to "take whatever measures they considered necessary for the salvation of the state."[13] The declaration of exception thus authorizes limitless arrays of fragments that can be deployed to re-draw the line and secure the life of the population. The graphing of the geo thus incorporates sovereign decisions that exceed and overspill the state—processes of scanning, screening, testing, and analysis whose results underwrite deportation or detention—and act beneath the threshold of the policing of the borderline itself.[14] In short, the visible enactment of the decision of the border guard conceals the multitude of petty judgments that is the floating imperium. In the discussion that follows I am concerned with specifying precisely how it is that the border comes to be written in and through the life signatures of what Gilles Deleuze terms a "dividuated" human subject.[15] I am interested particularly in two emerging sets of practices through which the contemporary borderline is written, each of which inscribes its lines within the mobile body, dissecting the subject into degrees of risk: mosaic lines and automated targeting and the lines of sight in biometrics and whole-body scanners.

Mosaic Lines: The Border and Automated Targeting

The Special Immigration Appeals Commission (SIAC) is the only court of appeal in the United Kingdom for foreign nationals facing indefinite detention, deportation, or exclusion from the country on the grounds that they may pose a threat to national security. Where there is insufficient evidence to charge an individual under the Terrorism Act (2000), the secretary of state may pass the suspect from the institutions of criminal justice to the immigration authorities in the form of the UKBA. In effect, an exception to the usual rule of law is in operation in SIAC hearings, where the principle that one must know of what one is accused is partially suspended. Intelligence material is heard in closed session as secret evidence and excludes the appellant and his or her legal representative from knowing the full case on which the sovereign decision rests.[16] As one senior barrister reflects on the gathered fragments on the basis of which inferences of future security threat are made: "Neither we nor our clients were ever given the 'ingredients' of the mosaic—we were simply given conclusions, expressed in the form 'we assess that X has been involved in attack planning.' This is the way it operates, piecing together fragments which in themselves are innocent."[17]

It is precisely this piecing together of otherwise contingent life signatures that produces the mosaic spatial form of the contemporary borderline. Though the SIAC hearings arguably represent the extreme case of where the borderline is written into the relations and associations of the mosaic—where counterterrorism and immigration blur irrevocably into one—in fact, the mosaic form is at the forefront of all contemporary border controls. Although the evidence heard in closed session is most commonly depicted as secret intelligence pertaining to terrorism planning, the disclosure of which could compromise the safety of intelligence officers, actually the mosaic is comprised of multiple mundane fragments that only become designated as "secret" or, indeed, as "intelligence" once they are assembled together in association. "That is the problem," explains one SIAC lawyer, "in order to represent them effectively I need to be able to understand those links that have been made, to retrace the steps. But to take the mosaic apart and rebuild it? It is increasingly impossible to do." If the borderline is drawn through a joining of dots and lines of associated elements, the many decisions on the assembly of the mosaic are, in effect, sovereign decisions that are untraceable and unrecognizable in the conventions of legal evidence and burdens of proof. The content of the mosaic that is sought by this lawyer is best understood as a set of relations between life signatures—between people and their "associates," between past travel to Yemen and a specified duration of stay thought to be necessary for terrorism training, between donations to a charitable agency and a particular money transfer agency, for example.[18]

While some of the elements of the mosaic are intelligence data gleaned by the security services, much of it is built on government and commercial material that is routinely collected for other purposes. In the case of the United States, for example, under the Intelligence Reform and Terrorist Prevention Act (IRTPA) of 2004, the category of what counts as "national intelligence" is vastly extended, such that the Office of the Director of National Intelligence "can designate information collected anywhere as national intelligence, which means it can be used in analyzing threats to the country."[19] The meaning of intelligence itself is expanded, with the effect that information that would be insufficient to allow for charges to be brought within the criminal justice system is deployed as a preemptive immigration and border control measure. As is the case with SIAC proceedings or with the use of DNA "snips," expanded national intelligence permits preemptive detention, deportation, or the revoking of citizenship by other means. The writing of a broader mosaic of possible life signatures seeks to bring into focus the unknown potential terrorist. As the former U.S. director of national intelligence Dennis Blair testified to the U.S. Senate Homeland Security and Governmental Affairs Committee:

> The most valuable national intelligence is the huge collection of
> databases of routinely collected information that can be searched by
> computer algorithm. An analyst may know that a *potential* terrorist
> attacker is between 23 and 28 years old, has lived in Atlanta Georgia,

and has travelled often to Yemen. That analyst would like to be able to very rapidly query the travel records, the customs and border protection service, the investigative records of the State Department. . . . We made important progress after the December 2009 attempted bombing of an aircraft over Detroit, but there remains much more to be done.[20]

Thus it is that what comes to count as the actionable intelligence behind a sovereign decision is a mosaic of overwhelmingly ordinary fragments of a life that become, once arrayed together, secret and sensitive evidence. The "potential terrorist attacker" subject is disaggregated and reassembled as a mosaic of elements that then become classified and, therefore, are not disclosed to the subject. How is the mosaic assembled? How do the lines of association hold together the fragments? When the category of national intelligence expands to assemble multiple ordinary elements, the security mosaic begins to have profound political effects. Let us now take one strand of the mosaic—travel and immigration records—to explain something of the making of this novel border geography.

Following the foiled plot to detonate liquid bombs in transatlantic airliners in August 2006, Michael Chertoff, the then U.S. secretary for the Department of Homeland Security (DHS), publicly made the case for the collection, integration, and analysis of "terrorist-related information" as a central measure of the war on terror. In an article for the *Washington Post*, Chertoff contrasted the use of credit card and telephone records to identify the associates of the 9/11 hijackers after the event with his desire to "identify such connections before a hijacker boards a plane."[21] "Ideally, I would like to know," he proposed, "did Mohammed Atta get his ticket paid on the same credit card. That would be a huge thing—and I would like to know that in advance, because that would allow us to identify an *unknown terrorist*." Hence, the relationship between two fragments of commercially derived data—an airline reservation and a credit card record—become a condition of possibility for preemptive security intervention.

Similarly, and also in 2006, the routine extradition of travel and financial data from the European Union to U.S. authorities for the purposes of identifying "potential terrorists before they arrive on U.S. soil" was uncovered and became the subject of European legal challenge.[22] On June 23, 2006, the *New York Times* disclosed the existence of the Terrorist Finance Tracking Program (TFTP) that had been initiated by the U.S. Treasury and the

CIA in the weeks following the 9/11 attacks.[23] Within the TFTP the U.S. authorities requested and analyzed financial transactions records held by the Belgian-based Society for Worldwide Interbank Financial Telecommunications (SWIFT) in order to "identify future perpetrators and facilitators."[24] For the security authorities, the SWIFT database was seductive because it held the records of some 80 percent of global financial transfers, thus offering a kind of "electronic footprint" of future terrorist intent. Similarly, the transfer of passenger name record (PNR) data from European carriers to the U.S. authorities, via the departure control systems, was perceived to offer a vast array of new data fields for security analysis.[25]

The PNR and SWIFT data represent significant sources of the life signatures that comprise the border mosaic. Indeed, the transactions contained within the SWIFT database and the PNR records are not merely the "traces" or "electronic footprints" of a known subject left behind in the residue of life in a global economy. They are more precisely life signatures in the sense that they are deployed to sift and assess forms of life in emergence, incomplete forms that do not map one-to-one onto an individual. In her discussion of René Dubos, the microbiologist who first used the term *emergence*, Melinda Cooper describes a biological evolution that could "never be predicted in linear terms" but that demands a response within the emergent itself, "long before it has actualized in a form we can locate or even recognize."[26] In a similar way to Dubos's sudden horizontal transitions in microbial life, the security life signature is thought to contain incipient disturbances that signal a future possible threat. Consider, for example, the U.S. assessment of the value of unverified fragments of PNR data in the absence of "complete and detailed information." The analysis of the fragments, as the U.S. attorney general proposes, serves to "fill in the gaps with inferences" and to "provide the best answer possible under conditions of uncertainty."[27] The partial and fragmentary content of the mosaic becomes a virtue, becomes the very means by which to grasp the contours of an emergent suspect who has not been actualized in a recognizable form. Thus the geography of what the U.S. and UK authorities have termed a "virtual border" is written in a series of "touchpoints" that "prevent potential threats prior to arrival."[28] Understood in this way, the life signatures of an emergent subject reach a physical international border crossing long before an identifiable and actualized subject does.

Where and how is the borderline written in the extradited data of emergent subjects? Where does the border materialize and how is it decided?

The existing and draft PNR agreements include the establishment of a network of passenger information units (PIUS), where the raw data are "flushed through" the analytics for the twinned purposes I discussed in chapter 2: for the "real-time risk assessment of the passengers," generating risk scores that are conveyed to the frontline border guards, and for the "purpose of identifying trends and patterns, to create new criteria."[29] The day-to-day creation of elements of the mosaic can be most clearly viewed in the more developed examples of the PIU system—the UK's National Border Targeting Centre (NBTC) and the U.S. Automated Targeting System for Passengers (ATS-P). As the designer of the data-push systems to both NBTC and ATS-P explains:

> So you are going to have match analysts, people in Newington Virginia or Manchester UK who are sitting in these terrible rooms looking at the screens. But the idea of these systems is that they're fully automated, . . . every flight into your country and in all likelihood every flight out of your country or maybe even domestic flights. You're capturing the data, you're processing the data, you're assigning a risk score. The one percent or less who are a concern you assign a risk score to them, in the interactive world of i-Borders, you may want to even detain because there's such a problem.[30]

The so-called match analysts within the PIUS watch the screens of data, judging the strength of the automated alerts and passing the coded risk score to border control, customs, law enforcement, or the intelligence agencies. It is in the anonymous buildings of Newington, Virginia, and Manchester in the UK that pixelated people, dissected into degrees of risk, begin to emerge on the screen. And yet the match analysts do not merely engage in one-to-one matching of known individuals on a watch list. Rather like the Madrid geneticists who differentiated their matching of a known suspect from the inference of "what a suspect may look like," the PIU draws inferences on the basis of possible links. In this sense the writing of the borderline via the PIU shifts from a border security modeled on the Fordist production line, with its linear series of finite tasks and decisions, to the fractured lines of the post-Fordist call center, with its differentiated flows and modulated responses.[31] Indeed, the border writing of the PIU echoes the commercial logics of the call center, where incoming calls are screened and differentiated according to the potential risks and opportunities they present, as "existing customers" or "new claimants," for example. Where the Fordist production line operates by the completion and signing off of a specific task in the series, with each worker responsible for their phase until it is passed to the next, the border crossing of the PIU is never complete, never signed off, always potentially in play. The vertical lines of Fordist integration give way to a horizontal line—a horizon of possibility where all incoming data may become significant in the future and, therefore, must be arrayed in view. The revised EU–U.S. PNR agreement, for example, maps two time horizons for the assessment of data in the PIU. The first sees the PIU retain "PNR in an active database for up to five years," where, after the first six months, it is "depersonalized and masked," present only as a set of relations in other possible mosaics.[32] Second, following the five-year active period, the PNR "shall be transferred to a dormant database for a period of up to ten years" and only "repersonalized" when the PIU cross-checks in connection with "an identifiable case, threat or risk."[33] The horizontal lines of the PIU maintain an array of possible future threats, delinking the PNR from a named subject ("depersonalizing"), discarding the known individual but preserving the possible future relation to new data.

The world of the PIU is a world of gathered fragments, of points and lines that are continually changing in relation to the "real-time" events of the border crossing. It is in this way that the writing of the mosaic allows for a different and distinctive kind of border control, a modulated border that imagines possible future links in its arrayed data. As the U.S. Director of National Intelligence James Clapper explains, the Obama administration advanced an "imaginative" program of linking partial data elements: "To develop security programs that take full advantage of the *fragmentary* intelligence information we need something else. For too long the only responses to the incomplete threat information we collected on Al-Qaeda operatives was a general colour coded terrorism warning or the no-fly list. We needed to do better. I engaged personally with Secretary Napolitano on this issue early in 2010, and the DHS developed several *imaginative* programs to take advantage of *partial intelligence* to guide the screening at border entry points."[34]

The more imaginative programs depicted by James Clapper consist precisely of the use of inference to make links between partial elements of information. Mosaics are assembled pieces of partial intelligence held together by the social network analysis that is automated within the PIU and by the expansion of some risk-scored relations to fill in the gaps. As I suggested in chapter 2, the fixed disciplinary criteria of the alert or the no-fly list does not readily fit with the fragmentary intelligence of the mosaic. In the imaginative programs of mosaic lines the border control ceases to be interested in individuals as such, instead attending to an incomplete subject comprised of elements. In what Gilles Deleuze calls the "societies of control," what is important is "no longer either a signature or a number," nor a "watchword," but rather the "password."[35] Like the Deleuzian watchword, the watch list is a distinctively disciplinary technique of prohibition, enclosing, and stopping. We see in Foucault's lectures that the project of an "exhaustively disciplinary society" gives way, as "on the horizon we see instead the image . . . of a society in which the field is left open to fluctuating processes."[36]

Unlike the watch list or the color-coded alert, the "password" of PNR is akin to a net that allows for the passing through of some elements of a subject, while others are drawn into new horizontal relations with the elements of other subjects. "Enclosures are moulds, distinct castings," writes Deleuze, "but controls are a modulation, like a self-deforming cast that will continuously change from one moment to the other, or like a sieve whose mesh will transmute from point to point."[37] To illustrate, indifferent to the properties of the "dots" to be connected, one might see that this passport number, or that visa waiver, would pass through unnoticed, while some other data "point" or fragment (a past event, a past transaction) is disaggregated from the remainder and becomes associated with others derived from other subjects. Such point-to-point techniques can never meaningfully be said to have failed. Though a critique might point to the multiple failures of the life signature—in the SIAC or in the HPP or at the border—the unmooring and reassembling of residual elements means that even the error is incorporated. So, for example, the pre-subjects that would later emerge as Najibullah Zazi (convicted in 2012 of the plot to bomb the New York City subway in 2009), Umar Farouk Abdulmutallab (sentenced in 2012 for the attempted bombing of an airliner in 2009), and Faisal Shahzad (sentenced in 2010 for the attempted Times Square car bombing) could be offered as evidence of the fallibility of the system—conventionally placed on the watch list and missed by the risk-based technologies. Yet in later analyses of counterterrorism by the U.S. attorney general, these subjects emerge not as named and identified individuals but as dividuals whose reassembled elements function as part of Secretary Napolitano's more imaginative programs. The subjects became "operatives with British or American passports or visas who had visited South Asia and had returned to the United States over [redacted in original] time period."[38] Thus, it is the modulated life signatures of their associations that write them into being and call them retroactively to attention.

How might we grasp the spatial character of these mosaic borderlines as they modulate from point to point, exceeding the sum of their constituent elements? The systems of enclosure that characterized Foucault's disciplinary societies, Deleuze reminds us, appear as a linear series of spaces of enclosure—school, factory, barracks, clinic, prison—through which "the individual passes" as though "independent variables."[39] In the logic of the series, "one was always starting again," moving from one enclosed and independent space to the next. Each stage in the series is signed off as the subsequent enclosure opens up—the signature marking the right of passage. In the "variable geometry" of the modulation, by contrast, "molecular engineering" and "genetic manipulations" exceed the analogue series of a life of enclosure, rendering the subject as "chains of variables torn from each other."[40] Though perhaps Deleuze was correct to declare the death of the signature in the sense of a one-to-one matching to the individual, it is precisely in the torn chains of variables that the contemporary life signature ceases to be attached to the subject as such and is released into the world in new ways.

If the contemporary border control acts through a mosaic comprised of modulated life signatures, then the linear series of checks, documents, and verifications becomes overwhelmed by the unanticipated element—from a PNR or a TFTP to a DNA "snip." In Manuel DeLanda's "partially aleatory series" we begin to see how an array of dots and lines defy serial causality and criteria in the strict sense: "The ideal events forming a virtual series must not be conceived as having numerical probabilities of occurrence associated with them; they must be arrayed using only ordinal distances, and be distinguished from one another exclusively by the difference between the singular and the ordinary, the rare and the common, without further specification. In other words . . . an information transfer should not be conceived as changes in conditional probabilities, but simple changes in the distribution of the singular and the ordinary within a series."[41]

It is just such an aleatory series that forms the information transfer of PNR data within a broader security mosaic. First, the composite elements do not have numerical probabilities of occurrence attached to them. The presence of a singular event—say, this transaction made in this place on this day—alone tells nothing of the probability of occurrence of some future event. What matters is solely the difference between the singular event and the ordinary. Second, the relation to other elements is defined only by ordinal distances point to point—the array of the social network analysis positioning possible association only by represented proximity within a diagram. The value of the element is not intrinsic to the number itself—not a cardinal number as such—but is derived from its position in relation to other elements, from its ordinal value. Third, the distinguishing marks of difference, unlike the criteria of a probabilistic series, are only those of the singular and the ordinary. What I termed the "mobile norm" in chapter 2 is the only mark of norm and anomaly that is at work in the mosaic. The information transfer represented by extradited PNR or SWIFT data does not signal a change in conditional probability; it cannot say "this individual element makes this attack more probable." Rather, the transfer of such information simply changes the distribution of possibility, the array of the normal and ordinary with the singular and anomalous that makes it possible to intervene on a future subject at the border. In short, the aleatory and variable geometry signaled by Deleuze and by DeLanda, and manifested in the border mosaic, allows for action on the basis of the improbable, the merely possible.

To clarify at this point, contemporary border controls no longer work strictly with a linear series of enclosed life events, attached to the individual as signatory. As it is for Richard Flanigan's fictional unknown terrorist, the Doll, the series of her life events that she might recount to protest her innocence (the circumstances of her childhood, the death of her own child, her job as a pole dancer, her friendships as more than associations) are torn apart as variables and reassembled as a chain of events signaling emergent dangerous intent. She becomes, in Deleuze's terms, a "dividual," divided at once within herself and from the others in her community. The dividuated elements of her life signatures, torn from their context, readily become attached to the gathered elements of other people and things. Where disciplinary society renders the individual and the population as "two poles," the society of control has the dividual and the "bank." As a dividuated subject living amid a bank of disaggregated indicators of risk, Flanagan's Doll does indeed become a subject in what William Connolly calls a "world of becoming," a subject of "sovereign decisions in a shadow zone."[42] The life signature I have outlined is the signature that persists, the signature of subjects severed from any linear series, written in and through the fragments of a life. "We are traversed by lines," write Deleuze and Guattari, "we are composed of lines," of "bundles of lines," each of them multiple and different in nature, "some of these lines imposed on us from outside" and "others that can be invented, drawn, without a model."[43] Just as the collection of spatial and geometric data was intrinsic to the genealogy of cartographic border writing—written and imposed from the outside but lived in the everyday signatures of immigration documents—so the new cartography of the borderline assembles the life signatures of transactions with airlines, DNA databases, travel agencies, banks and credit card companies. The Doll's life signature writes a future person, an unknown terrorist, into being, and this is precisely how the life signatures of PNR, ATS-P, and the PIU do their work.

Lines of Sight: The Border and the Unknown Subject

In a letter sent to members of the European Parliament in 2007, Michael Chertoff, the then U.S. secretary for the DHS, outlined the case for the use of software analytics and biometrics in the search for "hidden links that might reveal unknown terrorist connections."[44] This letter represents one of the very few instances where the case for new risk-based and preemptive border controls is made on the basis of specific examples of security interventions that have been made at, or in advance of, the U.S. border. As such, it reveals how a "person of interest" comes to attention: "the use of a shared credit card," "a reservation history," "a past travel itinerary," "a ticket purchased using cash and with certain changes to the reservation," "travel patterns exhibiting high risk indicators," "a split PNR," and "a Palestinian who had previously claimed political asylum." I have discussed how it is that these lines of association become actionable intelligence, and I have proposed that this has become a novel geo-graphing of the borderline. However, at the heart of these techniques is a particular way of bringing to attention emergent subjects who, as yet, are not fully in view. Thus in the examples presented to the European Parliament, what matters is not strictly what the technologies can do to identify known individuals but rather how previously unknown "dangerous" subjects come to attention, and how a security decision of detention or deportation might be made on that basis. Given that it is not individuals as such but fragments or elements of risk that are brought to attention, how does the contemporary border recognize a "person of interest"? And how does that risky subject come to attention in advance of the event?

Within the text of Michael Chertoff's speech before the European Parliament, one example illustrates vividly the logic of an emergent subject whose full-threat potential is only realized in a future event, but whose biometric imprint secures the link to the event: "In June 2003, using PNR data and other analytics, one of our inspectors at Chicago O'Hare Airport pulled aside an individual for secondary inspection and questioning. They took his fingerprints and denied him entry to the United States. The next time we saw those fingerprints—or at least parts of them—they were on the steering wheel of a suicide vehicle that blew up and killed 132 people in Iraq."[45] The lines of association that are drawn here are not linear and causal but temporally and spatially fractured. An array of associations between past events is assembled to create a "high-risk traveler" in advance of arrival at the U.S. border. Though the data elements are insufficiently strong as evidence to detain or to charge with a crime, the subject is denied access to the United States and his biometric is added to the database. The incomplete array of data elements persists long after the subject has receded from view. It is a future event yet to take place—a suicide bombing in Iraq—that retroactively becomes the justification for the intervention at Chicago O'Hare. In this way the vast expansion of biometrics in the military strategic control of flows of people in Iraq and Afghanistan is paralleled by biometric border controls with which it is interfaced.[46]

Unlike the watch list with its named individuals, or indeed the signature on a passport or immigration document, the biometric is one specific manifestation of the *life signature* of an emergent dangerous subject. Where the conventional signature serves to verify a series of data on an individual, the life signature authorizes access to an array of elements on an unknown subject. The biometric does not simply authenticate a one-to-one match with a named individual; it is not primarily a mode of identification but rather functions as a form of a "key" that unlocks the chain of variables of the modulated border control. Indeed, for the designers of border security solutions, the biometric is the key that unlocks the automated gate or "e-gate" of the contemporary border:

> To completely automate these systems means adding in biometrics.
> You go to security, you provide your biometric, you go through an
> iris type of system, a short cut through security, you use an e-gate.
> You're a citizen of, say, France or the UK, you're entitled to use this
> e-gate. It may not be available for foreigners or non-Europeans or

whatever, wherever you want to draw the line. Maybe you have one guy watching ten gates, that's what you have in Dubai, reduced head count, you still haven't dealt with an airline official. And then you go to the boarding gate and again you have a turnstile or some other device with a biometric reader, like the Heathrow MiSense programme. For a border solution to be fully effective, you want a biometric layer.[47]

The relationship between the biometric key and the analytics that tells the e-gate whether to be open or closed is fluid and contingent, the key never fitting the lock once and for all time. Because the so-called e-gate is modulated according to chains of variables, the biometric key may fit when the variables are arrayed in a particular way (for example, when this frequent flier data and this payment method and this hire car dropped off at airport), but it may fail to unlock the chain in other future forms (for example, when it is torn through this subsequent pattern of travel or by a booking with this high-risk associate). Understood in this way the "software sorting" of safe or "trusted travelers" from the dangerous or risky is never as simple as the judgments of surveillants against a series of criteria suggested by some commentators.[48] Perhaps even the depiction of biometric border controls as the biopolitical control of mobile bodies has underestimated the extent to which the biometric life signature divides the body even within itself. When Giorgio Agamben decried the "electronic scanning of finger and retina prints," the "subcutaneous tattooing" of the biometric, he characterized this "bio-political tattooing" as "the routine inscription of the most private and most incommunicable element of subjectivity—the biopolitical life of the body."[49] For Agamben there is a particular "taking outside" at work in the biometric enrollment of "good citizens" in the "gears and mechanisms of the state," wherein the most private and incommunicable elements of subjectivity are extracted and exposed to view. The governing of species life, one might say, takes place through the *exteriorization* of intimate and corporeal elements of life itself, of a subject in formation.

In fact, though, the biometric life signature writes its lines in ways that simultaneously *interiorize*, extending the dividing practices that would otherwise dwell outside the body to the inside. The subject in formation is dissected, penetrated not merely to expose to an external objective security gaze but also to significantly extend the dividing practices of discrimination at work in society into and through the body itself. In this sense the biometric as life signature is somewhat akin to Deleuze's genetic code, in which there is an "interiorization of the intensive individuating factors" that would otherwise remain external to the body itself.[50] The constitutive differences through which a society makes itself and its relation to others are, by means of the use of measures such as DNA analysis or biometrics, extended to the body itself, interiorized and "taken inside." So, for example, the complex systems of difference that make the establishment of citizenship and the noncitizen possible extend not only to the conventional objects of passport and visa but also are interiorized in the differentiation of snips on the Y chromosome or iris scans at the e-gate. As Irma Van der Ploeg has depicted the entwining of bodies with information systems, the "body as data" collapses meaningful distinctions between the interior or "body as matter" and the exterior or "body as representation," such that there is a rewriting of "the boundary between what is inside and what is outside the human body."[51] As the borderline enrolls the biometric, it does so with an intertwined corporeal inside and outside, a spiraling out of pictorial images of the inside coupled with an incorporation or incorporealization of digitized risk profiles and biometric databases within.

Prefiguring the contemporary desire to infer genetic provenance or locate biometric anchor points, the genealogy of biometry exhibits the coalescence of processes of interiorization and exteriorization—a drive to anchor identifiability in the uniqueness of the human body and to visualize and project future deviant tendencies through abstracted bodies. Francis Galton's nineteenth-century founding of biometry sought to correlate physical attributes and social and racial "types" with degrees of criminality and degeneracy. His "composite portrait" technique sought to overlay multiple exposed photographs of individuals within a group in order to produce a picture that "contains a resemblance to all [its constituents] but is not more like to one of them than to another."[52] Galton's composite is not a one-to-one match with an identifiable individual but a reaggregation of those underlying individual components that produces a picture of an unknown subject. Galton had twinned objectives for his composite portrait—to "exteriorize" judgment, banishing subjective error with mechanical imaging devices, and to "interiorize" difference, locating the indicators of deviance within the body itself. His composite portraits of groups of "murderers or violent robbers" visualized the statistical correlations between corporeal measurements and behavior, bringing propensity "into focus so that the archetypal killer could appear before our eyes."[53] Galton's biometry appealed to the belief that the inherited traits of degeneracy would threaten the very basis of social order and that statistical correlations could be usefully deployed to protect that order. The effort to visualize deviant tendencies from abstracted bodies and to locate identifiability in the body's specificity led to the fingerprint identification method pioneered by Galton, and it arguably persists in contemporary biometric techniques.

We can say that there is nothing intrinsically novel in the contemporary claim to secure the border through the apparently unique life signatures of DNA or digital fingerprint, nor even perhaps in the preemptive visualization of what someone not yet in full view "might look like." The genealogical story of biometry suggests that the body as data, or at least as statistical data, has never been a matter merely of the enumeration of individual bodies but rather the surface for the analysis of future propensities and proclivities. In Galton we can locate a historical moment where the life signature came to the fore—his composite not quite mapping onto any identifiable individual—a "true combination" of underlying tendencies.[54] And yet the question of how those underlying components are assembled together and, moreover, how they are made amenable to the senses and to judgment is not only a question of continuity. To address how the contemporary borderline deploys novel relations of the body to objectivity, another genealogy would have to be traced—the story of how *bodies in movement* become amenable to science and knowledge.

A particular form of objectivity, termed "mechanical objectivity" by historians of science Lorraine Daston and Peter Galison, characterized Galton's world of the mid-nineteenth century. The new methods of "making images untouched by human hands, neither the artist's nor the scientist's," write Daston and Galison, "aimed at automatism," the eradication of subjective judgment and the establishment of "blind sight, seeing without inference."[55] Certainly for Galton it was important that his composite emerged objectively from the mechanical merging of the component images. We might even see an echo of this mechanical objectivity in the unmanned e-gate of contemporary biometrics, where the fallibility of the border guard's judgment is replaced by the automation of biometric keys in digitized data locks. In Eadweard Muybridge's experiments with sequential photographs of galloping horses in 1879, though, it is possible to locate a line of sight, a regime of seeing, that reconfigures the perception of movement itself. Commissioned by the wealthy Californian financier and racehorse owner Leland Stanford to conduct motion studies of the horse, Muybridge took a

FIGURE 3.1. Eadweard Muybridge's modular segmentation of images of the racehorse Sallie Gardner, 1879. Courtesy of Kingston Museum and Heritage Service.

series of photographs of horses at the gallop. Segmenting his image stills as a series of "cuts" in movement, and displaying them in an array of columns and rows, Muybridge famously demonstrated to a disbelieving public that there is a moment in the horse's movement at the gallop when all four legs are suspended, hooves off the ground (see figure 3.1). The breakthrough of Muybridge's work, as art historian Jonathan Crary recounts, is "its deployment of machinic high speeds for the creation of perceptual units beyond the capacities of human vision," and their "subsequent abstract arrangement outside the terms of any subjective experience." Here we have an important moment in the making of a form of seeing—predating cinema—that precisely uses the gaps between the frames to visualize something beyond the capacity of human vision, to "radically rearrange perception itself." The arrangement of Muybridge's frames is a broken chain in Deleuze's terms, a chain of variables whose flow is not immediately causal or linear. The relations between the frames are relations point to point; their value ascribed only via the gaps between the frames through which the observer must infer movement itself. For Jonathan Crary there is a close proximity between the array of equine stills and the flows of financial capital that funded Muybridge's experiments: "The segmentation of Muybridge's work should be understood not simply as the breakup of a perceptual field. . . . It announces a vision compatible with the smooth surface of a global marketplace and its new pathways of exchange. Muybridge seems to present the semblance of a classical tabular organization, but what is arrayed in his columns and rows has none of the immutable identities on which the intelligibility of a table depends."[56]

So, the array of gathered images does not depend on a matrix of horizontal and vertical axes against which movement is made intelligible; rather, suspended movement becomes a new technique of vision compatible with the smooth surface of a global marketplace. The point-to-point movement of Muybridge's frames and Stanford's global capital flows definitively breaks with the series of periodized stages, offering a way of visualizing things in movement that does not require absolute identification or categorization. Describing the flows of capital as a "recording surface," a "body without organs," "fluid and slippery," Deleuze and Guattari depict a "strange subject with no fixed identity, wandering about over the body without organs."[57] Like Galton's ghostly composites and Muybridge's horses, the life signature is a strange subject with no fixed identity, and it proliferates within the spaces of the global economy. Consider, for example, the contemporary use of so-called whole body imaging scanners at international borders.[58] Like the biometric and the use of SNPS on DNA, the Backscatter X-ray has become one element in a broader assemblage of fragments to be mined, reassembled, and visualized. Described by its manufacturer Rapiscan Systems as "the most effective people screening solution available," producing "high resolution images that enable the operator to easily identify concealed threat," the whole body scanner holds out the promise of imaging the unseen, penetrating the surface, and making visible that which is hidden from view, opening up new visualizations of the unknown, potentially risky body, as well as new perspectives on its management.[59]

Far from the promised "whole body image," the Backscatter scan is actually a composite of dissected elements of a body, pixelated by X-rays that are "received by high resolution detectors and passed to advanced image processing software," then reassembled with the risk-flagged areas highlighted in red.[60] The resulting image resembles a shadowy negative imprint of body contours that can then be abstracted into what the Transportation Security Administration (TSA) refers to as "chalk lines," reminiscent of those drawn in outline of the evidential body at a crime scene. The image viewed by the screening operative at the border checkpoint is not a "copy" or picture of an individual as such but an abstraction and a recomposition of the dimensions and densities of the body. Dividuated and broken apart in this way, the unknown body is rendered knowable and amenable to security intervention. In effect the borderline is written within the body itself, the zones for security attention "visibilize the invisible," probing beneath what is immediately available to the perception of the observer.[61] Just as the nineteenth-century discovery of X-rays challenged the reliability of touch in medical "imaginations of the interior body," so contemporary arrays of biometrics, DNA, and whole body images reshape perception itself, altering the terrain of what we pay attention to, of who comes to attention.[62] Indeed, rather as the development of medical instruments for revealing somatic secrets challenged the credibility of the physician's touch to take a pulse or measure a foetus, so contemporary instruments make a virtue of what the TSA calls the "hands-off screening" that replaces the "invasive pat down search."

The line of sight that is at work in contemporary border controls is both a regime of perception and subjectivity and a set of practices by which the lines of discrimination and partition are concealed.[63] Put simply, the line of sight works hard to hide from view the very dividing practices it institutes. When, for example, the former secretary for the DHS appealed to the neutral lines, drawn without prejudice in new border controls, he asserted that "we use this data *to focus* on behavior, not race and ethnicity. In fact, what it allows us to do is move beyond crude *profiling* based on prejudice, and *look at* conduct and communication and actual behavior as a way of determining who we need to take *a closer look* at."[64] In one specific sense Chertoff was indeed correct that this line of sight is not strictly profiling. The lines that are drawn are not drawn according to fixed criteria that could be mapped one to one on racial characteristics or ethnic origin. But the particular governing of perception that such systems deploy allow precisely a "focus on," a "closer look at," such that, as we have seen, Chertoff himself offers the example of the Palestinian who has previously claimed asylum. Similarly, the UKBA's defense of the HPP appealed to the scientific objectivity of the underlying behavioral components. The lines of sight that are drawn are prejudicial in new ways that are not quite captured by conventional categories, but they are closer in form to what Jacques Rancière has called the "partitioning of the sensible."[65] For Rancière, politics and aesthetics are founded upon a partitioning of the sensible, a distribution of what can be sensed of the world, on the basis of which people are recognizable as part of community (or not) and sanctioned to take part within community. Understood thus, politics dwells in this very partitioning of the world into that which can be perceived and registered and that which cannot.

In the multitude of ways that software code, digitized images, or biometric scans partition the recognizable from the unrecognizable, they write a borderline that "partitions the sensible" and demarcates the politics of the body at the border. Where Francis Galton's composite images of incipient criminality relied upon a series of layered images of individuals—past criminality inferring the future via the inherited physiognomy of the deviant—Eadweard Muybridge's moving horses break up the series into variables that are torn from one another, arrayed out of series. There is an important distinction between the techniques, with Galton seeking objectivity from the mechanical displacement of the human eye, and Muybridge relying upon the very capacities of perception to "fill in the gaps" between the frames, to reconstitute movement. In both instances, though, the abstraction is underpinned by pictorial elements that are complete and individual photographs of a body in space and time. The line of sight that governs the border today, though it contains the residues of techniques such as those used by Galton and Muybridge, acts on the gaps in forms in a quite different way. The *pixel*, which so vividly creates the images of the unknown terrorist in Richard Flanigan's novel, derives its name from the picture cell or picture element. The composite image is produced not from the movement in a series from one still individual frame to the next but instead via plural dividuated points in play simultaneously. The spatial forms of the array and the mosaic allow for the altering of selected pixelated dots to change the overall composite, but, importantly, the last frame is not lost as the new one comes into view. As we saw with Deleuze's distinction between molds and castings in the society of control, Galton's composite is created from a series of molds, where contemporary borderlines work with castings that keep all other possibilities held together, altering only their relations. Of course, it is not that these castings are not prejudicial or discriminatory, and indeed the forms of concealed racial prejudice are profoundly troubling, but that they write their lines in a novel form that never quite lets go of other future possibilities.

To Be Written Out of This World

When the UK Court of Appeal overturned the judgment reached in the first SIAC case on Shafiq ur Rehman, it distinguished the cumulative effects of the arrayed mosaic from the probabilities of individual acts. "The cumulative effect may establish that the individual is to be *treated as a dan-*

ger," records the Court of Appeal, "although it cannot be proved to a high degree of probability that he has performed any *individual act* which could justify this conclusion." Put simply, the juridical treatment of the data mosaic distinguishes the "balance of probability" of the underlying elements of the mosaic from the aggregate "danger" that is to be inferred. Indeed, the SIAC hearings are replete with uncertainties around the probability of the underlying fragments—"do these activities pose a threat to public security?," "are these loosely connected individuals 'known associates'?," "does the personal conduct of the appellant represent a genuine, present and sufficiently serious threat?"[66] A juridical sense of evidence from past events, and an evaluation of those events on the basis of probability, confronts a set of security measures that are founded on the basis of possibility and not probability. As the former SIAC lay member Brian Barder reported following his resignation from the commission: "The rulings seem to me to establish that the Home Secretary may deport an immigrant without having to show that any single one of his *past activities* contributes towards a case for deportation. He may act in this way merely on the grounds of his belief that *future activities* of the person concerned *might* threaten national security."[67]

Barder's critical assessment of the SIAC regime gets to the heart of all contemporary forms of border and immigration control that deploy the life signature. Indifferent to the specific circumstances of any past activity, the border mosaic seeks out life signatures that appear to signal future intent. In the search for the improbable but catastrophic future event, the making of the mosaic embodies a specific form of biopolitics—it acts on life by writing the life of a dividuated subject, an unspecified life that is recognizable only in its coded degrees of risk. Even the associations of this life, with other people or places, are torn variables that leave only the residue of suspicious behavior or likely future infraction. While critical lawyers continue to demand evidence of one-to-one mapping of the accused individual (and to refute the inferences made by association), the border mosaic is written beyond the limits of the one-to-one match. Drawing some elements of past activities into the calculation, the mosaic nonetheless moves over the surface of multiple past subjects and events in order to imagine a future unknown subject.

As a mosaic of life signatures, the contemporary border is not merely a site of technology, where bodies become inscribed with code, but rather it becomes the sovereign enactment of possibility par excellence. Carried by mobile bodies as they encounter a chain of "touchpoints," the border simultaneously discriminates among and within bodies, dissecting into degrees of risk and visualizing as a series of elements. Where conventional forms of probability in intelligence gathering would discount the fragments as unverifiable, the expansion of intelligence into a world of possibilities lends greater weight to the fragments, making them actionable—in the SIAC or in the PIU or at the e-gate. As the partitioned elements become written, layer upon layer, into data visualizations, scanned images, screened profiles of past behavior and transactions, the singular uncertainty of the variables in the chain becomes less easy to see. In contrast to Galton's composite profiles and Muybridge's movement studies, and despite their conjoined histories, the singular elements of the contemporary mosaic can never be fully excavated or retrieved—the archive is lost. When the geneticists or lawyers or privacy advocates try to intervene, to demand the retrieval and evaluation of the elements, there can be no effective response.

And so, what is left for political response in the face of the sovereign writing of the border mosaic? As I have suggested, visualizations of the body at the border operate on and through dissected and partitioned fragments of a subject, and yet they never confront the aporia, the profound political difficulties of that which cannot be seen or resolved. Instead, like many other sovereign claims to visualize objectively, they bring us into a domain "we cannot see," and they "authorize us to make claims about what we cannot see."[68] The mosaic border gives the impression of a smart, side effects–free way of seeing, "without racial prejudice," the depths of an unknown subject, the hidden intent beneath the surface. But, like the nineteenth-century scientific devices Joel Snyder describes, the elements are stretched, expanded, and distilled in order to project a subject who could not otherwise be seen. The mosaic automates intervention at the e-gate border at the same time as it writes out any possibility of a decision as such, a decision that confronts the aporia of all border decisions. Thus, for Flanagan's *Unknown Terrorist*, the potentiality of the young woman's life is written out by the projection of her as a terrorist, as violent, as an extremist. Perhaps most tellingly of all, following a series of attempts to challenge the authenticity of the "complete picture," where she takes a particular pixel and tries to tell the real contingent story of how it came to look that way (her private tragedies, the deprivations of her youth, her precarious existence in the margins of the urban), she finds herself fully actualized as the thing itself. "The mistake can never be rectified," reflects the Doll; "maybe this is what people do when they get written out of this world, when they get turned upside down and remade into something people become afraid of, into something no longer themselves."[69] All aspects of her becoming, her potentiality to do something in her life is thwarted, and so she does the only thing that is left, she becomes what she is not, and she opens fire.

4. ON LOCATION
Reconciling Security and Mobility

Using a nearby facility belonging to Raytheon, a subcontractor on its team, the Accenture team constructed a mock border point kiosk at which the government team had an RFID tag attached to their passports. They also constructed a mock land border crossing where a scanner read the RFID passport tags of the government officials inside the car. Even though the car became momentarily airborne after hitting a speed bump—the scanner read the digital information contained on the RFID chips of all four government officials in the vehicle, displaying their pictures on an electronic billboard as they passed by. —Accenture, *Values, Driven, Leadership*, 242

"You won't get by the booth. . . . You look too young to be driving out of state." . . . But there is nobody in the booth built to hold a toll-taker. Nobody. A green light flashes E-Z PASS PAID and Ahmad and the white truck are admitted to the tunnel. —John Updike, *Terrorist*, 298

In a bid to secure the contract to provide new electronic border control systems for the U.S. government, a team of consultants from Accenture staged a mock border crossing in a Raytheon production facility. Inserting radio frequency identification (RFID) chips within the passports of the government officials, the team demonstrated the capacity of RFID to transmit the data of people within a moving vehicle as it crossed the border, displaying their facial images on a screen. And so it was that an industrial facility more accustomed to the production of missile systems became the site where the potential of RFID to secure people and things in movement was enacted—Accenture won the U.S. Smart Borders contract,[1] and, seven years on, RFID-enabled passports are standard in more than twenty countries. From the ticketing of the Olympics through road tolls, tracking military supply shipments to Afghanistan and urban transportation cards, to building access systems, RFID has become the locative technology of choice for contemporary security.

In a final scene of John Updike's novel *Terrorist*, the protagonist Ahmad drives his truck bomb to the entrance of the Manhattan-bound Lincoln Tunnel. His passenger and reluctant mentor Jack Levy urges him to stop, telling him that the security guard will stop him on the grounds that he looks too young to have a state license permitting him to drive out of state. At the boundary line of the city, Levy feels sure, their fatal journey will be halted, their movement intercepted. What Levy does not anticipate is the RFID transponder on the windshield of the truck. The barrier reader transmits its power supply to the RFID tag; the tag replies with an automated decision—yes, the truck is licensed; yes, the toll is prepaid; no, the vehicle has not been reported stolen—communicating the data stored on the chip; the barrier replies "have a nice day," the green light flashes, and the truck enters the tunnel, effortless and smooth.

In Updike's novel the sovereign desire to secure people and things in movement is revealed in all its contingency and unpredictability. When asked by his wife what the Department of Homeland Security's elevation of threat from yellow to orange might mean, Levy replies: "It means they want us to feel they have a handle on this thing, but they don't." The vigilant technologies of Updike's tale—designed for prediction and security intervention—have wholly unpredictable effects that exceed any specific intervention. One has the sense that it is not possible to know what security techniques will do, what meaningful consequences they may have, at least beyond securing the crucial impression that people and commodities will continue to circulate, will keep moving. As Ahmad's truck enters the Lincoln Tunnel, the contingency of the security event is writ large—had the RFID tag's conversation with the barrier reader shown the white truck to be on a watch list database, or the E-ZPass to be out of credit or expired or had a previous transaction flagged a risk, then it could have been the case that the device would had signaled a red light, that the movement of the truck would be intercepted. Yet these are the unknown elements, the indeterminacies of the relations among Updike's characters, their vehicle, their technologies, the urban infrastructure, the liveliness of a small coiled RFID tag that may do unexpected things with unanticipated effects. As Jane Bennett reminds us, there is an unheralded magic, an enchantment in "encounters with the mobility, even the agency, of matter."[2] Such enchantment, as Bennett understands it, dwells within and alongside the more strictly calculable and rational forms of scientific reason. The surface effect of locating technologically a mobile person or object contains a multitude of conversations, mistakes, assumptions, and whims on the part of other subjects and objects.

The active agency Bennett so compellingly ascribes to matter, and to the relations between people and things, invokes simultaneously a sense of wonder and a sense of foreboding. "How disturbing," notes Bennett, "that an inanimate machine, or an advertisement for jeans, is allowed to function as an active agent."[3] And yet this disturbance is itself also enchanting, inducing a sense of wonder and a "state of openness to the disturbing-captivating elements in everyday experience."[4] The active agency of the RFID, one could say, has just such disturbing and captivating elements, the capricious onward life of the small coiled tags showing itself to exceed the security design. When the Accenture mock border crossing demonstrated so clearly the capacity of RFID-embedded passport data to be read from a distance, and at speed, "even after becoming momentarily airborne," it signaled also the capacity of RFID to exceed the sovereign capture of data. Prone to interception and hacking, and to a desire to continue to circulate beyond the designed system, the RFID tag in U.S. passports is now encased in a foil lining (the UK passport RFIDs remain free to wander at will). A technology whose agency in the tracking of mobile people has been so widely adopted has shown itself to have mobilities of its own, a will to circulate and to continue to move.

It is precisely the capacity to cross back and forth between the apparent smooth spaces of global mobilities and the striated spaces of state security that characterizes contemporary technologies of location. As a technology with significant origins in the smooth spaces of capital flows and radio waves, and in the material fungibility of silicon and plastic, RFID works hard to render movement around the subways, highways, and superstores of the global economy as a frictionless experience. As the architect and director of CityLab Dana Cuff explains, locative devices are part of "an invisible web of digital technology" distributed across "the visible world," always "creating new space for work, data, advertisement, and danger."[5] In this sense RFID tags embody an agency that opens space to new possibilities, forging new relations between people and things in the world. And yet the capacities of RFID as a so-called turn-key technology, unlocking data streams, operate on a terrain of what Deleuze and Guattari call "striated space," where mobilities are governed by the directional grain of sovereign interventions.[6] A key characteristic of our contemporary politics of possibility, I suggest, is the locative device's movement between the sovereign security of the border and the space of a global economy of unimpeded movements, wants, and desires. Unlike historical conventions of address that seek to locate mobile things on a grid of horizontal and vertical indices—post codes, zip codes, barcodes, Morse code—locative devices address in and through mobility itself, navigating not by fixed metric locations but via the in-between spaces of transactions.

Of No Fixed Address: From Addressability to Locatability

The emergence of knowledges of location, what Nigel Thrift has called "our conventions of address," has followed a logic that one can govern space in such a way that one knows "what will show up where and what will show up next."[7] That is to say, a system of address has mattered to the capacity to locate events, objects, people, money, and so on in linear space and time. The history of the address can be understood as a playing back and forth of the movements and impulses of moving things and people, with the governing techniques instituted to know where they are, who they are, and in what sequence they will appear. Address, we might say, is one of the means by which space is navigated, rendered useable, or made safe. Deleuze and Guattari offer the space of the sea as "a smooth space par excellence," the "archetype of all smooth spaces" by virtue of its continuous variation with the tides, the lunar cycle, and the weather system.[8] The space of the sea is simultaneously, though, "the first to encounter the demands of increasingly strict striation," as the city-states' maritime demands of mapping and bearings are "gridding it in one place, then another, on this side and that."[9] The increased mobilities of maritime trade intensify the desire to know what will turn up and where on an intelligible grid. A smooth space becomes subject to striation as the demands of commercial trading insist upon the navigability of the open seas. Such is the genealogy of other systems of address—space is apportioned, divided, and parceled precisely in order that it can be navigated. Just as the city-states found ways to know what would turn up when and where on the high seas, so the logistics of movements of armies and troops and the trading routes of commerce required a system of address.

Consider, for example, the way that the Morse code communications of military logistics transformed and traveled into the locating of mobile objects in commercial environments. Historical records of early barcode systems describe a young graduate student, Joseph Woodward, whose dissertation assignment was to devise a more efficient means of identifying products at point of sale. Marking out the dots and dashes of Morse code as a series of marks in sand, Woodward began to experiment with the spatial relationships between the dots and lines. Extending the dots and lines to a series of parallel wide and narrow bars in the sand, he devised the first barcode system on the basis of patterns of lines, later successfully patenting the first binary barcode system. Said to have been tested first in the sale of packets of chewing gum at a local store, Woodward's system was extended to the location of rail freight, his barcodes affixed to the railcars as they passed by a static track-side scanner. The location of moving vehicles proved to be more difficult than the scanning of consumer products, the "bounce" of the freight trains on the tracks often taking the code out of range of the reader. It was in Woodward's development of barcode technologies that we first began to see the attempt to locate objects in movement in a way that does not stop, inhibit, or prevent mobility.

It was not until the late 1950s that mechanized postal sorting in the United States and Europe began to use code to identify addresses. As delivery systems required ever more finite locatability, the identifiers of location that had resided in named householders, local landmarks, and, later, numbered buildings became encoded in the zip and postal code systems of the 1960s.[10] By the 1970s the advent of the laser scanner, designed to resolve the problems encountered in the relationship between code and reader, brought barcodes into the labeling of goods in the postal system. The historical problem of addressability not only implied a means of identifying a fixed set of coordinates of address or the "destination" for an object but also the search for a means of recognizing, verifying, and authenticating location in movement.

As computing technologies began to enable the electronic reading and recognition of patterns, and the storage of those patterns in a form of memory, new relationships between the identifier (postal code, zip code, barcode, personal identifiers such as date of birth) and the identified

FIGURE 4.1. Reconstruction of a 1930s punched card office with Hollerith machine. Courtesy of the Science Museum, London.

(people, places, parcels, vehicles, and so on) became possible. Consider, for example, IBM's punch cards of the 1950s—patterns of punched holes in a card to be fed into the pattern recognition programs of IBM machines (see figure 4.1). Each of the holes in the punch cards corresponded to a particular item of data so that, for example, the recording of census data on an individual would be translated into a particular pattern of holes in the grid form. A woman, aged forty, with three children, whose husband was an automotive worker, for example, would have a particular pattern of dots. Significantly, the punch card system opened up the possibility that data records could be stored and cross matched—the Hollerith machines that read the data were able to identify common patterns of holes across the "database."[11] In IBM's Hollerith machine we find perhaps the archetypal "striated" system of address—its "series of points" serving to "plot everything onto a grid."[12] Indeed, the technological genealogy of the punch card system of early computing lies in the use of loom cards to guide the complex patterns woven into Jacquard cloth.[13] The loom cards guide the weft of the woven thread, its movement "determined by the frame of the warp," and "the necessity of a back and forth motion" implying a "closed space."[14]

Understood in Deleuze and Guattari's terms, as the "supple solid" of weft threads on a loom, the unpredictable mobilities of people and things are rendered governable through the punch card that marks out life events as a series of data holes. The "patterns of data on the IBM cards," writes the architect Reinhold Martin, "made visible what was invisible," the machine's ability to "read" the cards extending beyond the mere cataloging of data and into the almost magical realm of animating a life unseen.[15] In a publicity brochure in 1955, IBM reminded the American public of how their lives were locatable in the traces of actions and transactions left in the card and "read" by the machine: "IBM first came into your life when your birth was recorded on a punched card. From then on many such cards have been compiled, giving a lifetime of history of your important decisions and actions. If you went to school, entered a hospital, bought a home, paid income tax, got married or purchased an automobile, the chances are that permanent records were made of these and other personal stories."[16]

While even rudimentary systems of address involve recognizing identifying markings, whether these are numbers, features of the natural landscape, or codes, the computer reading of markings and the recognition of patterns begin to make possible novel forms of locatability. The IBM punch card matters to contemporary practices of security because it is the first example of locating people and things through the patterns and traces they are thought to leave behind in their daily transactions and life events. The world of Fordist production and consumer households in the 1950s ushered in a more mobile and agile mode of address, one that does not "stop at the door" but instead dwells inside, making visible, readable, and locatable the traces of daily life. With the rise of what Jerry Kang and Dana Cuff call "computer addressability," the fixed grid location of the address is loosened via "unique identification codes."[17] With digital forms of address the governing of population ceases to be a matter of mapping against fixed census-based criteria, becoming instead a more supple form in which the movement of bodies is locatable in and through movement itself.

Where the conventions of address made possible new forms of relation between state and population, so in the shift from strict addressability to locatability the direction of a body is inferred from its relations with its environment. No longer solely identifiable via the fixed coordinates of mapped space, the address is derived through mobile correlates between a body and its milieu. As Jerry Kang and Dana Cuff suggest in relation to ubiquitous computing, the ability to track and trace things in movement is achieved by animating the physical environment so that it is able to "respond directly to what it sees."[18] Thus the automated reader of traces, markings, or transactions, established via the early technologies of punch cards and barcodes, becomes ever more important to the system of location as "addresses move with human and non-human actants."[19] The early computers produced by IBM divided and cataloged people's life histories from the patterns punched into the cards and from the intervals between them. By contrast, contemporary readers of location, as a group of RFID researchers at Intel have put it, "infer people's actions from their effect on the environment, especially on the objects with which they interact," thus scattering the distributed intervals and encounters.[20] The striated breaks of IBM's punched holes are "defined by a standard," organized on a grid system of dimensional space, while locative devices map directional spaces that deploy "irregular and undetermined" intervals and breaks.[21] In the animated RFID-enabled environment, movement and direction are inferred from multiple location queries between device and reader.

Locating in Smooth Space

In Deleuze and Guattari's account of the distinctions between smooth and striated space, they definitively do not position these forms in opposition. Indeed, for Deleuze and Guattari there can be no smooth space without striations, no striations without smooth space. "There are many interlacings," they write, and "we must remind ourselves that the two spaces in fact exist only in the mixture." Any example one might identify as archetypal of a form of space is always already troublesome and is always also implicated in what it is not: "smooth space is constantly being translated, transversed into a striated space; striated space is constantly being reversed, returned to a smooth space." It is precisely this complex intermingling of smooth and striated spaces that is so crucial to the technologically animated worlds of the politics of possibility. The blending of smooth and striated space, however, does not "preclude an abstract distinction between the two spaces."[22] As such, the striated grid of an address system of horizontal and vertical coordinates in space is distinct from the locative technologies that locate in smooth space, in and through movement itself. In sum, where conventions of address index mobile things and people to fixed elements, locative devices such as RFID operate through continuous variation. In contrast to a mode of address that allocates sequences and rhythms evenly, RFID devices are distributive; they distribute pauses and interventions across space. Finally, the dimensional logics of punch cards and barcodes give way to what Deleuze and Guattari term "directional" logics that subordinate the position on a grid to knowledge of trajectory.[23]

Like the barcode, the origins of contemporary RFID technology also find some roots in military communications and logistics, with the earliest writings on the problem to be found in research by radio engineers seeking more efficient readability of signals. Harry Stockman's finding that radio waves possessed sufficient electromagnetic energy to power a remote transmitter was, in many ways, the condition of possibility for RFID devices.[24] Contemporary RFID technologies deploy miniature tags, emitting a radio signal with a unique numeric identifier that can be received by a reader up to twenty-five feet away. Composed of a silicon chip and coiled antenna, usually embedded within a plastic tag, so called passive RFIDs use the power supply from the reader to send their signal and are, therefore, smaller and require closer proximity to the reader than active tags that carry their own power supply. For example, a passive RFID application such as a machine readable passport that is read at the border checkpoint is, in effect, inert until it is in range of the reader that activates it. Once in range of the reader, the RFID's numeric identifier allows the reader to locate the tag and to correlate it with an array of other data, biometric measures, and transactions. In this sense the RFID definitively does not locate a person or an object against a grid of fixed and allocated elements, but rather they are located on a field of distributed transactions. So, for instance, an RFID-enabled Secure Electronic Network for Travelers Rapid Inspection (SENTRI) card holder, crossing the U.S.–Mexico border at San-Ysidro, is not checked against a fixed grid of coordinates but against an array of databases and transactions that are unlocked by the transmitted identifier as it passes through.

The capacity of the RFID to move between the striated spaces of international borders and the apparently smooth spaces of global circulation is, in part, afforded by its materialization in the lived and everyday objects of our lives. When the vice president of the Philips Corporation, global market leaders in RFID, testified to the U.S. Congress on the potential for RFID in national security, he appealed to the already existing ubiquity of the devices in everyday life. "Consumers are already likely to encounter RF-enabled personal identification devices in their daily lives," he argued; "it is unavoidable, think of secure access cards for building entry, speedy gasoline purchasing such as the Exxon Speedpass, vehicle anti-theft systems, and transportation systems all over the world."[25] For states and organizations who seek new modes of locatability, RFID offers a system of address that dwells within the material entity itself. Thus, for the Organisation for Economic Co-operation and Development (OECD), "compared to the barcode system, RFID promises long-term gains in supply chain management, transportation, defence and health care."[26] When things and people are moving around in space, RFID locatability implies that one can know more than the referent points of where they began their journey and where they show up next. "Over the next few years," concludes the OECD, the ability of RFID's mobile address to move around will advance "as RFID migrates to item level."[27]

It is exactly this potential, for RFID to become incorporated at item level within all consumer products, bank notes, and so on, that exhibits its "fit" with the smooth spaces of global economic circulation. As Deleuze and Guattari insist, there is a plasticity to smooth space, a potential "to draw an open space in all directions."[28] RFID labels have made a significant step toward replacing barcode—now printable as nano-injected ink that replaces the circuitry of silicon, they can be incorporated into packaging as print. "RFID can be printed directly onto cereal boxes or potato chip bags," report the electronic engineers; "the tag instantly transmits information about a cart full of groceries, no more lines, you just walk out with your stuff."[29] The device transmits with no fixed elements, a continuous variation of streams of data that do not have the striated characteristic of being "delimited, closed on at least one side."[30] The migration to a malleable material, and to item level, is arguably the critical moment in the potential for RFID to locate in smooth space, to "keep things moving," and to coalesce the "no more lines" of the grocery store with the "no more lines" border crossing. As *Science News* reports on the incorporation of RFID into commodity labels, "it brings closer the prospect of RFID tags becoming as common as barcodes, or perhaps even more so as plastic tags make novel electronic tracking and transactions possible, from computer monitoring of what is in the refrigerator to mail routing by means of smart address labels."[31]

The historical system of address that has enabled things and people to be accounted for while on the move is giving way to a system of ambient locatability that moves with the trajectories of mobile entities. Where barcodes represented a label on the surface of a body or object, RFID penetrates into the transaction itself, routing the reader to integrated databases that "tell a story" of other transactions made in the past, in process, or planned for the future. As people interact with RFID-enabled, self-describing objects (whether these are travel documents, food packaging, medications, or vehicles, for example), they inscribe the traces of their transaction. In this way the system of address does not strictly seek to account for a particular mobile body in space, or to locate on a grid, but rather it urges that one gives an account of oneself, an account in relation with other people and things. When our transactions with the physical world are locatable in this way, Jerry Kang notes that "the exception becomes the norm, every transaction becomes like a credit card."[32] The already present possibilities of economic transactions begin to suggest a means by which sovereign power can locate in and through those transactions. If RFID has begun to live in the very fabric of the global economy—from the wheat-flakes box on the breakfast table to the smart card swipe of the border-crossing card—then it has capacities to smooth out the striations of the borders and boundaries of sovereign decisions, to capture things on the move and to let them continue to move. As RFID-enabled smart cards replace cash in the so-called enacted environment kiosks of the London Underground, the address dwells within the transaction itself, an address that is specified in the transaction—the "trans-action," the passing through of a mobile body.

Security's Freedom

A young city worker stands at the elevator doors of his apartment block in New York City. As the doors open, a roller coaster stands waiting to take him on his daily commute to work, corkscrewing on an exhilarating ride over the horizon of the cityscape, pausing only for seconds to pick up his breakfast at a bakery, paying for his goods with his Barclaycard "contactless" chip—no standing in line, no waiting at the subway, no traffic, no stopping (see figure 4.2). It is the dream of the security apparatus, as seen through Foucault's eyes: departing a city that "encloses," "checks," and "regulates" and embracing an urban world that "is given freedom," the "possibility of movement," and "the freedom of circulation."[33] It is also the advertising campaign unveiled in 2010 for Barclays' "contactless payment technology"— credit cards with embedded Philips RFID technology that allows for payments of less than £10 or $10 with "one touch" between card and reader. The roller coaster commute embodies the contours of the politics of possibility and the place of locative technologies within it. On the one hand,

FIGURE 4.2. Barclaycard contactless payment "roller coaster" advertisement, set to the soundtrack of Boston's "More Than a Feeling," January 2010.

Barclays' advertising campaign for contactless transactions promises "a liberating world where customers' lives are made easier." This is a world in which the disciplinary actions of stopping, waiting, and verifying are removed from the experience of the daily commute. On the other hand, the replacement of small cash transactions with traceable databases of registered card transactions promises a more secure city where petty crime, money laundering, and other infractions are driven out. The smooth and the striated, the free and the secure, appear to be reconciled for a moment. "In contrast to the sea," write Deleuze and Guattari, "the city is the striated space par excellence," the urban environment being a "force of striation."[34] And yet the Barclays' roller coaster commuter exhibits some of the movements of smooth space that Deleuze and Guattari more readily associate with the sea, a smooth space within which the striations of data integration and algorithmic checking continue to reside.

If the history of address can be characterized as a series of moves from coded locations in space—departure points, destinations, depots, and stores—to the metric gaps between points (holes in an IBM punch card), then contemporary locatability is no longer strictly a matter of metric points in space. In technologies like Barclays' contactless payment, there is something of the realization of Foucault's sense that "freedom is nothing else but the correlative of the deployment of apparatuses of security."[35] The freedom of circulation thus becomes a means of securing, the capacity to move point to point a precondition for "the possibility of movement, change of place, and processes of circulation of both people and things."[36] In effect, the "points" of historical addressability were disciplinary, following Nigel Thrift's formulation of the necessary knowledge of what would turn up when and where. The techniques of liberal economy, though, do not necessarily wish to know exactly and predictably what will turn up when and where—an element of uncertainty being essential to profit. As Frank Knight famously observed, "profit arises out of the inherent, absolute unpredictability of things, out of the sheer, brute fact that the results of human activity cannot be anticipated and then only in so far as even a probability calculation in regard to them is impossible and meaningless."[37]

It is here in the absolute unpredictability of things, in the impossibility of a probability calculation, that the correlation between freedom and security becomes visible. For the entrepreneur to make profit on the future, her wager on the present must be subject to unpredictability—for it is in her navigation of the unanticipated surprises that the entrepreneurial spirit is revealed. As David Campbell writes, "were it possible to bring about the absence of movement," that would represent "pure security," yet it would be at that moment, where no movement were possible, that "the state would wither away."[38] Understood thus, the unanticipated human activity that is so central to Frank Knight's entrepreneur adventurer is also of the essence of the state itself—the state would wither in the absence of movement. The reconciliation of sovereign power and security with economy and freedom takes place on a terrain of embracing movement, governing in and through mobility itself. Where the indexed points of absolute address get in the way of economic circulation and state authority, what is sought is the relations among multiple points or the milieu—"the space in which a series of uncertain elements unfolds."[39] If, as Foucault proposes, the milieu is what is needed to account for action at a distance of one body on another, then such action takes place precisely in the movements and correlations among "a set of natural givens—rivers, marshes, hills—and a set of artificial givens—

an agglomeration of individuals, of houses, etcetera."[40] Significantly, if the state is to act and intervene, if the security apparatus is to be instituted, then it must do so "by acting on the milieu."[41] Security and freedom meet on the terrain of the milieu.

The ambient locatability afforded by technologies such as RFID effectively animates the relations of the milieu—the border crosser swipes the card, the card talks to a reader, the reader reaches into databases of multiple other encounters between people and things. The "no stopping" experience shared by the RFID-enabled border crosser and the contactless city consumer may appear to embody the smooth space of global economy, but it simultaneously affords a more dispersed and distributed mode of sovereignty, what William Connolly calls the "migration of sovereignty to a layered global assemblage."[42] In a world of animated things that talk to one another, the state need not confront the impossibility of complete knowledge of everything that happens within its territory, it need not know the address, as it only requires trajectory and direction—and that can be supplied. In this sense the migration of sovereignty echoes the dispersed elements and transactions of the global supply chain.

The Tracking of Things: Tales from the Supply Chain

Like the border itself that becomes governed as a broken chain of events and not a series of enclosures (see chapter 3), the contemporary supply chain eschews enclosed inventory and seeks out an unimpeded flow. How is the supply chain reimagined as a milieu? How does the flow of goods in the supply chain occupy smooth space that is governed only by movement itself? The integration of a chain of RFID-enabled objects has made possible a space where things talk to other things, things communicate with people, and people communicate with things. The emergence of RFID applications in the commercial supply chain has been closely associated with corporations seeking simultaneous distance and proximity. On the one hand, commercial entities look for efficient "off-shore" zones in distant places, yet on the other they want proximate and precise control of the flow of work and products.[43] Similarly, contemporary sovereign power seeks a dispersal of responsibility for security—outsourcing to consultants, deploying biometrics, replacing border guards with e-gates—while simultaneously desiring tightened control of borders and immigration.[44] The problem of dispersal and control is precisely the problem that Foucault identifies in the liberal art of government—the question "am I governing at the border of the too much and the too little," with the answer coming back "I accept, wish, plan, and calculate that all this should be left alone."[45] For Foucault a "new type of calculation" emerges, a form of governmental rationality that says "laissez-nous faire," let us alone.[46] To leave things alone, to allow things to move, is to render the dispersal of people and things as a productive resource to sovereign power. One of the things that is allowed to happen is that the things in movement talk, yield data on their transactions and trajectory, and feed the capacity of the risk calculations.

Turning to the laissez-nous faire of the supply chain, when, for example, U.S. retail giant Walmart began a trial of RFID tags at the pallet level across the supply chain, it codified the shipments of objects with numeric identifiers that rendered them locatable as they moved from production, through transit, and into the warehouses of stores.[47] What is significant here is that by means of the locative devices, Walmart was able to minimize inventory—they did not need to hold stuff, stop stuff, or store stuff; they only needed to keep it moving. In the movement of the commodities multiple forms of data are produced and communicated—not merely address-oriented data on what will turn up where and when but also directional data on trends and stock levels. Tagging at item level with "smart shelving," trialed by Gillette in its packaging for the retailers Tesco and Walmart, animates individual objects in the supply chain. Such tagging has shifted the balance of the calculus "governing too much or too little," so that the object itself will tell the supply chain when to supply more. In effect, when the last product is removed from the shelf, the RFID tag communicates to a reader interfaced with store databases and the shelves are restocked. Similarly, the development of "smart refrigerators" extends the continual flow of consumer things to a world of interfaced production and consumption. As the levels of particular items in the family refrigerator are depleted, the RFID labels on the products talk to the reader on the shelf, initiating an automated Internet order to the online supermarket.[48]

The idea of an animated supply chain, making its own calculations and judgements, incorporates the bodies and objects of the circuits of production and consumption, from the growers, pickers, and producers of raw materials to manufacturing and supply logistics. In the most vulnerable offshore spaces of the global economy, where commercial firms seek only the most fleeting of finger holds in a specific territorial space, we begin to see how the appearance of a smooth space of unimpeded flows of things is made possible through intense striations and control of other people in other spaces. Thailand's export processing zones—or free zones—for example, have become "e–free zones," using RFID to track the movement of imported materials, deliveries, exported goods, and, significantly, the bodies of workers as they traverse the boundaries of the zone. The fortified security fences associated with export processing zones are augmented by equally carceral, the less obviously visible lines that track and trace the movements of workers via "contactless" smart cards, and the mobility of objects via RF-enabled smart labels. Similarly, the extension of RFID into border crossing cards and immigration documents promises rapid no-stop crossing in smooth space, while it simultaneously institutes new sovereign lines and striations. There is a growing resonance between apparently economic *and* sovereign systems of securing circulation. As Jordan Crandall envisages the techniques deployed to track things in movement: "It plays out in new systems of production that aim to narrow the intervals between conception, manufacturing, distribution and consumption—shrinking the delays between detecting an audience pattern and formatting a new enticement that can address it. It plays out in pre-emptive policing and warfare systems that aim to close the gap between sensing and shooting."[49]

To specify the form of the resonance between economy and sovereignty, it is the embracing of the opportunities of things in movement, the capacity to disperse the supply chain and replace inventory with "a series of events," and to diffuse the security decisions of the sovereign in the same way.[50] As commercial locative technologies enter the sphere of security— RFID passports, "smart" national ID cards, RF-enabled immigration and visa documents, the tagging of detained asylum seekers, "contactless" access cards that enable employees entrance to buildings—it is not precise geometric address that is sought but rather locatability in variable space at some possible point in the future. The deferral of commercial decisions on stock, store, and inventory into the relations among things that, once left alone, give an account of themselves is mirrored by a dispersal of sovereign decisions into plural relations between people and things who must give an account. The locative device will encounter other contact points on other future journeys, giving multiple future accounts, long after the border itself is crossed.

Targeted Desires

In Stephen Spielberg's film *Minority Report*, released in 2002, the protagonist John Anderton is the chief arresting officer in a futuristic Washington, D.C., "pre-crime" unit that detains and incarcerates suspects identified as committing a future crime. Though, as Michael Shapiro suggests, Anderton's "body in motion" exhibits the "suborned body controlled by the state's apparatus" and then "a subversive body" who subverts the surveillance practices, there is another, less documented body in motion in Spielberg's film.[51] For Anderton is not only a sovereign subject fleeing the police but also a consumer whose wants and desires are arrayed in data on his past transactions. Entering the spaces of shopping malls and transit stations, Anderton's iris biometrics are read by scanners on smart advertising screens that ask him about past purchases and target his desires for future products and experiences. "Need to escape? Blue can take you" calls a woman from the American Express Blue Card screen. "John Anderton, you could use a Guinness right now," urges another. Of course, the film is a piece of science fiction based on a Philip Dick short story of the same name. The shopping mall and subway scenes, however, were put together in consultation with advertising agencies, RFID technologists, and software engineers. Indeed, the advertising boards of San Francisco's highways read the RFID signals embedded in the key fobs of passing Mini Cooper drivers, targeting their messages—"'Mary, moving at the speed of justice,' if Mary is a lawyer, or 'Mike the special of the day is speed,' if Mike is a chef."[52] Such exchanges exemplify the transformed relationship between people and space that is made possible when the physical world is animated to become a nonlinear sequence of actions and reactions of people and things. Objects and identities become intimately connected as mobile bodies walk past objects that can make identifications and respond. As I illustrated in chapter 1 in the context of data mining that targets future consumers yet to enter the space of the store, in the case of RFID the "backroom" data of sequenced transactions also become a means of visualizing future actions.

Significantly, the figure of John Anderton is not definitively targeted by the surveillant practices of the state; he is only targeted as a consumer with desires and habits whose outlines can offer a picture of a person that far exceeds conventions of surveillance. Where the visuality of surveillance is one of a centralized form of watching, "control is no longer the necessary counterweight to freedom, as in panopticism: it becomes its mainspring."[53] Quite contrary to disciplinary modes of surveillance, freedom and security are co-implicated in the movements of bodies and objects in space. In terms of forms of vision and seeing, Anderton's movement through the smart advertising spaces of the city subway is a sequence of projections of possible future needs and desires. An important distinction between RFID and past systems of encoded address is that movement is freed up by the capacity to read transactions, past, present, and future. So, for example, barcodes on products require direct scanning in order to be read and to enter a transaction, but RF-enabled smart labels can be read at a distance, enabling customers at a fuel station to record and pay for a transaction from their vehicle or airline passengers to scan their passports as they walk past a sensor. The affectivity of RFID, we might say with Mark Hansen, is embodied and exciting, tuned to our sensibilities and desires as consumers in a global economy.[54]

Consider, by way of example, the decision by Transport for London to upgrade the contactless technology in its Oyster card system, migrating to an apparently more secure encryption system in preparation for the London Olympics of 2012.[55] Oyster uses the Philips MIFARE system of RFID, which is common among most urban transit card systems in the world. The decision to upgrade to MIFARE DESFire cards will substantially transform the capacities of the smart card, incorporating a microprocessor onto the chip so that multiple applications can be supported. It is already possible for London Underground passengers to incorporate their Oyster card within a Barclaycard contactless system—recall our roller coaster commuter—and the extension of MIFARE DESFire will provide the additional capacity to all card holders. The experience of the visitor to the London Olympic Games, via contactless MIFARE, is envisaged as one of a smooth space of movement through the city, into the subway, across the mall space of Westfield London, and into the Olympic village and stadiums with integrated security smart cards.[56] Of course, the expansion of distributed contacts between chip and reader considerably extends the available data for risk analysis, twinning the impulses of freedom and control.

It is precisely this entwining of consumer practices, sport and games, desires and experiences, with security systems that is the promise held out to the state by mobile locative devices. Where RFID appears to render movement around the subways, highways, and superstores of the global economy as a smooth and seamless experience, it aligns the security practices of the state with the mobilities of the consumer:

Despite its use in criminal trials and as a means to track the movement of people under criminal investigation, E-ZPass remains a highly successful RFID application in terms of consumer acceptance. This alignment of consumer and state interests results from the benefit of not having to stop, roll down the car window, get out the money, hand it to the toll-collector, get the change and receipt, put it in the ashtray, roll up the window, and start driving again being greater than the potential risk that the computer records showing I left Manchester on Tuesday at 8:24 P.M. will someday be used against me.[57]

It is not strictly the case that mobile locative technologies represent some form of a post-9/11 deepening of political economies of surveillance, where we understand surveillance to function on a striated grid of prohibition and prevention.[58] The RFID within Oyster and E-ZPass is locatability of a different order; it does not say no, or prohibit, but it at least appears to say yes: "The sovereign is the person who can say no to any individual's desire. . . . Now through the economic-political thought of the physiocrats we see a completely different idea taking shape, which is that the problem of those who govern must absolutely not be how they can say no, up to what point they can say no. The problem is how they can say yes; it is how to say yes to this desire."[59]

Confronted with the need to "say yes to desire," the sovereign is no longer establishing limits or restricting movement but is in fact establishing the impossibility of limits and finding novel ways to, as Foucault describes it, "live dangerously."[60] The UK Home Office's embracing of contactless technologies as a means of governing the space of the city for the Olympics in 2012, for example, became a means of "inviting unprecedented numbers of guests to our city," "let them play, we want them to play." The appearance of smooth space, of course, conceals the intense striations of the integrated databases and fractionated risk scores I discussed in chapter 2. As Matthew Sparke has shown in his study of the biometric RFID cards used in the U.S.–Canadian border NEXUS program, the mobile body is broken into risk data as the RFID communicates via a reader to the border guard's screen.[61] The stitching together of playful, leisurely RFID encounters with security interventions and risk analysis trades locatability for expedited movement. In some of the most playful forms of RFID, subcutaneous RFID chips are inserted into the arms of VIP members of a Barcelona nightclub, so that they can pay for their drinks without the encumbrance of cash or cards. In the flagship New York store of luxury clothing brand Prada, the RFID tags inserted within clothing are interfaced with plasma screens on the walls of the fitting rooms. When the items are taken into the fitting room, the tag emits a signal to the reader, triggering footage of the clothing as it was seen on the catwalks of Milan—past images and future desires mingling together in the present consumption decision. The experience of the consumer is tightly interwoven with the security of the object itself—the locative tag affording both a space of play and the capacity for a future security intervention. Where RFID "pleasures and anxieties cohabit," the economy of circulation meets security so that, for some, "the edges are smoothed" as they "blend seamlessly into the crowd."[62] For others, of course, the locative device targets heightened exposure to visibility—to stop and search, to continually verify identity, to have movement in public space checked and intercepted.

Contactless Security

In the contemporary politics of possibility the location of mobile people and things in space is not strictly a matter of knowing exactly what will turn up when and where, but instead it is concerned with capitalizing on the uncertainty of movement itself. Thus the laissez-faire techniques of economic liberalism yield to sovereignty the capacity to smooth out the striations of impediment, prohibition, and enclosure. In February 2010 the U.S. ambassador to London announced the winning architects for the design of the new U.S. embassy in London. The Philadelphia-based architects Kieran Timberlake had been awarded the contract to design the new building, to be relocated from its central London site in Grosvenor Square to a location south of the river in Southwark. The striking impression of Kieran Timberlake's glass cube, surrounded by apparently open parkland, is the absence of fences and walls. As the U.S. authorities explained as the contract was awarded: "Viewed from the north at the proposed plaza, the embassy grounds will provide the prospect of an open park, with the required secure boundaries incised into the hillside and out of view. Instead of a perimeter-walled precinct, the site to the north and south is a welcoming urban amenity, a park for the city that fuses the new embassy to the city of London. Alternatives to perimeter walls and fences are achieved through landscape design."[63]

And thus it is that the overtly striated Cold war walls and fences of the Eero Saarinen U.S. embassy building are to be replaced by the appearance of a smooth space whose security capacity lies in its relations to a surrounding landscape. It is in this way that the architecture of contemporary security space fuses the "prospect of openness" with "secure boundaries." To welcome, to walk around, to say yes, to invite, to play—these are the invocations of the contemporary sovereign in light of the political economy of circulation and mobility. Of course, it is not the case that embedding locative devices in moving objects smooths out the political striations of the spaces of city and capital. Instead, the incorporation of locatability in space within mobile bodies works hard to conceal the deep striations that result. There are moments when this is acutely visible in the architecture of crossings, as for example, in the empty, contactless SENTRI Lane in San Ysidro, immediately north of the U.S.–Mexico border. And there are other moments when striations are embedded deeply within the security landscape. When architect Stephen Kieran explained his firm's vision of contemporary security, he appealed to the landscape architectural form of the ha-ha or sunken ditch: "Instead of having fences, we've tried to invert the process, so we've developed forms that have a first reference to landscape features—the pond, a ha-ha, a meadow, a long curved bench—which secondarily have a security function."[64]

The inversion of the process of dividing up open space in order to secure it, contemporary security deploys techniques of embedding within and beneath in order to bury striation in smooth surfaces—in effect, to secure through open space itself. As with the RFID embedded within a plastic card, so with the ha-ha embedded in a landscape—a technique of medieval castles and Victorian landscape design that submerges an invisible ditch beneath the surface of an unimpeded vista to the horizon. As Deleuze and Guattari have it, "smooth space subsists, but only to give rise to the striated," the encompassing element "becomes a horizon."[65] The ha-ha was the design par excellence of affording smooth lines of sight to the horizon, while simultaneously preventing animals from roaming and enemy forces from invading. Deployed also in the nineteenth-century design of the asylum, the ha-ha presented a secure wall to those viewing from the inside while affording the impression of an open space to those outside. Now reappearing in the design of the U.S. embassy in London as well as in the parkland surrounding the Washington monument in Washington, D.C., the ha-ha reconciles security and openness via landscape form. To develop forms with a first reference to landscape (milieu) and a second reference to security is to work with the plasticity of space in such a way as to rewrite the borderline. Indeed, the embassy need not have a border as such in its relation to its urban milieu, for its milieu may become its border. The forms of the ha-ha, the curved bench, the lake, and the pathways, as the architects explain, gather the vigilant and watchful eyes of the public within the security apparatus. Just as the RFID tag animates the relations between people and their physical environment, allowing things to talk and respond, so the architecture of the embassy lets the environment talk, allows for the features of the landscape to have agency, to be both security devices and places of freedom, leisure, and pleasure.

Yet the means of locating mobile bodies and things in otherwise open vistas will always also produce unexpected consequences and effects. The object to be tracked and located can never be strictly controlled or foreseen. Within the interwoven stories of new systems of address are tracks and traces that, at least momentarily, reveal the violence that is more usually buried and concealed beneath the surface. In January 2004 Italian prosecutors began gathering evidence of CIA agents involved in rendition flights between Morocco, Afghanistan, and Algeria. The twenty-two agents left behind the traces and transactions of luxurious mid-rendition breaks at Milan hotels, as they "had frequent flier numbers and hotel loyalty cards so they could earn points during their stay in the Italian fashion capital."[66] The coalescence of consumption and security that has become so central to homeland security unexpectedly opens up a glimpse of other offshore spaces of torture and rendition. The CIA agents' interactions with hotel services, credit cards, and retail purchases became an animated story of where they had been and what they had done. Contactless security, one might say, is not contactless at all—it contains contingencies and indeterminacies that can never be strictly foreseen.

Part III
EFFECTS

5. ON AESTHETICS
Security's Objects and the Form of Data

Let every object under our consideration be imagined to have its inward contents scooped out so nicely, as to have nothing of it left but a thin shell, exactly corresponding both in inner and outer surface, to the shape of the object itself: and let us likewise suppose this thin shell to be made of fine threads, closely connected together, and equally perceptible, whether the eye is supposed to observe them from without or within . . . the imagination will enter into the vacant space within this shell, and there at once view the whole from within. —William Hogarth, *The Analysis of Beauty*, 8

It is not easy to say how I know which elements to work on. If it doesn't feel right, I mean it needs to look pretty, then I . . . well, then I write another line of code. —Comment from observations and interviews carried out with designers of security software, Paris, May 2009

In an unremarkable industrial building in a Paris suburb, the graded colors of a screened display shift and change. The software engineer at the keyboard—he has called himself an "imagineer"—runs a test on a new software system destined for the South African government and designed to identify people who pose a potential security threat before they arrive into the country for the 2010 FIFA World Cup. Asked how he knows when the lines of code he has built are complete, when his analytics are ready to identify correlative links between multiple data sources, his reply is not the expected appeal to mathematics and computer science. Instead, he suggests an aesthetic judgement—"it needs to look pretty"—a tacit and affective sense of the appearance of a complete entity or whole object. As contemporary analytics gather together new elements, correlating data elements to produce new things that go out into the world and have effects, the objects of security materialize in new forms. In the systems deployed across multiple domains, from the detection of anomalous transactions in casinos or involving insurance claims or retail banking to the identification of future risky associations for airline security or counterterrorism, data are no longer strictly the stuff of the statistical knowledge of population. The aesthetic sensibility of the software engineer signals a different kind of object that emerges in a world of data mining, "mash ups," link analysis, social network analysis, and data fusion.

Data occupy an important position within contemporary security measures, appearing as the gathered fragments of an otherwise ungovernable global space of mobile people, money, and objects. As expressed by the U.S. President Barack Obama in the *National Security Strategy of 2010*, for example, "within global systems of transportation and transactions," data gathering at "key nodes—points of origin and transfer, or border crossings" represents "an opportunity for the interdiction of threats" as they emerge.[1] In this sense data are represented as security's *objects* that are emptied of their materiality, rendered as the essentially objective measure of the inner lives and future intentions of subjects. In their objective form, data are all but invisible to us, falling away from the register of an identifiable security apparatus. As a reading of Heidegger reminds us, the ubiquitous environment of technology and equipment renders the material object radically unperceived.[2] And yet, simultaneously, data appear as *things* with a curious vitality that exceeds their usability and with a lively capacity to travel in the world, to gather, to talk, to "be pretty," to exceed their objectness and to have effects, whether violent, unexpected, benign, or mundane. It is in these moments, where data are animated not by the design of an algorithmic line of code but by what the political theorist Jane Bennett calls "thing-power," that they become things with a life that is never quite caught by the design of a security measure itself. "Thing-power," writes Bennett, "gestures toward the strange ability of ordinary, man-made items to exceed their status as objects" and to "animate, to act, to produce effects dramatic and subtle."[3] To return to our writer of code, imagining himself to be the creator of effects on his screen (and animator of future acts of security screening as his model goes out to work), he responds to the aesthetics of form as such, his capacity to act and decide altered by the thing itself.

In this chapter I juxtapose the ontology of data as it is emerging in contemporary security with two other moments when objects were thought to alter the judgements and capacities of other objects and subjects assembled around them, other moments, in short, when objects became things. I do this because critical theoretical treatment of data, as it is deployed in security, has most often considered data as technologies or techniques of subjectivation—as central to the formation of knowledge of the modern subject and the governing of population. As I proposed in chapter 1, possibilistic security measures act upon the subject and population in a quite distinctive way. Put simply, when the partial elements of an unknown subject gather with other elements, some of these are parts of *things*. The dividuated subject, we might suggest, is composed of an amalgam of elements of other subjects and objects, held together by associations. Though work on data's historical classification of subjects is important, data were always also lively, vital things that did work beyond their designed intentions. To juxtapose historical moments when the life-form of data comes to the visible surface is to suggest how we might access the world of data as things. In this way I begin to open up the potentiality that exceeds a politics of possibility, the unexpected and unanticipated effects that are not in the design of the security apparatus itself.

The first of my moments is drawn from art's objects: William Hogarth's eighteenth-century depiction of the serpentine "line of beauty" as the definitive "figure of beauty" whose perfectly arranged correlates were "the whole order of form."[4] In Hogarth's treatise on artistic perfection in physical form, we see a crystallized moment in the modern struggle for an objective aesthetic whose properties could be made knowable and replicable. The "line of beauty" Hogarth depicts is a form in which the whole of the object is graspable to the observer by virtue of its perfectly arrayed parts. The object is emptied of its materiality, its "contents scooped out," its inner and outer surfaces perfectly corresponding, "fine threads closely connected," the better for the observer's "imagination to enter the vacant space" and "view the whole."[5] To be clear, it is not that the Hogarthian sense of form is strictly analogous to contemporary data forms but rather that it opens up a way of thinking about those forms that would otherwise be distant and difficult to reach. The Hogarthian emptying out of the matter of the object is akin to the emptying that must take place for data to be represented as an objective measure of security. Similarly, in the second of my object stories, drawn from the physical sciences, the much contested quantum thought of the early twentieth century attended to the correlative effects of objects in movement, even when distant and separated. In the principles of indeterminacy and uncertainty of Werner Heisenberg and John Bell, there is a capacity to imagine the properties of objects without recourse to fixed physical properties and mechanical laws.[6] In quantum theory we begin to see a science of noncausal relations among objects, a credibility afforded to "discontinuous existence in space," as Alfred North Whitehead conceived it, that is "very unlike the continuous existence of material entities which we habitually assume as obvious."[7]

Lines of Beauty: Data and Objectivity

The beauty of data in contemporary security is assumed to lie precisely in its capacity to reveal an objective and emergent picture through the arraying of its various elements. As, for example, Tom Black, the chief executive of the software company Detica, explained to UK authorities, citing the American novelist William Gibson: "It's impossible to move, to live, to operate at any level without leaving traces, bits, seemingly meaningless fragments of information that can be retrieved, amplified."[8] Such retrieval and amplification amounts to what Black calls a "digital footprint—a trail of ones and zeros" that can provide a picture of a person. This sense of data as the essentially objective traces left in the wake of the lives of subjects, though, Black describes as increasingly futile amid the "data deluge" of the Internet, telecommunications, and financial data. The key innovation, as Black explains to his audience, is the development of social network analysis to produce "hypothetical threatprints" of emergent dangers. The disaggregation and reassembling of data in social network analysis "breaks down into component parts" the bodies of mobile subjects and objects, such that the possible threat can be "continually reenvisaged and incorporated."[9] The lines that are drawn between elements of data are mobile lines that continually define new potential outlines and forms of future threats. To give a visual sense of the form of social network analysis, Valdis Krebs, a leading computer scientist developing software for counterterrorism, has mapped the correlating social networks of the bombers of the USS *Cole* in October 2000 and the nineteen 9/11 hijackers, concluding in his work for IBM that "the assembled data maps enough of the 9/11 conspiracy to have stopped it in advance."[10] A distinctive spatial map of data points and correlated lines of association, the social network analysis produced in Black's Detica software and Krebs's counterterrorism analytics has an aesthetic form in and of itself.

The deployment of data for identifying future security threats is concerned less with what it calls the "nodes" of specific items of data (the "dots") than it is with the inferred relations across those nodes ("connecting the dots"). Understood in this way, the detection of *emergent* threats takes place within form itself, in the links and patterns that materialize and take shape. But how might we understand the capacities of form itself as an object? To an extent, the capacities of a malleable emergent form is familiar to us, particularly in light of Michel Foucault's security mechanism that "sifts the good and the bad," ensuring always that "things are in movement, constantly moving around, continually going from one point to another."[11] If what is calculated is movement from point to point, then the outline of a form can shift and change for as long as the points are held together. Indeed, one might say that today's techniques of social network analysis are the very technological embodiment of the continual movement from one point to another, never quite settling on one point or element of data but perennially seeking new relations from point to point. And yet the form that emerges in the fine threads that connect the points also embodies a capacity to affect and to be affected—to leave a software designer looking for beauty or to amplify the response of the security analyst as viewer.[12] "We know nothing about a body until we know what it can do," write Deleuze and Guattari, until we see "what its affects are, how they can or cannot enter into composition with other affects, with the affects of another body."[13] What data can do, their very capacities to act, to affect, and to be affected, thus substantially exceed their design as objects. The software engineer who sits before the screen to demonstrate what his software can do does not know completely what it can do. His affective relation to the software exhibits its very capacities as a thing. The sifting and arraying of elements is not limited to the capacity of the data as security instruments but extends to the aesthetic form of data itself.

William Hogarth's presence on the English art scene of the 1720s and 1730s witnessed the art world engaging a nascent modernity, in which the search for moral codes of conduct and public order, as well as the scientific search for mechanical laws, became reflected in his works. In his *The Analysis of Beauty*, published in 1753, Hogarth devised what Frederic Ogée and Olivier Meslay describe as an "aesthetic program" revealing the code of beauty—a means of ordering the infinite variety of forms in a "compositional grammar," at the heart of which is his famous "line of beauty."[14] Hogarth's treatise on beauty led him to "consider more minutely than has hitherto been done, the nature of those lines, and their different combinations, which serve to raise in the mind the ideas of all the variety of forms imaginable."[15]

Hogarth's pursuit of the properties of the serpentine line led him to consider the aesthetic properties of form in human bodies alongside those of household objects, architecture, and landscape design. In the context of a world of proliferating material objects, Hogarth locates his line of beauty in human and nonhuman forms alike, reflecting on the aesthetics of the curve of a woman's body in stays alongside the curve of a carved chair leg. In the "legs of chairs" and the "row of stays" there is, for Hogarth, but one "precise line, properly to be called the line of beauty."[16] Arranging his images in a series of progressively shifting curves, Hogarth locates his aesthetically ideal line in relation to others in a linear series. As the art theorist John Bender writes on Hogarth's capacity to bring to attention the forms of everyday things, there is a "staging of ordinary objects and bodily forms" such that principles and laws of objects could be derived.[17] It was not only the nascent modernity of human acquisition of knowledge and material things that could be discerned in Hogarth's *Analysis* but also, significantly, a Newtonian world of the determinable properties of physical objects.[18] Indeed, like the cause–effect laws of Newtonian mechanics, Hogarth proposed that his lines are "like those of the mathematician's pen," depicting the true outline of physical form. In what follows I outline three sets of resonances across Hogarth's works on the properties of *objects as form* and the contemporary rise of *data as form*.

The Emptiness of the Object

In Hogarth's *The Analysis of Beauty* he contemplates the allure of objects to the eye of the observer through a specific method of the visual hollowing out of an object so as to leave only its inner and outer surfaces. This "conceit," he writes, permits the viewer to experience "any particular part of the surface of an object" and, thus, to "acquire a more perfect knowledge of the whole."[19] By "scooping out the contents" of objects in his drawings, Hogarth invites the viewer to become a "master of the meaning of any view of the object, as we walk around it, and view it from without."[20] It is precisely the emptying of the materiality of the object that, for Hogarth, creates the necessary space for the imagination of a whole. Thus, in his reflections on the aesthetic form of a candlestick, for example, it scarcely matters whether the object is carved from wood or cast from metal. What matters instead is the capacity to imagine the whole form from within and without, or to visualize a complete picture from the standpoint of every point on the surface. For Hogarth, it is the dense filigree of connected points that forms the outline of an object—and it is the position of those points in a series that govern aesthetic form. A small movement in the surface points can shift the curve into what Hogarth considered to be "ugliness" or "deformity."[21] Displaying his lines in a series, Hogarth identifies the precision of a specific line as against those that "bulge too much in their curvature" or "straighten, becoming mean and poor" (the line of beauty is line 4 in figure 5.1).

Hogarth's treatise on the emptied out form of the object provides conceptual purchase on how data points are assembled to create what are thought to be precision judgements. In order for form to be grasped in its entirety, the materiality of the object is emptied out. The substance of the object—it's dense content—is stripped away the better to grasp the elegance of form itself. And so it is with contemporary data modes such as social network analysis, in which the materialization of data, or the content of data nodes, is of less significance than the form of their assembly. As the content of a particular data field is hollowed out, the analytics allow for points "on the surface" to infer a view of the whole.

The Profile of the Object

In Hogarth's method the hollowing out of the object was essential to the exercise of achieving a true sense of the outline or profile. "Another advantage of considering objects merely as shells composed of lines," he writes, "is, that by these means we obtain the true and full idea of what is called the *outline* of a figure."[22] As we have seen, Hogarth's emphasis on the surface outline of objects, and on the lines that connect points on the inner and outer surface, equates his line of beauty with the object's profile. Writing on the dissatisfaction he felt with the symmetries of objects viewed full front, he states that "the profile of most objects, as well as faces, are rather more pleasing than their full fronts."[23] Describing the actions of a painter who, viewing a building, "takes it on the angle rather than in front, as most

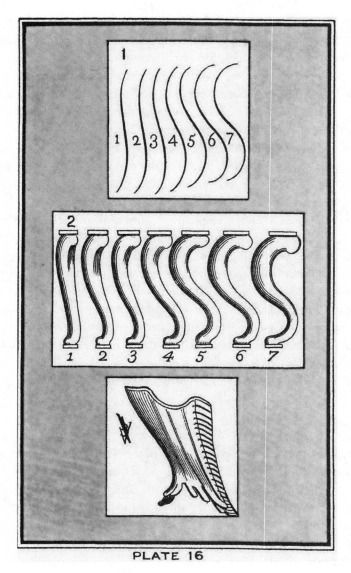

PLATE 16

FIGURE 5.1: William Hogarth's line of beauty, plate 16, 1753.

agreeable to the eye," Hogarth is interested in the composition of the profile as a pleasing aesthetic form.

What is the relationship of Hogarth's aesthetic sense of *profile* to the late eighteenth- and early nineteenth-century statistical techniques of *profiling*? Of course, in the social sciences the selection of data points in the profile of faces or bodies has been central to the genealogy of techniques of biometry and the statistical calculation of deviance. The nineteenth-century Belgian statistician Adolphe Quetelet, for example, was intrigued by the regularities and patterns copresent within the data on proportions in a single body and in large volume social data.[24] Observing the Gaussian distribution, or bell curve of the physical sciences, he applied the clustering around the mean to human and social phenomena. The behaviors, physical attributes, and habits of people, for Quetelet, adhered to a similar bell curve with an identifiable average man, "l'homme typique."[25] As Ian Hacking has described Quetelet's contribution to the making up of human subjects through data, "he gave us the mean and the bell-shaped curve as fundamental indices of the human condition."[26] By the nineteenth century, the mathematics of statistical normalization, the bell curve, and standard distribution had become the techniques for deploying data to manage uncertain futures. As Michel Foucault describes the operation of the bell curve and standard distributions in birth rates, mortality rates, and crime, they became the "first objects of knowledge of biopolitics."[27] No longer strictly a matter of governing man as body, the statistical regularities of man as species allowed for population to be governed as though it were Quetelet's l'homme typique. The profile of the individual body that Foucault identifies with "anatamo-politics" becomes a profiling of population that attends to a mass of bodies and their relations.

Prefiguring Quetelet's statistical identification of patterns and regularities by some one hundred years, Hogarth too was interested in the retrieval of patterns in otherwise scattered data points. Indeed, the bell curve itself appears in Hogarth's illustrations, albeit in the form of the outline of an actual physical and touchable bell (figure 5.2). What is interesting is that Hogarth's search for the precise principles of form are entirely aesthetic and not at all interested in statistical regularities. This is notable because in contemporary manifestations of the bell curve there is a significant move to invite aesthetics back into statistical calculations. The Gaussian distribution of the bell curve produces what Nassim Taleb calls a "precipitous decline" to the tail of the curve—the "outliers" of low probability.[28] It is,

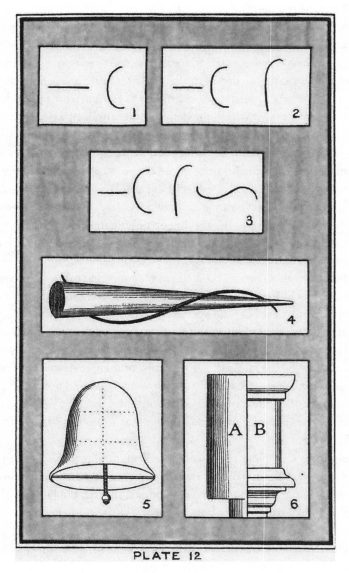

PLATE 12

FIGURE 5.2: William Hogarth's inclusion of the bell curve within his illustrations of the waving line, plate 12, 1753.

of course, precisely the outliers that are now thought to contain the potentially catastrophic "low probability, high consequence" event. Thus aesthetic judgements and inferred correlations, already present in Hogarth but evacuated by the growth of statistics, are invited within calculation. Aesthetic judgements on the pleasing quality of particular forms, though they did eschew strict statistical distribution, nonetheless inferred correlations among apparently disparate objects. "How pleasingly is the idea of firmness in standing conveyed to the eye by the three elegant claws of a table," writes Hogarth, and how this aesthetic quality is found also in "the three feet of a tea lamp, or the celebrated tripod of the ancients."[29]

Notably, in Hogarth's sense of patterns in form there is no distinction made between the lines of beauty in the curve of the bell, the lamp, or table and those of the human face, where his comments on the curve of a nose or forehead echo his ideas about the profile of other objects. What Hogarth allows us to see, in this nascent period before what Ian Hacking calls the "avalanche of numbers" in the growth of data as a means of making up subjects, is that the arraying of forms as data points is implicated in the *twinned emergence* of the modern subject and the modern object. Thus, for Hogarth, a concern with the *outlines* of a figure leads him to the points and lines of all forms, human and nonhuman: "He who will thus take the pains of acquiring perfect ideas of the distances, bearings, and oppositions of several material points and lines in the surfaces of even the most irregular figures, will gradually arrive at the knack of recalling them into his mind when the objects themselves are not before him."[30]

The form of the object—once conceived as points and lines—can precipitate effects even when the body of the object is itself absent. Even the most disorderly and chaotic of vistas, for Hogarth, can be rendered orderly by its conversion to the profiles of faces and the outlines of everyday objects. And so it is with the outline form of contemporary data analytics, where concern that the Gaussian distribution makes it difficult to attend to low probability "tail events" brings a rejection of strict adherence to statistical probability.[31] Like Hogarth's observer who "acquires perfect ideas of the distances and bearings," the software engineer is afforded a greater space for imagination to enter into the data object and infer from within. "Link detection software," explains the designer of security software in an interview, "finds nonobvious associations across huge databases," the points and lines of the analytic form having effects on the screens of match analysts and security officials. Like Hogarth's observers of points and lines, these experts in inferring from visual form have the capacity to act, "to assign a risk score to the data." Even where the data objects themselves are absent, they have effects and precipitate a response. The contemporary use of data to assign risk profiles and to enact security decisions takes material form in the outline of an object conceived as a shell composed of points and lines.

Objects and Movement

A dominant theme in Hogarth's works is city scenes of ribald street life and chaotic and cacophonous crowds. Though in many ways his scenes appear as anathema to the supple grace and parsimony of his line of beauty, in fact his analysis of the beauty of forms is present in his captured scenes of everyday urban spaces. As Mark Hallett proposes in his reading of Hogarth's satirical images of Georgian London: "The fragmented, crowded and cluttered forms . . . not only effectively translated the rush of signs encountered in the city, but also offered a pictorial language which helped make that rush of signs legible. Through these processes of mediation, places such as Covent Garden, Soho, Islington and Charing Cross were turned into malleable environments."[32]

The aesthetic grammar of Hogarth's line of beauty extends also to his depiction of city scenes. At first glance a chaotic and overwhelming rush of figures, the composition of his scenes follows the points and lines of his analysis of beauty, such that the crowd becomes legible and the environment malleable. In his *Southwark Fair* of 1734 (figure 5.3), the crowd of theatrical performers and street entertainers suffuse the scene as the stage (left of picture) collapses onto the street stall below. Amid the crowd, the striking profile of a woman, her head turned at an angle, displays the line of beauty within the anatomy of the single human body. Meanwhile the flow of the crowd—once conceived as points on a line—itself follows a perfect serpentine, from bottom right to top left of the frame. The apparently random distribution of figures and objects in the crowd scene is made legible by the regularity of the serpentine line that the eye observes. Indeed, converting the figures of the scene into correlating points on a line, Hogarth invites the viewer to infer movement in the otherwise static frame. It is the data points within the multiplicity that "invite the beholder" and "leads the eye a wanton kind of chase."[33] For Hogarth, the aesthetic beauty of the serpentine line is not separable from the sense of movement it instills in the eye that views it and the hand that draws it. "The eye hath this sort of en-

FIGURE 5.3: William Hogarth's *Southwark Fair*, 1734. Courtesy of Museum of London.

joyment," writes Hogarth, "in winding walks, and serpentine rivers, and all sorts of objects, whose forms are composed principally of waving and serpentine lines."[34] In the Hogarthian sense, the object possesses the property of beauty precisely by means of its affective capacity to invoke movement.

In part, the search for aesthetic appeal in contemporary security is motivated by the invocation to movement that we find in Hogarth's crowd scenes. By contrast with past modes of statistical data, characterized by periodic fixity of data elements, contemporary analytics seek to produce something beyond the sum of its elements, something emergent and mobile. Hogarth's technique of ordered points of reference within a disorderly crowd resonates strikingly, for example, with the gathering and analysis of data elements for security in crowded places. The UK Home Office's commissioned Innovative Science and Technology in Counter-terrorism (INSTINCT) "crowded places technology" converts the movement and signs in urban space into a series of data points that detect emergent properties of the form of the crowd. Amid the crowd, "these technologies take crowd volume and flow data at specific points (such as ticket barriers or retail outlets) and use it to predict how the crowd will flow through the location."[35] Somewhat resonant with Hogarth's struggle to locate an emergent civic order in the chaotic streets of Georgian London, making legible the sense data of the rushing crowd, the generation of new knowledges of the crowd as emergent data forms make the environment malleable precisely in the way that the art historian Mark Hallett suggests.

Indeed, the "malleable environments" that Hallett proposes Hogarth makes of Covent Garden, Soho, and Islington, find resonance with the modulated securing of contemporary crowded places. Consider, for example, the public vigilance programs initiated on the city streets and subways of New York, London, or Madrid. Programs such as "see something, say something," and the U.S. TSA's "highway watch" appeal to the everyday observer to report something that feels out of place or that is out of the ordinary. The affective judgement on the look and feel of a place with which one is familiar is enlisted into security practice because it overrides the probability of particular events, ushering in aesthetic senses of possible anomalies amid the crowd. The crowd may be cacophonous and indeterminate, but its modulated outlines can be detected as they emerge. In the London Metropolitan Police campaign "If You Suspect It, Report It," for example, the scene of the crowd in a public square is secured by the observer who reported a suspicion: "a bomb won't go off here because weeks before a shopper reported someone studying the CCTV cameras" (see figure 5.4). What I have elsewhere called the "vigilant visuality" of homeland security techniques embodies a hybrid of aesthetic inference ("something looks out of place") and algorithmic calculation (the antiterror hotline operator who follows a decision tree for "effective response").[36] Like Hogarth's collapsing stage amid the cacophonous Southwark Fair, the emerging event is visible only when the movement from point to point is discernible.

The problem, of course, with the resonance of lines of beauty with the aesthetics of security is that in both instances we continue to talk of objects, to sustain the inertness of objects, and to conceive of them as hollowed out instruments in the making up of subjects. If the object is emptied of its materiality in Hogarth, if beauty is present by virtue of this hollowing to a shell-like form, is it the case that the aesthetics of security is one of outlines, profiles, and emptied out objects? For, wherever we follow it, the life of security data is a lively one, an alert life that moves, travels, and has effects in the world. As Lorraine Daston has described so beautifully in her histories of the objects of science, the material of science laboratory and archive is

FIGURE 5.4: Metropolitan Police "If You Suspect It, Report It" campaign poster, 2009.

also the stuff of "potentially active agents that engage with viewers as if they were persons and the viewers were mere things."[37] For Daston, even those instruments most closely associated with the quest for scientific objectivity are also things with capacities, lives, and influence.

Things That Talk: The Vitality of Data

To acknowledge the agency of data in terms of its capacity to have security effects, violent and banal, and to understand data as having a potential to act, is to take a significant step toward understanding data as elements within a broader assemblage of human and nonhuman entities introduced in this book—risk scores, credit cards, travel tickets, lines of code, border guards, risk consultants, scanners, and screens. But, the life force of data, its materiality and vitality as *a thing in itself*, is much less understood and analyzed. As Jane Bennett reminds us, we are accustomed to thinking of objects always in relation to a subject, as instrument or as designed or built, when, in fact, "things, too, are vital players in the world, existents in excess of their association with human meanings, habits or projects."[38] Bennett's insight casts new light on the problem of how data come into being and dwell within the security landscape, precisely because data are *represented as objects* in association (and in algorithmic association rules) with human beings, habits, and projects. Consider, for example, the allure of a model of data analytics that is designed, built, and can be "retuned," as explained by the designers of i-dentify software: "Maybe they're worried about illegal immigration or maybe there's a terrorist attack and their focus is on terrorism. If they want it we can give them the source code, they can retune the algorithms or we can do it for them."[39] Here, the data analytics are represented as objects with origins in a source code without which they are nothing. They are objects to be retuned by agencies of the state or private companies for the fully instrumental purposes of security. Their "objectness" is a function of their representation as objective measures, far removed from the fallible senses of the human observer. Yet look a little closer and the data exist, as Bennett proposes, in excess of their association with data subjects and data users. Returning to our software designer, who here explains the capacities of the data system: "Biometric identifiers that can talk to a departure control system, that can talk to the risk algorithm, that can talk to the border guard."

What is intriguing about this tension between the object that is "tuned" and the thing that "talks" is that the potentiality of the life of data itself is not exhausted by the careful man-made arraying of dots and lines, but instead the potentiality exceeds and overflows the bounded object. Data are never merely instruments tuned to the needs of a sovereign whose focus is immigration control or terrorism, given life only by a source code. As the historian of science Lorraine Daston argues, "things talk" in ways that are inventive and creative, and they categorically "do not merely repeat" as though "instruments for recording and playing back the human voice."[40] They have capacities to attract attention, from people and from other objects, to gather listeners and observers around them, to intervene in scientific discourse, to change the terms of the debate. Writing on the Harvard Museum of Natural History's Ware Collection of nineteenth-century glass botanical models created by Leopold and Rudolph Blaschka, Daston describes a world in which these "unclassifiable" scientific models or works of art show their capacities as "things" that have relations with other people and things. "The capacity to call a society of friends into existence," writes Daston, "is as much a part of a thing's thingness, of its reverberations in the world, as its material properties like weight and chemical composition."[41] Though their human design was somewhat instrumental—to devise accurate and durable botanical models—the Blaschka models significantly exceed and transform their design, having an onward life that could not be designed in or determined in advance. The glass flowers' thing-power lies in their propensity to affect and to be affected, to travel in the world and to induce others to travel to see them.

And so, though we are comfortable with objects that have identifiable outlines—the shell-like profile so important to Hogarth—the things that talk tend often to be "composite" beings that "straddle boundaries between kinds. Art and nature, persons and things, objective and subjective are brought together in these things."[42] For Daston, the fusions and composites that emerge mean that "all these things threaten to overflow their outlines, to have reverberations in the world."[43] While outlines and point-to-point forms have become so central to contemporary security aesthetics, there remain gaps between the points that exceed calculative relations. To reread the software engineer's search for beauty in the form of the analytics, or Hogarth's analysis of beauty, through Daston's scientific objects "that talk" or Jane Bennett's "thing-power" is to find a way to understand data as things that overflow their crafted outlines and live on to reverberate in the world.

The idea of data, as it has been treated in the social sciences at least, has been all but inseparable from the notion of collection. Arguably a pre-occupation of all matters of method—how one collects, in what way one samples, what work the data archive does—has been this question of data collection. I argued in chapter 2 that contemporary techniques of data analytics fundamentally alter the meaning of collection, such that the constant movement and discarding of data become of greater significance than collection itself. It is not my purpose here to dwell on collection, but suffice to say that one significant aspect of the problem of collection is that the verb *to collect* solidifies the object that is collected. Daston's glass flowers, we might say, are represented as objects in the Ware Collection, but everything that they do, all of the effects that they have, defy collection in favor of gathering. The processes of contemporary data mining and analytics for security are more about *gathering* data elements in malleable forms than they are about data collection.[44] Certain properties of this gathering—form, pattern, fungibility—could be said to be possessed by the data things themselves. Indeed, one might say that it is possible for data to gather *themselves* together, as for example in the crowdsourcing of digital data or the self-organizing capacities of the social network. In his essay "Das Ding," Martin Heidegger insists upon a clear delineation of the "thing" from Kant's "object," with objects made possible only insofar as they are representations of the thing.[45] To interpret data, for our purposes here, as objects and as objective security measures of the lives of subjects, they exist only insofar as their "thingness" is occluded by representations of objectivity. The representation is not a stable one, always and all of the time the things will overflow their objectified outlines. This is because, as Heidegger conceives it, the thingness of the "thing" derives from its capacity to gather other elements around it (*das Dingen versammelt*).

Though in his essay on the thing Heidegger stops short of specifying how it is that the thing assembles together and gathers other elements around it, in his work on building and dwelling he asks "what is a built thing?," reflecting on the building of a bridge. "The bridge does not just connect banks that are already there," writes Heidegger, but rather "designedly causes them to lie across from one another" such that "the bridge *gathers* to itself, *in its own way*, the earth and sky, divinities and mortals."[46] The bridge is designed and it is built, but it is never merely a bridge; it is a thing that gathers or assembles other elements—the harvest wagon, the flow of the river, the castle, the city square, and the horse teams—in ways that bring something else into being:

Bridges lead in many ways. The city bridge leads from the precincts of the castle to the cathedral square; the river bridge near the country town brings wagons and horse teams to the surrounding villages. The old stone bridge's humble brook crossing gives to the harvest wagon its passage from the fields into the village and carries the lumber cart from the field path to the road. The highway bridge is tied into the network of long distance traffic. . . . Always and ever differently the bridge escorts the lingering and hastening ways of men to and from. The bridge gathers.[47]

We can build or make something, but it will then bring forth other things, unanticipated and surprising—new vistas, new relations, new crossings, altered perspectives.

As a bridge between items of data, the algorithm gathers the elements differently and in ways that could not be anticipated. Though the presence of data elements guide the design of the algorithm (like Heidegger's banks that guide the building of the bridge), once built it is a thing that gathers, and gathers beyond its design, such that even the data "banks" look quite different. Indeed, the form of data itself exhibits the power to gather the gaze of the designer, a kind of affective pull that Jane Bennett has described as the "sex appeal of the inorganic" or "a shimmering, potentially violent vitality intrinsic to matter."[48] I propose that the apparent tuning of the algorithm takes place, materializes, in the more durable life of lines of code that are things going out into the world. Data, and their software bridges, are things with capacities. Data are not only gathered in the strict sense of data collection, but they assemble themselves with multiple other elements and things. Data do unexpected things with unanticipated effects: stop the wrong person at the border, fail to stop the right person, gather the false positives and then let them loose into the world, invite some intuitions and inferences from observers and banish others. As Heidegger reminds us, it is when the apparent object breaks or fails that its "thingness" becomes visible and the fragility of its status as an object is momentarily exposed. "When we discover its unusabilty," he writes, "the thing becomes conspicuous" and amenable to philosophy and thought.[49] Could it be that the apparent objective mastery of security by data-driven technoscience, precisely because "things talk" to other things and to people, can never quite account for the durable life of data as things?

Quantum Things: Emergence and the Object

It seems we may be witnessing a distinctive turn in contemporary philosophy and the social sciences, simultaneously toward an ethos of engagement with fractionated and dispersed subjectivities and toward a reconsideration of the object as not merely an "actant" or a "device" circulating in a world of human subjects but also as a self-sufficient thing with capacities in and of itself.[50] One of the many things that is interesting about these multiple turns, their affinities and dissonances, is the way in which they flesh out the specific deployment of "life" as the means of governing in late modern capitalism. Put simply, the *bio* in biopolitics is much disputed. What form of life is manifest within the governing of species life? Can we usefully conceive of things as having emergent life that is both flourishing within, and targeted by, biopolitics? In an essay reflecting on the late work of Michel Foucault, Giorgio Agamben suggests that the thinker had gestured to "a point of departure in the concept of life" that remained unexplored but left open a new terrain for a generation of scholars to roam within.[51] Thus, in Foucault's last written essay, "Life: Experience and Science," he writes that "at the most basic level of life, the processes of coding and decoding give way to a chance occurrence that, before becoming a disease, a deficiency, is something like a disturbance in the information system, something like a 'mistake.'"[52] In this, Foucault's obliquely signaled research never to come, he places emergence, contingency, and disturbance at the heart of this markedly "different way of approaching the notion of life."[53] It would have been, Gilles Deleuze proposes, "like a new axis, different from the axes of both knowledge and power."[54] Understood thus, life ceases to be attached to an identifiable subject or, indeed, to population or species life, but perhaps signals a form of life that is common to the emergent properties of plural elements of people and things.

The question of emergence—the heterogeneous and contingent properties of a whole system, network, or assemblage that exceeds its composite parts (its mistakes, its reversals, its mutations, and so on)—has become critical to a range of debates on the governing of life at the edge of catastrophe or crisis.[55] Mainly, the material of the study of emergence has been the stuff of the biological sciences, the dynamic and complex forms of organic entities. Certainly the genealogies of emergence in the biological sciences offer plentiful bounty of lively, vivacious things that cross so readily and productively between the lives of subjects and the lives of things. In

Melinda Cooper's compelling account of recombinant DNA and its capacity to mobilize "transversal processes of bacterial recombination," she locates within the life forms of genetic matter a broader biopolitical process, a "new science of life" that seeks to respond to "the emergent, long before it has actualized in a form we can recognize."[56] Like our security techniques that seek out the emergent threat preemptively in form itself, long before it is actualized, Cooper's microbial life makes "field transitions" that could never be predicted and can only be formed speculatively and imaginatively. And yet, as Manuel DeLanda reminds us, "while organic materials and organic creatures serve as good illustrations of nonlinear causality, biology does not have a monopoly on nonlinearity."[57] Could it be the case, perhaps because species life itself has so dominated our thinking, that the *bio* in biopolitics has had a blind spot with regard to the lives of objects? Perhaps even in Foucault's late signaling of a "different way of approaching the notion of life" there might be the possibility of a form of life that is shared by human and nonhuman beings? I will suggest here a second story of the relations between things, their observers, and other things, this time one to be found in the physical sciences, in the vibrant lives of quantum things.

In contrast to Hogarth's Newtonian-influenced art world of physical properties possessed by objects, the post-Newtonian world of quantum physics speaks of entangled objects. Here there are subatomic particles, mysterious and vibrant, that do unexpected things, take unexpected courses, and act on one another at a distance. As Louisa Gilder explains in her careful biographies of the quantum physicists, the objects of quantum theory are the stuff of *entanglement*: "Any time two entities interact they entangle. It doesn't matter if they are photons (bits of light), atoms (bits of matter), or bigger things made of atoms like dust motes, microscopes, cats or people. The entanglement persists no matter how far these entities separate, as long as they don't subsequently interact with anything else—an almost impossibly tall order for a cat or a person, which is why we don't notice the effect. But the motions of subatomic particles are dominated by entanglement."[58]

Of course, superficially, we might say that it is the entanglement of things—people, money, information—that is the guiding principle of the forms of security that seek to exploit distantly correlated associations. More accurately, though, it is the scientific treatment of subatomic particles as mysterious and lively things that has contributed a language of form and attraction—present in the commercial data mining domain, for example—

that is a significant condition of possibility for the active life of data we witness today. In his remarks on quantum theory, Alfred North Whitehead notes that "a problem is handed over to the philosophers." The "electrons, with the correlative protons, are now conceived as being the fundamental entities out of which the material bodies of ordinary experience are composed," such that we have to "revise all our notions of the character of material existence."[59] Kant's "object," then, was "saturated with Newtonian physics," a view of material existence that was to be fundamentally challenged by the idea that the movement of an electron has "a series of detached positions, on not a continuous line."[60] As with Deleuze's chains of variables that are torn one from the other, Whitehead's appreciation of quantum theory was that it would tear the causal lines of mechanical space and time. There are three aspects that I will focus on here, each suggestive of a form of data that allows for the line of beauty to be achieved even where the outline is overflowed: cause-effect relations, action at a distance, and movement and form.

Objects and the Cause-Effect Relations

Much of the early controversy surrounding quantum physics centered on the question of the cause–effect relations between objects. Challenging the determinist laws of Newton's classicism, the relations between objects at the quantum scale were the subject of much dispute, most notably in the exchanges between Albert Einstein and Niels Bohr. It was not until the second half of the twentieth century, though, that a new theoretical language for noncausal relations among subatomic particles began to be advanced. In a keynote address to philosophers and physicists at the Còllege de France in 1980, the physicist John Bell contrasted the correlative relations among objects in everyday life with the "mysterious" correlative relations among spinning particles. On the matter of the everyday perception of correlation, he famously used the allegory of a fellow physicist's socks:

> The philosopher in the street, who has not suffered a course in quantum mechanics . . . can point to many similar correlations in everyday life. The case of Bertlmann's socks is often cited. Dr. Bertlmann likes to wear two socks of different colours. Which sock he will have on a given foot on a given day is quite unpredictable. But when you see that the first sock is pink, you can be quite sure that the second

sock will not be pink. Observation of the first, and experience of Bertlmann, gives immediate information about the second.[61]

Bell goes on to explain that, though the observation of two spinning particles may appear to be correlative in the same way—"when one goes up the other always goes down, after a while it is enough to look at one side to know also about the other"—in fact, these peculiarly correlative relations are "inexplicable" in strict terms of local causality.[62] Where, in the case of Bertlmann's socks, there is a local cause (his penchant for odd socks), Bell's particles in the "singlet spin state" correlate in spite of there being no local causality.

The implications of the contested rise of quantum correlative reasoning for linear time and prediction are considerable. Contemporary forms of data mining and analytics (risk algorithms, link analysis, social network analysis) celebrate the correlative relations among elements. Consider, for example, the consumer loyalty card data that correlates grocery purchases to online car insurance to times of day to forms of payment. In a sense such correlations between data items are like Bertlmann's socks; that is to say, they are not mysterious at all, they have local causality. In contemporary forms of data analytics for security, though, it is the inexplicable and emergent correlations that are sought. Could it be that the correlated future states proposed by John Bell in his theoretical physics have made a particular world of data thinkable and actionable—one in which data elements are correlated and not locally causal? As Peter Galison reminds us, quantum mechanics' "renunciation of classical determinism and causality in favour of strictly probabilistic predictions" has had significant impact on the way we think and act today.[63] The advent of quantum thought contributed to the condition of possibility for thinking beyond linear causality to explore the emergent properties of relations among objects.

Objects and Action at a Distance

In a letter to Max Born in 1909, Einstein described critically the "spooky action-at-a-distance" or "sort of telepathic coupling" implied by quantum thought.[64] For Einstein, there was a troubling element to the inexplicable effect that one individual particle appeared to have on another in the absence of relays or other observable mechanical relations. It is not my purpose here to recount the century of contested thought on action at a distance that has followed. Rather, I am interested in the relationship between knowledge of action at a distance in quantum theory and the "governing at a distance" that has become commonplace in social and political thought. Some seventy years after Einstein's letter to his friend and colleague Born, Michel Foucault depicted in his lectures a security apparatus that acts upon "an indefinite series of elements, circulations, movements" and upon "an indefinite series of events that will occur" in the context of "action at a distance of one body on another."[65] Equating the problem of security with what he calls "the problem of the series," Foucault sees that the actions are not serial in the sense of a linear series of causes and effects but are instead an "open series" that cannot be predicted.

The things of quantum worlds—subatomic particles, their spin, their direction, their observation, their recording as data—are things with capacities that exceed observable action. They have effects upon each other, but these are actions at a distance, effects across vast spaces. The series of Newton's world, exhibited also in the visual representations of Hogarth's series of objects, is segmented in quantum thought, scattered and arrayed differently. The drive to locate causal relations between objects remains present in quantum thought, but it becomes arrayed differently, perhaps something like what Quentin Meillassoux describes as a "contingent causality" where "in the future, completely different effects could follow from exactly the same causes."[66]

Things, Movement, and Form

In William Hogarth's lines of beauty, the objects of his interest were understood to have fixed properties of form. In his series of curved chair legs, for example, the serpentine line of beauty has a fixed geometry. Indeed, for Hogarth it was precisely the capacity of the object to have a clearly defined profile or outline that was intrinsic to its aesthetic properties. Even where Hogarth sought to represent the movement and flow of a crowd or a river, it was via the identifiable surface data of points on a line. The lines of the post-Newtonian world of quantum science, by contrast, blur the edges of objects and overflow their outlines. Werner Heisenberg's identification of the uncertainty principle—that the more that is known and measured of the momentum of a particle, the less that can be known of its position— marked a significant break with mechanical laws. The properties of p (momentum) and q (position) were everything to the Newtonian system, knowing the position and momentum of objects meant one could predict exactly what would happen next. Observing the experimental electron within the cloud chamber, Heisenberg posited that one could never have absolute determinable knowledge of both p and q. Put simply, to have a definitive and precise point for the position of a particle is to render indeterminate its momentum, to blur the edges of its outline.

In a world of the global circulations of people, objects, and money, the question of indeterminacy of mobility and position has come to dominate political thought and practice. The rise of the uncertainty principle in quantum physics made it thinkable that data on the movement of objects in space could be indeterminate, contingent even, but still useful in telling us important things about the nature of the universe. The politics of possibility that seeks to secure unknown futures, identifying correlations between people and objects and making interventions from a distance, has significant origins in the contested quantum thought of early twentieth-century mathematics and physics. Not only do contemporary security techniques deploy the technological progeny of post-Newtonian science—from risk algorithms to biometric identifiers and backscatter scanners—but they precisely draw on ways of thinking about the capacities of objects that may not have been possible without Heisenberg's uncertainty principle and Bell's correlations.

The Life Form of Data

Returning to my starting point, when the software engineer sits before his lines of code, running the test data through his incomplete analytics, there is a certain Hogarthian reverence before the object that appears on the screen. In the aesthetic capacity to appear as a beautiful thing, there is space for the imagination to enter into the object, to stretch its outline until "it looks right" as a form. Likewise, affixed to the white-tiled wall of the Leicester Square tube station in London, a heavily outlined graphic line drawing dominates a poster for the antiterror hotline campaign. Urging the everyday observers of the passing crowd to notify about the thing that "feels out of place," the images depict only the outlines of a human eye and an exclamation mark in a simple aesthetics of security. In one sense there is an aesthetic relation between the many subjects and objects that assemble in the judgement of dangerousness. Yet there is also an undeniably political set of questions—these forms have effects, some of them violent or prejudicial (to report someone to the police, to freeze someone's assets, to risk profile and add to a watch list, to detain, to deny entry, and so on). As objects, the data appear technoscientific, hollowed out or shell-like. But, as a thing, it also lives, moves, has unintended consequences. How does one get at this life, capture it analytically? Isabelle Stengers has called for another vocabulary or narrative that can somehow access the complexities of a world of multiple beings, human and nonhuman, subjects and objects: "I am convinced that we need other kinds of narratives, narratives that populate our worlds and imaginations in a different way . . . to make present, vivid and mattering, the imbroglio, perplexity and messiness of a worldly world, a world where we, our ideas and power relations, are not alone, were never alone, will never be alone."[67]

For Stengers, the "wonder" and "alarm" with which we greet new scientific practices is to be connected with multiple other struggles. These are struggles that do not definitively oppose or overturn a "wrong" science, as we will see in chapter 6, but rather, struggles that make vivid a contingent and teeming world in which the sovereign decision itself is built on a shifting terrain of aesthetic judgements that can be challenged and disputed. The appearance of an objectivity of point-to-point calculations is shown to be an appearance as such, an appearance of wonder and alarm that also brings forth new effects beyond its design.

In juxtaposing the turn to new modes of data in contemporary security with Hogarth's world of points and lines, and with the indeterminate things of quantum theory, I have sought a different way of thinking about the perplexity Stengers alludes to. While as represented objects of science and technology new modes of data resonate with Hogarth's lines; as things they are more proximate to the emergent forms that have been depicted predominantly in the biological sciences. The capacity within science, and particularly within twentieth-century quantum thought, to imagine a world of indeterminate data that do things and have effects (but not causes) has been a significant condition of possibility for a new world of data things. The life of data dwells uneasily here, moving back and forth between the object-centred Hogarthian lines of beauty that are sought by the designers of security measures and the mysterious actions at a distance that are never fully incorporated by the measure itself.

6. ON A POTENTIAL POLITICS
Toward an Ethics of the Unanticipated

> The effects of the book might land in unexpected places and form shapes that I had never thought of. . . . I can't help but dream about a kind of criticism that would try not to judge but to bring an oeuvre, a book, a sentence, an idea to life; it would light fires, watch the grass grow, listen to the wind, and catch the sea foam in the breeze and scatter it. It would multiply not judgements but signs of existence; it would summon them, drag them from their sleep. Perhaps it would invent them sometimes—all the better. All the better. Criticism that hands down sentences sends me to sleep; I'd like a criticism of scintillating leaps of the imagination. —Michel Foucault, "The Masked Philosopher," 174

What are the effects of the politics of possibility on the capacity for critique? Confronted by a technoscientific security politics that acts on the very basis of future possibilities, indifferent to whether they come to pass, how does one begin to map the "condition of possibility" of such a politics, or to show how things might be otherwise? Is the possibility of critique effaced by a political program that precisely takes possibility as its object? In this chapter I propose that the contemporary politics of possibility poses a specific and unique problem for the capacity of critical response and intervention. That is to say, the politics of possibility appears to occupy the same terrain—of unknown subjects, acting upon the excess, thinking nonlinear relations—that has for so long provided resource for politics and critique. In the previous chapters of this book I have focused on how the politics of possibility targets preemptively, acting upon emergent and fractionated subjects yet to come fully into view. From the passenger information units (PIUS) ascribing numeric scores to border security risks to the so-called turn-key technologies of biometrics and radio frequency identifiers (RFID), the conventions of the archive and the watch list give way to the visualization of unknown future subjects. As I have described, the technologies devised in the late twentieth century to identify the commercial retailer's dream of the unknown consumer yet to arrive with unfulfilled desires have become the state's means of identifying the unknown security threat, a risky body yet to come. From partial fragments of the data of everyday transactions, a subject is dividuated into degrees of risk, scored and projected as a possible future economic opportunity or sovereign threat.

Understood thus, the politics of possibility appears to incorporate every element, even its own mistakes and errors are folded back into the capacity to write new code and locate new correlations. At least on the surface, this appears as a mode of governing that is capable of reconciling the smooth surfaces of the opportunities of globalization, the market *possibilities*, with the exercise of sovereign power, the ever present *possibility* of a security decision. And so, how can a diagram of the power of this emergent security terrain be excavated, and at the same time, how can a critical space for the political, for critique itself, be opened up?

In an interview for *Le Monde* in 1980, Michel Foucault requested anonymity—the "masked philosopher," nostalgic for a time when "being quite unknown" meant that there remained the potential that "the effects of the book might land in unexpected places and form shapes . . . never thought of."[1] The potential of the book lies in some future effect that had not been expected or anticipated in advance. Not all of the future relations, lives, and connections of what is written, Foucault suggests, could be established within the text itself; there will always be gaps, in-between moments, open to the creativity and inventiveness of the reader. What matters is not the pronouncement or judgment on something, a judgment that would forever curtail the imagination. Instead, Foucault "could not help but dream" about a form of criticism that "would try not to judge" but would bring "an idea to life," a criticism he described as having "scintillating leaps of the imagination."[2] This mode of critique beyond judgment was present also eleven years earlier when, in his lecture "What Is an Author?," Foucault similarly invokes potential future subjects, asking "what are the places in it [discourse] where there is room for possible subjects."[3] Let us keep the threads of this form of critique and weave them together: to land in unexpected places, to form shapes not yet imagined, to make leaps of the imagination and room for possible subjects, subjects as yet unknown.

The question of such a form of critique has become one of crucial significance to our times, not least because the contemporary politics of possibility is written also on the terrain of gaps and unknown subjects. The politics of possibility says that no person or thing may land in unexpected places, no person or thing may arrive anywhere unless they are already anticipated, risk scored, and biometrically anchored. All life in the politics of possibility has, in Gilles Deleuze's terms, a definite article—*the* life—identifiable, locatable, securable.[4] The life that is the object of technologies of possibility is life as it is manifested in the individual, properly belonging to specified moments. The shapes not yet imagined are imagined by means of inferring definitive life—rendered thinkable by association rule, linkage analysis, data mining, and risk visualization. The bell-shaped curve of probabilities is replaced by the imagination of the possibilities that dwell in the "tail risk," the unknown is made amenable to knowledge.

Yet, though acting on possibilities and proclivities is becoming the means of governing security beyond probability, this is a form of governing that can only act on a potential future that is already actualized as a possibility—a plane that would have been boarded, a border that would have been crossed, a bomb that would have gone off, a future violence that would have been fully realized. There is an important difference between the technoscientific risk-based politics of possibility that I have depicted in this book and what Gilles Deleuze has termed "immanent life," a life of pure potentiality comprised only of "virtualities, events, singularities."[5] The distinction between life with a definite article, the life, and life indefinite or immanent is a productive difference, one that is fertile ground for the imaginative, critical form envisaged by Foucault. In short, where the politics of possibility actualizes the unknown in material forms—risk scores, visualized networks, decision trees, protocols—the potential of people and objects is never fully actualized and, therefore, never meaningfully incorporable. The question for critique becomes how to sustain potentiality itself, how to keep open the indeterminate, the unexpected place and the unknowable subject.

In part, this form of critique is, as Foucault suggests, the pursuit of the very conditions of possibility of a particular security apparatus: How did it emerge? What is the specificity of its techniques? What are its effects?

How might things have been otherwise? This form of critique does not set out to uncover the wrongs in a system, to denounce the "mistake," the "lie or error" in an apparatus, but instead to bring to light "the conditions that had to be met for it to be possible."[6] In the preceding chapters I have sought to uncover the conditions that had to be met in order for risk-based, preemptive security measures to be possible. Within a form of critique that can work with indeterminacy and the unexpected, however, there is also an element of the conditions of *impossibility*. That is to say, as Deleuze and Agamben differently ask, under what conditions is there the potentiality not to write, not to inscribe the line, not to act, not to judge?[7] Under what conditions might a potential subject never quite come into view, never fully match with the characterization of the life? The significance of this potential not to act is that we live in times where the injunction is to render the future actionable, where all "high impact, low probability" events are imagined and acted upon as certainties. In such times critique must be able to think a potential that is not acted upon, to imagine leaving an incomplete picture of a person who will never be fully visualized, to conceive of living with the unknown and the uncertain, that potential being the very liveability of life itself. There are other forms of potential politics flourishing in the interstices of the programmatic politics of possibility, forms of potentiality that are incipient, never fully grasped or actualized in tactics or strategies.

Drawing on the work of installation artists and novelists who have depicted the unanticipated movements and spaces of the city amid the security techniques of a post-9/11 world, in this chapter I map the contours of a distinction between a politics of possibility and the terrain of a potential politics. Beginning by identifying the limit points of the politics of possibility across three axes—imagination, judgment, and life—I then suggest that the actions of possibilistic security can be critically interrupted along these same three dimensions.

Imagination 1: Guilt by Association

Jennifer Egan opens her Pulitzer Prize–winning novel *A Visit from the Goon Squad* with lines from Marcel Proust's *Á la Recherche de Temps Perdu* (*In Search of Lost Time*): "The unknown element of the lives of other people is like that of nature, which each fresh scientific discovery merely reduces but does not abolish."[8] It is precisely this "unknown element" in the lives of others that is present throughout Egan's novel—each of the nonlinear chapters connected to the next in sequence only by the fragile relations between the characters. In each of Egan's chapters, a character who appears fleetingly, half-glimpsed, ghostlike at the edges of the narrative, in the subsequent chapter becomes the protagonist at the center. The reader is unable to anticipate the association in advance, the future figure present only by a remote connection to a past story, one among multiple other possible associations. As in Proust's unknown element of the lives of others, Egan's novel deftly displays the persistence of the indeterminate elements, even in the face of a science and technology that would otherwise gather every fragment in the form of network analysis or semantic web. The subject at the edges of perception is felt as an unspecified presence—we know little or nothing about them, nothing, that is, until they become actualized as fleshed-out characters with history, consequences, and effects in a chapter yet to come.

The politics of possibility I have depicted in this book has no such tolerance for the emergent or half-seen figure at the edges of perception, no such interest in an unfulfilled future potential. It is precisely at the edges of what is visible in probability where contemporary security measures seek to render the associative connections of possible future risk. As I have described, the algorithmic association rules of possible links are wrought precisely to mitigate the unexpected arrival of a new subject. The "failure of imagination" that was said to contribute to the security failings of 9/11 in the United States and July 7 in the United Kingdom has led to the imagination of "all possible links" to identify "potential terrorists" and to "build a complete picture of a person." Imagination thus plays an important and specific part in the capacity to anticipate all future possible arrivals, all possible movement from the edges of a network to its hub. In the correlative relations that are drawn between bodies (human and nonhuman), as they are disaggregated into degrees of risk, in effect there can be no stranger at the edge of the narrative. Techniques such as social network analysis and risk mapping, in contrast to the incipient potential subjects in Egan's novel, are designed to develop the characterisation of all future elements. All potential must be actualized and fulfilled. One of Egan's characters, the music promoter Bennie Salazar, laments the effects of the digital world on the capacity for surprise and improvisation in music. "The problem with digitization," he muses as he listens to a manufactured pop track, is that it "sucked the life out of everything that got smeared through its microscopic mesh."[9] Through the mesh of digitization, as Salazar sees it, all of the gaps and potentials of the relations hips among musical phrases are filtered out, leaving a preprogrammed and already decided "automated" piece of music. Like the filtering of derivative data through the mesh of algorithmic software, the digitization of music, at least for Salazar, leaves little capacity for the unanticipated.

Egan's character Salazar's sentiment is echoed in Brian Massumi's insistence on the distinction between the virtual and the digital, in which "digital technologies in fact have a remarkably weak connection to the virtual, by virtue of their systematization of the possible." It is this systematization of the possible that takes place also in the deployment of digital techniques to identify possible future security threats. They do not imagine potential futures in the sense of incipient and emergent virtualities but rather "array alternative states for sequencing into alternative routines." Everything must be in association with something else, even the most partial and fragmented elements incorporated as possibilities. Understood in this way, the correlative relations of the security algorithm—if x in association with y, where w is copresent, then z—act to systematize the possible in an array of possible connections. In Massumi's terms "the medium of the digital is possibility, not virtuality, and not even potential," with digital coding being "possibilistic to the limit."[10]

In the digital arraying of risk factors, the missing elements and the gaps between data items are drawn into the array of the possible. Like Salazar's sense of digital sound as precoded and systematized, the algorithmic security technology "programmatically prearrays" all possible links.[11] There is an important critical distinction between the imaginative programming of the possible future and the imagination of the potential future. The coded arrays of risk software can only actualize the possible—visualizing an array of risk scores and making them actionable—while any potentiality could not be "contained in the code" but is "entirely bound up with the potentializing relay."[12] To consider one of Massumi's examples, while the digital arrays of code in word processing or in digital photography remain bound by the programming of possibilities, the reading of the resulting text or image reintroduces the "analog process" and with it the potentializing relay of "fleeting vision-like sensation, inklings of sound, faint brushes of movement."[13] Like our software designer's affective responses to the image of the code in chapter 5, the digital array of possibility does not close off the capacity for potentiality, but the resulting analogue relay is beyond incorporation by the code itself. Similarly, in the reading of Egan's novel, one becomes attentive to the sensation of an incipient character at the edges of perception, every stranger always also a potential future protagonist. In contrast to the arraying of possible links in order to actualize a character in advance, the incomplete subjects in Egan's novel retain their potentiality beyond any sense of a programmed plotline.

In this first mode of imagination, possibilistic techniques are active in the arraying of associations, such that they can be actualized and acted upon. All links are possible correlative relations, all associations possible evidence of guilt by association. Why does it matter, though, that the politics of possibility acts on the basis of systematized arrays and not potentialities? In part, the significance is that the politics of possibility does not eviscerate completely the terrain of resistance and the space for critique. The preprogrammed actions of the automated gate and the risk protocol, though they incorporate elements of affect, imagination, and intuition, do not act upon potentiality itself. Indeed, calculative risk protocols could not act upon potentiality as such, for at that moment it would cease to be potentiality and become rendered as possibility. And yet despite the impossibility of their acting upon potentiality, such calculations remain acutely vulnerable to the effects of potentiality. As we have seen, when the technologies of security fail—as they often do—they are vulnerable to the effects of the subjects and objects that could never be anticipated. As Massumi has put it, "the coding is not the whole story"; the preprogrammed array must always also be received, translated, transformed "in a way that intensifies, creating resonances and interference patterns."[14] The terrain of potentiality is slippery and evasive; it is the domain of the unanticipated effect, surprise event, and chance encounter. We have seen glimpses of it in the previous chapters, when the effects of a measure exceed and evade its design. Massumi warns that "perhaps the day is not far off" when the digital can "integrate the analog into itself" or, through ubiquitous computing, "multiply its relays into and out of the analog."[15] Certainly, the feedback loops and automated learning of machinic security seek out such an integration. The potentiality remains eluded though and, as we will see, retains the capacity for imagination in a different political mode—a mode that can imagine that things could be otherwise, that other claims could be made.

Judgment 1: Deferred Decisions

A software engineer reflects on the similarities that mark the codes he has written for the missile guidance systems for unmanned aerial vehicles (UAVs) or drones and the design of systems to identify incipient threat in crowded places:

> Well, for me, I mean the scripts are the same. . . . One way to say it is that both applications look for small anomalous movements in an intensely crowded environment, I mean crowded visually. It could be to look for insurgent targets in Afghanistan, or could be for somewhere that is, somewhere like Olympic village. Maybe even it is better, better that such decisions [on targets] do not get made by a pilot, or a police officer in a busy sports stadium? The margin of error is reduced I would say, yes it is reduced almost to zero. And if there is error, this system will learn instantly. It will not take, you know, the three years for a review of procedures.[16]

As the politics of possibility distributes sovereign decisions of many kinds into an assemblage of subjects and objects—the designers of code, a risk score, a handwritten warning passed from match analyst to border agency, a shift in color on a screen, the intuition of a customs officer—what happens to the decision itself? Who or what constitutes responsibility for a decision and its effects? Where the risk calculus, as we saw in chapter 2, seeks to act on the very basis of possibilities, the security decision appears to embrace a neutral, objective, and side-effects free form of knowledge. As the software designer here proposes, the intelligence-based correlations that guide the writing of code appear to underwrite a responsible and automated decision that is free of the fallibilities and impulses of a pilot, border guard, or police officer.

The politics of possibility seeks to eradicate the aporia of all decision making. The risk-based security technologies I have described in this book appeal to an expansion of forms of knowledge that can always be rendered as actionable intelligence. In the search for almost imperceptible movements in a guidance system or crowd security scanner, even the merest fragment of an element can be used to refine the data. Anything could be the basis for action within the systems that are increasingly known as *actionable analytics*. On the basis of a series of past events that are cast as catastrophic "failures to join up the dots," all dots can be joined, all elements could be grounds for a judgment. A responsible decision, in this formulation, is one that can be made even on the basis of incomplete knowledge. It is precisely this fraught relationship between necessarily incomplete knowledge and decision that has for so long challenged the philosophy of decision:

> Saying that a responsible decision must be taken on the basis of knowledge seems to define the condition of possibility of responsibility (one can't make a responsible decision without science or conscience, without knowing what one is doing, for what reasons, in view of what and under what conditions), at the same time as it defines the condition of impossibility of this same responsibility (if decision making is relegated to a knowledge that is content to follow or to develop, then it is no more a responsible decision, it is the technical deployment of a cognitive apparatus, the simple mechanistic deployment of a theorem).[17]

While the politics of decision resides precisely in its difficulty, in the impossibility of a form of knowledge that could resolve all claims, algorithmic security decisions deploy a theorem that appeals to a decision without politics. The technologies of the politics of possibility promise sovereign decisions that appear to be knowledge-based, objective, and free of the fallibility of human judgment. In Derrida's terms there are no decisions made at all or, more precisely, no decisions as such, no decisions that dwell in the uneasy state of aporia. The proliferating faith in apparently neutral and objective technologies actively conceals the perennial deferral of any meaningful decision. The algorithmic security decision, we might say, is no longer a decision as such but only the application of a body of knowledge. Indeed, as the UK Home Office says in support of the automated security decisions of e-gates, these "convey decisions to the frontline" and "engage action."[18] And so, if decisions are simply relayed to the frontline, where they are enacted, where is the agonism and the difficulty of all of the decisions that are confronted? Does it lie within the selection of data elements or the writing of code? Is it in the real-time stress testing that seeks to push the security system to its limit point? Does it take place when the data are assembled by a match analyst within a data processing center? Is it in the reading off of a screened risk score by a border guard?

While contemporary security techniques work hard to annex judgment from politics—to replace visual profiling with algorithmic profiling or to evacuate the touch of the pat-down search with whole body imaging, for example—they deny the politics of all decision. Rather as the actions taken on the basis of possibility eviscerate all potentiality, so the automated decision is equipped to make judgments but never to decide. "Judgement," as Gilles Deleuze has expressed it, "prevents the emergence of a new mode of existence," inhibiting the potential for anything new, any new beginnings or unscanned horizons.[19] To impose expert judgment is to act upon future worlds yet to come, to inhibit the potential for new horizons that are not already scanned. When a judgment is made there can be no unforeseen singularities or events, no moments when a meaningful decision, a "decision worthy of the name" can advance without reference to precoded protocols, can "advance where it cannot see."[20]

Lest we should think of this limit point—the impossibility of a decision worthy of the name—as only a philosophical limit of the politics of possibility, let us consider for a moment why it limits even the capacity for response to the unanticipated event. In Joseph O'Neill's *Netherland*, a novel of a post-9/11 New York, his protagonist Hans van den Broek considers the difficulty of establishing clear links and incontrovertible associations between people, places, and events. "To make a link," he reflects, "to say that one thing led to another, I've never found such connections easy."[21] He considers the many encounters, relationships, and moments of play that he has experienced in the city, concluding that these are matters of chance—the lively and unanticipated elements of a life lived in association with multiple other people and things. He is confounded by the calculative search for causes and threats after September 11, likening it to any rule-based judgment. "It's not a problem I have at work, where I merrily connect dots of all kinds," he ponders, "but there the task is much simpler and subject to rules."[22] In his everyday life, the making of connections is difficult; it is politics itself, relying on no preprogrammed calculation or body of knowledge. It is when the connecting of dots is subject to rules that the task of judgment is more simple to undertake, the protocol readily replacing the need for a decision as such.

It is precisely this sense of making the task of judgment simpler and subject to rules, merrily connecting the dots of many kinds, that actively marks a limit point in the politics of possibility. For the automation of judgments within security technologies can only ever conceal and mask the difficulty of decision that actually is always already present. When this difficulty, this politics, is exposed, we can begin to see the dilemmas of the politics of possibility. Consider, for example, the London firefighters who responded to the events of the Aldgate tube bombing of July 7, 2005. The established body of knowledge of risk protocols actively inhibited the capacity of the firefighters to enter the tunnel and to respond to the suffering of those injured and dying within the train. As fire fighter Neil Walker testified to the coroner's inquests into the London bombings, in order to respond effectively he had to be a "maverick," a "firefighter who thinks for himself," breaking with the risk protocols and making decisions that departed from the rulebook.[23] His decisions were profoundly agonistic—whether to walk on the tracks without confirmation that the power was off; confronted with injured people marked with the ambulance service's triage "priority cards," deciding who to help first, saying "we are not allowed to pronounce anyone right or wrong are we?"[24] In order to make decisions "worthy of the name," decisions as such, Neil Walker had to depart from the risk protocols in which he was trained and confront the radical difficulty of a decision that could be the wrong one. To put it simply, for all of its talk of imagining the unimaginable and anticipating the unexpected, the politics of possibility's risk-based judgments impede actual decision and response in the face of the event.

Life 1: Definite Possibilities

In the preceding chapters I have mapped some of the elements of a politics of possibility as biopolitical, as acting upon species life, seeking to govern in and through life itself. However, the life that is taken as the object of the politics of possibility is a specific and limited form of life. It is life with a definite article—the life—the locatable, identifiable life than can only be readily ascribed to the agency of human subjects. The life, one could say, is a life that can be possessed; rather like "my life" it belongs to an individual or to a group thought to share a "way of life." The life, borrowing from Gilles Deleuze, is life that "refers to an object, or belongs to a subject."[25] The life is determinate in the sense that it has identifiable moments and, as such, leaves its traces, material evidence of its passing through, behind it.[26] It is just such definite life that is the object of the forensic aesthetics depicted by Thomas Keenan and Eyal Weizman in their reading of the scientists called as expert witnesses in the analysis of Mengele's skull.[27] Within the politics of possibility, life has a definite article because it is securable via the residue of its transactions—this subway journey, that credit card transaction, this travel booking, these materials contained within human remains. The writing of security, to use David Campbell's terms, becomes a matter of securing definite life via the data that are the very imprint of life itself—all of the given moments of the life measured in the data that can be derived. Perhaps it is the very essence of the comfort of the promise of security that it is capable of acting to secure definite life, that there is something tangible and identifiable to be secured.

In Egan's novel *A Visit from the Goon Squad*, she depicts the multiple moments of a life course as it is inscribed in subjects and objects:

> Thirty-five years from now, in 2008, this warrior will be caught in the tribal violence between the Kikuyu and the Luo and will die in a fire. One of his grandchildren, a boy named Joe, will inherit his *lalema*: the iron hunting dagger now hanging at his side. Joe will go to college at Columbia and study engineering, becoming an expert in visual robotic technology that detects the slightest hint of irregular movement (the legacy of a childhood spent scanning the grass for lions). He'll marry an American named Lulu and remain in New York, where he'll invent a scanning device that becomes standard issue for crowd security. He and Lulu will buy a loft in Tribeca, where his grandfather's hunting dagger will be displayed inside a cube of Plexiglas.[28]

Projecting the life of the warrior thirty-five years into the future, beyond death itself, Egan preempts the future potential of her characters. As the life of the warrior becomes actualized "in all the moments that a given living subject goes through and that are measured by given living objects," it exceeds the "single moment when individual life confronts universal death."[29] The warrior's life dwells in moments, like those inside the relations to his grandson and to the object of the inherited hunting dagger that is enclosed in a display case. This life that is actualized in association with others and objects that are left behind is akin to the life that becomes the object of contemporary security. Like Joe's security scanner that identifies threat via the data points of the crowd, the politics of possibility can target only actualized life that attaches itself to bodies and objects, human and nonhuman. All potential futures must be fully actualized in the life signature that is left (see chapter 3). Significantly, though contemporary security writes its subjects of interest on the basis of what is not yet known of the future, it projects that future through actualized elements—this transaction, that associate, this journey. The human potential that Egan so vividly portrays of

Joe's future life—this university, that career, this life, that city, that inherited object—is annulled because it is so fully realized in advance. We can see only the connections that are made point to point and almost nothing of the between times. It is these "between times," as we shall see, that are so very significant to an indefinite form of life, where potentiality can flourish.

Imagination 2: Leaps of the Imagination

How might we engage a different mode of imagination, one that does not annul the potential that things could be otherwise? What would a criticism of leaps of the imagination, as Foucault describes it, look like? Let us begin with an example. The New York artist Meghan Trainor is a multimedia artist who invites her audience to confront anew the lively potential of digital technologies and ubiquitous computing. In their *With Hidden Numbers*, a media project from 2005, Trainor and her collaborator Michelle Anderson placed RFID tags inside tactile handcrafted objects that invite a playful interaction in which the artwork is never fully completed. When scanned, the objects trigger audio playbacks that place the work in the hands of participants, continually adapting and creating new possibilities and variations. The objects foster what Trainor calls a "nostalgia for the new," in which people feel an affective pull toward the object.[30] Enclosed within the tactile, smooth ceramic objects, like preserved amber insects, the RFID devices or "arphids" are encountered as enchanting and vaguely familiar objects. To touch one of Anderson and Trainor's objects is to feel a sudden sense of doubt about their location in our lives. They look and feel old, like a thing we once played with in our grandmother's house, something for which we feel nostalgic. And yet, in their orientation to Trainor's digitized sounds, they suggest something of a future world yet to come. Our sense of the place these technologies have in the world, of where they dwell, is momentarily interrupted. In one sense they seem to echo our everyday encounters with RFID: the movement of the hand on the reader at the subway station, the sound of the verifying "bleep," the tactile feel of the Oyster card in the hand. Yet the potentiality of RFID, otherwise subsumed in the security application, is newly visualized, experienced, and attended to.

In Trainor's project *16 Horsepower*, RFID tags are similarly integrated within tactile objects and a networked soundscape. The visitors to the installation hold sensor-enabled graphite objects that leave their traces on the white walls, triggering sounds in response to their movement. As they play with the objects, the movements and actions of people echo some of the movements of passengers in the subway or at the border crossing but also, strangely, the movement of dancers to the hands of a DJ on the decks. The imaginative play with these RFID objects is never predictable, always surprising and renewed. As Michel Foucault has observed of acts of play, the element of playfulness and curiosity exceeds what can be known or knowable about oneself and the world. To play, he proposes, is to "play the same hand differently, or playing another game, another hand, with other trump cards."[31] Rather as Trainor and Anderson's audience play the hand of commercial and security technologies differently, with different effects, for Foucault the act of playing nurtures a "sharper sense of reality, a readiness to find what surrounds us strange and odd; a certain determination to throw off familiar ways of thought and to look at the same things in a different way."[32] To encounter something in play is to make strange those things that are otherwise so mundane as to be all but invisible. Installing her work in a disused bank in New York's Lower Manhattan, Trainor invites her audience to enter spaces they thought familiar, places they thought they already knew to be rational and calculable, and to play with objects they may think they have seen somewhere before, encountering them afresh. Experimenting with the imaginative potentiality of RFID—a potentiality that is never fully actualized in a final form of art—Trainor's work suggests that a leap of imagination can indeed open a critical space for alternative becomings.

There is a sense of this imaginative mode of potentiality in the hybrid "crossings" Jane Bennett describes between human and nonhuman bodies, crossings that "invoke the exciting sense of travelling to new lands," creating a "space for novelty" in the imagination of futures.[33] Of course, one might reasonably ask at this point, how precisely a space for novelty can be created in the crossing from self to the RFID tag in one's newly issued passport. Perhaps one answer is that the definitive verification of identity of the passport, which we "play" at the border, closes down any possibility of unanticipated arrivals or new beginnings. The point is illustrated by the moment in 2008 when Meghan Trainor's incongruous ceramic objects (carefully packed in her cabin luggage) drew the suspicions of border security officers at Charles de Gaulle Airport. Unconvinced by Trainor's appeal that the RFID devices embedded in the ceramic were ordinary—"like the one in your security pass, like the one in my passport"—the border guards asked to see "what they do." The very potentiality of the objects was troublesome for the border guards, all potential demanded to be actualized, to be shown "what they do." Trainor's work reveals for us an alternative mode of imagination, one that unsettles security's orientation to unanticipated surprises, one that is, as Jane Bennett describes, "enchanting." "To be enchanted," writes Bennett, "is to be struck and shaken by the extraordinary that lives amid the familiar and the everyday."[34] For Bennett, enchantment "can propel ethics," at least in the sense that the magic of future potential, the promise of life not yet lived, remains open. Where the incorporation of imagination into the risk calculus of possibility actively annuls the potential for the unanticipated, to momentarily be enchanted by "nostalgia for the new" is to live with the unknowability of the future, even where it may contain dangers or fears. Unscanned horizons open up in a world that is otherwise searching out, screening, and scanning the horizon of all possible futures.

Judgment 2: Decisions against the Grain

If, as I have suggested, the politics of possibility annuls all decisions as such, even while it focuses vast resources and attention on automating sovereign decisions of many kinds, then how might the terrain of decision be opened to critique? Let us begin by considering what a meaningful and responsible decision would look like. Given that responsibility within the politics of possibility has become a matter of acting on the basis of even the most incomplete intelligence, what form of response would be required to reinstate an ethics of decision? "The only responsibility worthy of the name," writes Thomas Keenan, "comes with the withdrawal of the rules or the knowledge on which we might rely to make our decisions for us."[35] To withdraw the rules, the association rule or algorithm, and the risk protocol, we might say following Keenan, is to fully confront the difficulty of all decision. For Keenan, this difficulty is paramount—"politics is difficulty." If the decision were to be rendered easy, automated, or preprogrammed, then not only would the decision be effaced, but politics itself is circumscribed. To decide, Keenan suggests, is to take a more difficult route, what he describes as a "politics on the bias."[36] The bias cut of a piece of cloth is a cut against the grain of weft and warp, a perpendicular cut that is not guided by the direction of the threads of the weave. To decide against the grain is to "reopen the question of politics," Keenan says, for "the frontier, with its questions and answers, is not simply something bad or to be avoided";

rather it is a "chance for politics, the chance of the political, the possibility of the other, of the one who arrives."[37] If the decision at the border frontier is to be political, Keenan's insights remind us, then it must decide without reference to risk score or algorithmic judgment. It must decide against the grain, in face of the other, the one who arrives.

It is this capacity to make a cut against the grain or on the bias of prevailing logics that captures something of the capacity of some forms of art and literature to engage differently the politics of decision. As the art historian Jonathan Crary has said of the capacity of installation art to stand in the way of our passage through space, to interrupt direction and flow, this "experimental activity" works by creating "unanticipated spaces and environments in which our visual habits are disrupted."[38] Suspending the usual terms of reference on which we depend to inform our decisions, we confront an unanticipated world, a world as yet unforeseen. Edward Said, in his own late works, proposed that the great works of music and literature are those that run "against the grain," that proceed with "intransigence, difficulty and unresolved contradiction."[39] For Said, what is significant in such forms is that they cannot be readily interpreted within prevailing sensibilities of what counts as art or what is culturally valued. Works against the grain interrupt the flow of forms and demand new ways of thinking about the world.

In contrast to a mode of decision that seeks to codify and automate decisions, gathering together fragments of knowledge as the very basis for action, there are forms of knowledge available to us that nurture what Derrida calls "a decision in the dark," a leap of faith or imagination that "takes place beyond any theoretical determination."[40] One of the places that we may find just such an interruption of conventions of thought is in literature that leaves us without clear grounds on which to stand. In some of the novels written after the events of September 11, we encounter the politics of possibility not as a set of necessary measures of science and technology but as a curious and confounding difficulty, an undecidability of what risk and security may actually mean in daily life. Returning to Joseph O'Neill's *Netherland*, the protagonist Hans reflects on what it might mean to move to a place of safety in a post-9/11 America: "We talked about moving to Brooklyn or Westchester or, what the hell, New Jersey. But that didn't meet the problem of Indian Point. There was, apparently, a nuclear reactor at a place called Indian Point, just thirty miles away in Westchester County. If something bad happened there, we were constantly being informed, the 'radioactive debris,' whatever this might be, was liable to rain down on us. (Indian Point: the earliest, most incurable apprehensions stirred in its very name)."[41] Confronted with the circulating judgments on the relative risk of some possible future catastrophe, Hans finds himself unable to reach a decision on anything. He knows not where to stand or on what grounds of knowledge to base his decision. He is left with the difficulty of advancing where he cannot see:

> I was almost completely caught out. I found myself unable to con-
> tribute to conversations about the value of international law or the
> feasibility of producing a dirty bomb or the constitutional rights of
> imprisoned enemies or the efficacy of duct tape as a window sealant
> or the merits of vaccinating the American masses against smallpox
> or the complexity of weaponising deadly bacteria, or indeed any
> of the debates, apparently vital, that raged everywhere. . . . In this
> ever-shifting, all-enveloping discussion, my orientation was poor. I
> could not tell where I stood. If pressed to state my position, I would
> confess the truth: that I had not succeeded in arriving at a position.
> I lacked necessary powers of perception and certainty and, above
> all, foresight. The future retained the impenetrable character I had
> always attributed to it.[42]

In the figure of Hans the decisional logics of the politics of possibility are inverted. Where the automated decisions of the politics of possibility are equipped to reach ready judgments but never to decide as such, the disorientation of Hans exposes the undecidability of all matters of security. While orientation, position, and foresight matter greatly to algorithmic security, what is at stake is a capacity to respond, as for Hans, in a way that is dis-oriented toward the uncertain future. It is precisely this disorientation that holds the capacity for creative interruptions of preemptive logics.

The interruption of security logics both confronts us with the curiousness of systems, techniques, and knowledges that had come to be mundane and prosaic and opens a space for alternative imaginings. As Walter Benjamin writes of the epic theater of Berthold Brecht, it "interrupts the plot, by means of the interruption of sequences," arresting action in its course, and "alienating" the public "from the conditions in which it lives."[43] The plotlines of security calculations are similarly interrupted in the novel *Netherland*, as the sequence of associations between risky places, people, and objects are arrested and made strange. We can find similar devices in

Egan's *A Visit from the Goon Squad*, where the security sequences of "daytime security in Central Park" are interrupted via a letter to the *New York Times*:

> To the Editor,
>
> In the earnest spirit of your recent editorial ("Vulnerability in Our Public Spaces," Aug. 9), allow me to make a suggestion that is sure to appeal to Mayor Giuliani, at the very least: why not simply erect checkpoints at the entrances to Central Park and demand identification from those who wish to enter? Then you will be able to call up their records and evaluate the relative success or failure of their lives—marriage or lack thereof, children or lack thereof, professional success or lack thereof, healthy bank account or lack thereof—and using these facts, you can assign each person a ranking. . . . The rest is easy: simply encode each person's ranking into an electronic bracelet and affix it to their wrist as they enter the park, and then monitor those encoded points of light on a radar screen, with personnel at the ready to intervene.[44]

Rather as Benjamin suggests of Brecht's plays, the author's intervention is made via the interruption or arresting of sequences, "to allow for a circumstance which has been too little noticed" and "to expose what is present."[45] Egan's account of her character Jules Jones's ironic call for risk-based security in Central Park interrupts the flow of a New York that "looked frictionless," exposing the conditions of possibility of the appearance of a smooth surface.[46] In this book I have proposed that it is not the decision on the exception per se that produces sovereign power but the multiple repetitive acts that write the very possibility of security. To interrupt the sequence is to withdraw the knowledge on which we rely to found our decisions, leaving only politics, leaving only difficulty, leaving only the undecidability of the action.

Life 2: Indefinite Potentialities

It has been my case that the contemporary politics of possibility acts upon definitive life—life with a definite article, as it is actualized in subjects and objects. Indeed it is part of the seductiveness of the techniques of governing possibilities that they promise to make present a future life yet to come, to materialize definite life through the arrays of data it leaves behind. Yet for all the action that the politics of possibility conjures on the basis of potential futures, it is part of its logic that it must actualize that life in the form of data, make it present, make it amenable to a security intervention. Perhaps curiously, the politics of possibility cannot live with potentials that are not actualized—a possible immigration infraction is actualized as a visual risk alert; a possible threat in a crowded public place is actualized as a series of linked data points; a possible national security threat is actualized in associations between people, objects, and events. This vulnerability to the potential that is not fully realized contains within it a space for critical response. Like Foucault's book that may land in unanticipated places, where he did not intend, having effects that were not written in the text itself, or like Anderson and Trainor's RFID objects whose life exceeds their design, potentiality is a promise that ceases to be once it is fully realized. In the world of a politics of possibility, potentiality is fugitive because it signals a form of life that is not quite the subject of biopolitics, not the life of species life.

In his essay on immanence, Gilles Deleuze gives character to a form of life that does not have a definite article, "a life" that is indefinite. "A life is everywhere," he writes, "an immanent life carrying with it the events or singularities that are merely actualized in subjects and objects." This indefinite life, he proposes, "does not itself have moments, but only between-times, between-moments," such that "the singularities and the events that constitute *a* life coexist with the accidents of *the* life that corresponds to it, but they connect with one another in a manner entirely different from how individuals connect."[47] Let us interpret Deleuze's indefinite life within the frame of the associations, links, and connections that are made in the politics of possibility. Coexisting with the definitive writing of the life between data points across the gaps, dwells an indefinite life that transcends the individual points, living in the "between-times" as pure singularities.[48]

Dwelling within the politics of possibility's determinate life, whose "electronic footprint" can be gathered and actualized via its interaction with subjects and objects, is an indeterminate life, what William Connolly calls "partly formed potentialities."[49] When algorithmic security couples together an array of moments that precipitate an action, they close down what is partly formed and render it actual. According to Connolly: "At the time the moment was in play, it contained several potentialities—or half-formed trajectories of development. This array of uncertain potentialities thus escapes the attention of most who participate in the moment. Sometimes, as Deleuze says, one figure has a premonition that others miss. It suggests a seer dwelling within a nest of partly formed potentialities jostling against and upon each other during a forking moment, with no potentiality settled enough to be foreseen with certainty."[50] Here, Connolly is reflecting on the "forking moments" in film, when critical moments seem to distill an array of unformed potentialities. Most of the characters participating in the moment, Connolly proposes, are unaware that such a fork in the road has been reached, but the viewer or reader is afforded a glimpse of the partly formed potentialities courtesy of the seer. The fork in the road that Connolly depicts is systematized in the politics of possibility via the decision tree or algorithmic logic—if this, in association with this, where this is also present, then this. The algorithmic fork could not be more different from the cinematic potentialities, for the array of uncertain potentialities will always escape the attention of the security measure itself. The indeterminate life that we see in Deleuze's and Connolly's cinema, Said's and Crary's art and literature is, as yet, not incorporable within the politics of possibility.

If life with an indefinite article—a life—resists the systematized arrays of algorithmic security, then how precisely does it do so? Within a number of works on the potentiality of a life, the figure of Herman Melville's *Bartleby, the Scrivener* embodies something of the capacity of potential. As a scribe who has stopped writing, Bartleby's formula in response to those who command him to write is "I prefer not" or "I would prefer not to." His potentiality, as Giorgio Agamben captures it, is not strictly to write or to express his will but precisely his potentiality not to write, such that he "neither accepts nor refuses, stepping forward and stepping backward at the same time."[51] What is striking about the formulation is that it avoids an absolute "no," a refusal that would echo the demand itself. Consider, for example, the difficulties that legal advocates are currently encountering in challenging the inferences of mosaic data (see chapter 3). Is there a way of responding to the charge "this is your intent, this is the risk you pose" in a way that avoids "that is not my intent, I do not pose that risk"? As Deleuze understands Bartleby's formula, the power of "I prefer not" is that "it disconnects words and things," it responds in a way that does not adhere to the yes or no logic of the demand. Bartleby's refusal, for Deleuze, is one of "a man without references, someone who appears suddenly and then disappears, without reference to himself or anything else."[52] The politics of possibility demands that all subjects have references, referent data points, that no one appears or disappears without reference to risk. Bartleby's formula evades the referent point and defies actualization in an act (writing) or a subject (the scrivener).

The indefinite potentialities that are glimpsed in Deleuze's observations of the gestures of children or in Bartleby's "evoking the future without either predicting or promising" are also present, I suggest, in the unrecoverable stories that emerge between the lines.[53] A critical response to the politics of association rule and algorithmic judgment would invoke an associationism that can never be known, a life of associating with other things and people that is not amenable to calculation. It would not, as Foucault reminds us, "hand down sentences," but it would imagine the forks in the road, the potentialities as yet unrealized. An indefinite life, because it exceeds the individual and dwells in the energies, rage, shame, and enchantment that circulates in relations one to another, is not subject to the calculation of probability or likelihood.

To excavate the stories between the lines need not imply making counterclaims to the inferences of security technologies—this pattern of travel was not for that purpose but for this private family purpose; these associations with these people are wholly coincidental; that financial transaction was not for that purpose but for this. Instead, the Bartleby-inspired stories between the lines could appear more like the emergent characters in Jennifer Egan's novel, connected by lines untraceable, unrepeatable, indefinite. The copresence of *a* life with *the* life would mean that wherever contemporary security seeks to write the life of the subject through data items, a life that is otherwise—evasive, slippery, unknowable—is always already present. At the close of her novel, Egan describes a crowd of people moving through a future New York to gather together for a concert in Lower Manhattan. The politics of possibility is present in her depiction of "two generations of war and surveillance" written into the security architecture of the city:

> Before them, the new buildings spiralled gorgeously against the sky, so much nicer than the old ones (which Alex had only seen in pictures), more like sculptures than buildings. Approaching them, the crowd began to slow, backing up as those in front entered the space around the reflecting pools, the density of police and security agents (identifiable by their government handsets) suddenly palpable, along with visual scanning devices affixed to cornices, lampposts, and trees. The weight of what had happened here more than twenty

years ago was still faintly present for Alex, as it always was when he came to the Footprint. He perceived it as a sound just out of earshot, the vibration of an old disturbance. Now it seemed more insistent than ever: a low, deep thrum that felt primally familiar, as if it had been whirring inside all the sounds that Alex had made and collected over the years: their hidden pulse.[54]

The vibrating resonances of risk and security in the city are vividly portrayed here as a "hidden pulse," a background rhythm against which their daily lives are conducted. And yet, just as the architecture of risk and security vibrates across the spaces between buildings, crowd, reflecting pools, police, security agents, handsets, scanning devices, lampposts, trees, so the relations among the people in the crowd exceed and interrupt that rhythm. The reach of the security technologies is exceeded by the capacity of those technologies to reach people across the crowd, to connect and gather together. Egan's young music "mixer," Alex's "handset had no trouble locating his wife's handset, but it took many minutes of scanning that section of the crowd with his zoom to actually spot her." He "kept his zoom trained on her face until he saw her register the vibration, pause in her dancing, and reach for it."[55] Even amid the technoscience of contemporary security, the capacity to recognize, to connect, and to associate in ways that are not preprogrammed is not eviscerated. There are potentialities that dwell between the data points that are so readily gathered and projected.

In a world where security works by writing the subject between the lines, prejudging and preempting, there is another writing between the lines that is copresent. Working in the absence of certainty, indeterminate and without quest or endgame, it offers a crucial space in which to respond. The politics of possibility exhibits one mode of suspension or deferral—a suspension of the normal rule of law in favor of force perhaps but also a deferral of fraught decisions into preprogrammed calculations. In the lively technologies, half-glimpsed subjects, and indeterminate lives I am pointing to, there is another deferral at work, a more imaginative writing between the lines that suspends the rules on which we might rely, opening an unanticipated space for response.

Notes

Introduction

1. There is too much good work on the novel forms taken by contemporary sovereign power to cite here exhaustively. William Connolly's *Pluralism* (Durham, NC: Duke University Press, 2008) and *Capitalism and Christianity, American Style* (Durham, NC: Duke University Press, 2008) offer important insights on the ambiguity of sovereignty. See also Judith Butler, *Precarious Life: The Powers of Mourning and Violence* (London: Verso, 2004) and *Frames of War* (London: Verso, 2009); Brian Massumi, *Parables for the Virtual: Movement, Affect, Sensation* (Durham, NC: Duke University Press, 2002); J. K. Gibson-Graham, *A Postcapitalist Politics* (Minneapolis: University Of Minnesota Press, 2006); Michael Dillon and Julian Reid, *The Liberal Way of War: Killing to Make Life Live* (London: Routledge, 2009).

2. Brian Massumi, "The Future Birth of the Affective Fact," Conference Proceedings, Genealogies of Biopolitics, 2005, http://browse.reticular .info/text/collected/massumi .pdf, 5–6.

3. Gregorio Agamben, *State of Exception* (Chicago: University of Chicago Press, 2005), 48.

4. Jacques Rancière, "Who Is the Subject of the Rights of Man?," *South Atlantic Quarterly* 103, nos. 2–3 (2004): 307.

5. On the matter of the productivity of power, see Michel Foucault, *Discipline and Punish: The Birth of the Prison* (London: Penguin Books, 1977); and on the copresence of relations of power and resistance, see Michel Foucault, "Governmentality," *The Foucault Effect: Studies in Governmentality,* ed. Graham Burchell, Colin Gordon, and Peter Miller (Chicago: Chicago University Press, 1991), 87–104.

6. Michael Chertoff in a speech delivered to the European Parliament's Committee on Justice, Civil Liberties, and Home Affairs, May 15, 2007, accessed April 24, 2013, http://useu.usmission.gov/may1407_chertoff_ep.html.

7. The Chertoff Group "provides strategic security advice and assistance, risk management strategy and business development solutions for government and commercial

clients on a broad array of homeland and national security issues" (http://www.chertoff group.com, accessed May 10, 2010). Among the Chertoff Group consultancy team is John Reid, UK Home Office secretary from 2006 to 2007. It was with Reid that Chertoff negotiated the initial agreement on the transfer of passenger name record data for security risk analysis in 2006.

8. Eric Lipton, "Former Antiterror Officials Find Industry Pays Better," *New York Times*, June 18, 2006.

9. Department of Homeland Security, "Transcript of Secretary of Homeland Security Tom Ridge at the Center for Transatlantic Relations at Johns Hopkins University," September 13, 2004, https://www.hsdl.org/?view&did=475404.

10. Statement made in May 2004 by Asa Hutchinson, under secretary for border and transportation security of the U.S. Department of Homeland Security, on the award of the US-VISIT risk-based borders contract to the consultants Accenture (http://news.cnet .com/Accenture-lands-Homeland-Security-deal/2100-1029_3-5223851.html, accessed April 24, 2013).

11. Gilles Deleuze and Félix Guattari, *A Thousand Plateaus* (London: Continuum, 1987), 247.

12. Connolly, *Capitalism and Christianity, American Style*, 39.

13. Connolly, *Pluralism*, 54.

14. Michel Foucault, *The Birth of Biopolitics: Lectures at the College de France, 1978–1979* (Basingstoke, UK: Macmillan, 2008), 282.

15. Foucault, *The Birth of Biopolitics*, 285.

16. Foucault, *The Birth of Biopolitics*, 283.

17. Though there are others who do take the politics of economic authorities as their focus, and I owe a great debt for their novel insights. See Tony Porter, "Private Authority, Technical Authority, and the Globalization of Accounting Standards," *Business and Politics* 7, no. 3 (2005): 427–40; Mark Blyth, *Great Transformations: Economic Ideas and Institutional Change in the Twentieth Century* (Cambridge: Cambridge University Press, 2002); Jacqueline Best, *The Limits of Transparency: Ambiguity and the History of International Governance* (Ithaca, NY: Cornell University Press, 2005).

18. Butler, *Precarious Life*, 56.

19. See also Jenny Edkins, Veronique Pin-Fat, and Michael Shapiro, *Sovereign Lives* (London: Routledge, 2004).

20. On the political and spatial forms of the drawing of lines and borders between inside and outside, see Didier Bigo, "The Möbius Ribbon of Internal and External Security(ies)," in *Identities, Borders, Orders: Rethinking International Relations Theory*, ed. M. Albert, D. Jacobson, and Y. Lapid (Minneapolis: University of Minnesota Press, 2001), 91–116; R. B. J. Walker, *Inside/Outside: International Relations as Political Theory* (Cambridge: Cambridge University Press, 1993); Derek Gregory, *The Colonial Present* (Oxford: Blackwell, 2004).

21. Ulrich Beck, *World Risk Society* (Oxford: Wiley-Blackwell, 1999), 4. See also Ulrich Beck, *Risk Society: Towards a New Modernity* (London: Sage, 1992) and Ulrich Beck, "The Terrorist Threat: World Risk Society Revisited," *Theory, Culture and Society* 19, vol. 4 (2000): 39–55.

22. Barbara Adam and Joost van Loon, "Introduction: Repositioning Risk," in *The Risk Society and Beyond: Critical Issues for Social Theory*, ed. Adam and van Loon (London: Sage, 2000), 1–32; Pat O'Malley, "Uncertain Subjects: Risk, Liberalism and contract," *Economy and Society* 29 (2000): 460–84.

23. Judith Butler, *Gender Trouble: Feminism and the Subversion of Identity* (New York: Routledge, 1990) and *Bodies that Matter: On the discursive Limits of Sex* (New York: Routledge, 1993).

24. The UK's National Security Strategy of 2010 addresses "an age of uncertainty" in which the greatest risk is to fail to imagine possible future threats. François Ewald reminds us that political programs that state an increase in risks do, in effect, understand the world in terms of risk (Ewald, "Insurance and Risk" in *The Foucault Effect: Studies in Governmentality*, ed. G. Burchell, C. Gordan, and P. Miller (Chicago: University of Chicago Press, 1991), 138–61.

25. Louise Amoore, "Risk, Reward and Discipline at Work," *Economy and Society* 33, no. 2 (2004): 174–96; de Goede, "Repoliticising Financial Risk," *Economy and Society* 33, no. 2 (2004): 197–217; Pat O'Malley, *Risk, Uncertainty and Government* (London: Cavendish Press, 2004).

26. Beck, *World Risk Society*, 32,

27. Beck, *World Risk Society*, 58; Beck, "The Terrorist Threat," 44.

28. Marianna Valverde and Michael Mopas, "Insecurity and the Dream of Targeted Governance," in *Global Governmentality: Governing International Spaces*, ed. W. Larner and W. Walters (London: Routledge, 2004), 239.

29. Gilles Deleuze, "Postscript on the Societies of Control," *October* 59 (1992): 3–7.

30. Paul Langley, "Sub-prime Mortgage Lending: A Cultural Economy," *Economy and Society* 37, no. 4 (2008): 469–94; Rob Aitken, "Capital at Its Fringes," *New Political Economy* 11, no. 4 (2006): 479–98; Louise Amoore, "Biometric Borders: Governing Mobilities in the War on Terror," *Political Geography* 25, no. 2 (2006): 336–51; Marieke de Goede, "Hawala Discourses and the War on Terrorist Finance," *Environment and Planning D: Society and Space* 21, no. 5 (2003): 513–32.

31. Richard Ericson and Aaron Doyle, "Catastrophe Risk, Insurance and Terrorism," *Economy and Society* 33, no. 2 (2004): 151.

32. Ericson and Doyle, "Catastrophe Risk, Insurance and Terrorism," 130.

33. François Ewald, "The Return of Descartes' Malicious Demon: An Outline of a Philosophy of Precaution," in *Embracing Risk: The Changing Culture of Insurance and Responsibility*, ed. T. Baker and J. Simon (Chicago: University of Chicago Press, 2002), 296.

34. RAND, *Forging America's New Normalcy: Securing Our Homeland, Preserving Our Liberty* (Arlington, VA: Rand Corporation, 2003), 2.

35. Melinda Cooper's account of the idea of emergence in her book *Life as Surplus: Biotechnology and Capitalism in the Neoliberal Era* (Seattle: University of Washington Press, 2008) is simply compelling.

36. Ericson and Doyle, "Catastrophe Risk, Insurance and Terrorism," 138.

37. Interview with Trusted Borders consortium members, London, June 2009.

38. Ewald, "The Return of Descartes' Malicious Demon," 288.

39. Frank Knight, *Risk, Uncertainty and Profit* (Boston: Hart, Schaffner and Marx, 1921), 311.

40. Knight, *Risk, Uncertainty and Profit*, 237.

41. Baker and Simon, "Embracing Risk" in *Embracing Risk: The Changing Culture of Insurance and Responsibility*, ed. Baker and Simon (Chicago: University of Chicago Press, 2002), 1–22.

42. Louise Amoore and Marieke de Goede, "Governance, Risk and Dataveillance in the War on Terror," *Crime, Law and Social Change* 43, no. 2 (2005): 149–73.

43. McKinsey & Company, "Strategy in an Uncertain World," *McKinsey Quarterly* (New York: McKinsey, 2002): 5.

44. Ron Suskind, *The One Percent Doctrine: Deep inside America's Pursuit of Its Enemies since 9/11* (New York: Simon and Schuster, 2006), 62.

45. McKinsey & Company, *Increasing FDNY's Preparedness*; *Improving NYPD Emergency Preparedness and Response*.

46. Documents accessed in the McKinsey archive, New York, November 2004.

47. McKinsey & Company, *Improving NYPD Emergency Preparedness and Response* (New York: McKinsey, 2002), 105.

48. McKinsey & Company, *Improving NYPD Emergency Preparedness and Response*, 57.

49. James Der Derian, *Virtuous War* (New York: Routledge, 2002).

50. Edkins and Pin-Fat, "Life, Power, Resistance," in *Sovereign Lives*, ed. J. Edkins, V. Pin-Fat, and M. Shapiro (London: Routledge, 2004), 1–22.

51. Agamben, *State of Exception*, 2.

52. Agamben, *State of Exception*, 26; Agamben, *Homo Sacer: Sovereign Power and Bare Life* (Palo Alto, CA: Stanford University Press, 1998), 9, 20.

53. Agamben, *State of Exception*, 35.

54. Agamben, *State of Exception*, 48.

55. See Claudio Minca, "The Return of the Camp," *Progress in Human Geography* 29 (2005): 405–12; Derek Gregory, *The Colonial Present* (Oxford: Blackwell, 2004); Rens Van Munster, "When the Exception Becomes the Rule," *International Journal for the Semiotics of Law* 17, no. 1 (2004): 141–53.

56. See David Lyon, *Surveillance after September 11* (Cambridge: Polity, 2003); Matthew Sparke, *In the Space of Theory: Postfoundational Geographies of the Nation-State* (Minneapolis: University of Minnesota Press, 2005); Mark Salter, "When the Exception Becomes the Rule: Borders, Sovereignty, Citizenship," *Citizenship Studies* 12, no. 4 (2008): 365–80.

57. Bülent Diken and Carsten Bagge Laustsen, *The Culture of Exception: Sociology Facing the Camp* (London: Routledge, 2005).

58. Giorgio Agamben's writings on the "coming politics" in *The Coming Community* (Minneapolis: University of Minnesota Press, 1990) and his work on the "potentiality not to write" in *Potentialities: Collected Essays in Philosophy* (Palo Alto, CA: Stanford University Press, 1999) are of particular significance here.

59. Jenny Edkins, "Whatever Politics," in *Agamben: Sovereignty and Life*, ed. M. Calarco and S. Decordi (Palo Alto, CA: Stanford University Press, 2007), 70–91.

60. Connolly, *Pluralism*, 145.

61. Connolly, *Pluralism*, 141.

62. William Connolly, "The Complexity of Sovereignty," in *Sovereign Lives: Power in Global Politics*, ed. J. Edkins, V. Pin-Fat, and M. Shapiro (London: Routledge, 2004), 30–31.

63. Butler, *Precarious Life*, 61.

64. R. B. J. Walker, "Sovereignties, Exceptions, Worlds," in *Sovereign Lives: Power in Global Politics*, ed. J. Edkins, V. Pin-Fat, and M. Shapiro (New York: Routledge, 2004), 248.

65. See Marieke de Goede, "Beyond Economism in International Political Economy," *Review of International Studies* 29 (2003): 79–97; David Campbell, *Writing Security: United States' Foreign Policy and the Politics of Identity* (Minneapolis: University of Minnesota Press, 1998), 6–7.

66. Peter Miller and Nikolas Rose, "Governing Economic Life," *Economy and Society* 19, no. 1 (1990): 1–31; Miller and Rose, *Governing the Present* (Cambridge: Polity, 2008).

67. Michel Foucault, "Questions of Method," *The Foucault Effect: Studies in Governmentality*, ed. G. Burchell, C. Gordon, and P. Miller (Chicago: University of Chicago Press, 1991), 92.

68. Foucault, "Questions of Method," 93.

69. Foucault, *The Birth of Biopolitics*, 293.

70. Foucault, *The Birth of Biopolitics*, 293.

71. Foucault, "Questions of Method," 99.

72. Nigel Thrift, *Knowing Capitalism* (London: Sage, 2005), 4.

73. Slavoj Žižek, *The Ticklish Subject: The Absent Centre of Political Ontology* (London: Verso, 1999), 61.

74. Slavoj Žižek, *The Universal Exception* (London: Continuum, 2006).

75. Michel Foucault, *Society Must Be Defended: Lectures of the Collège of France, 1975–1976* (London: Penguin, 2003), 19.

76. Michel Foucault, *Security, Territory, Population: Lectures of the Collège of France, 1977–1978* (Basinstoke: Macmillan, 2007), 62.

77. Jacques Derrida, "Nietzsche and the Machine," *Journal of Nietzsche Studies* 7 (1994): 37.

78. Derrida, "Nietzsche and the Machine," 37.

79. See Nigel Thrift, "Movement-Space: The Changing Domain of Thinking Resulting from the Development of New Kinds of Spatial Awareness," *Economy and Society* 33, no. 4 (2004): 582–604; Lewis Pinault, *Consulting Demons: Inside the Unscrupulous World of Corporate Consulting* (New York: Harper Business, 2001); Michael Power, *The Audit Society: Rituals of Verification* (Oxford: Oxford University Press, 1999) and *Organized Uncertainty: Designing a World of Risk Management* (Oxford: Oxford University Press, 2007).

80. Jenny Edkins, *Poststructuralism and International Relations: Bringing the Political Back In* (Boulder, CO: Lynne Rienner, 1999); Žižek, *The Universal Exception*.

81. Michael Dillon, "Correlating Sovereign and Bio Power," in *Sovereign Lives*, ed. J. Edkins, V. Pin-Fat, and M. Shapiro (New York: Routledge, 2004), 57; Didier Bigo, "Se-

curity and Immigration: Toward a Critique of the Governmentality of Unease," *Alternatives* 27 (2002), 74.

82. Foucault, *Society Must Be Defended*, 16.

83. Agamben, *State of Exception*, 41.

84. Agamben, *Potentialities*.

85. Agamben, *State of Exception*, 43.

86. Dillon, "Correlating Sovereign and Bio Power," 50.

87. Agamben, *State of Exception*, 50.

88. Bigo, "Security and Immigration," 64.

89. Full text of the testimony was available at http://www.house.gov/reform/tapps /hearings.htm, accessed May 9, 2010.

90. Power, *The Audit Society*, 139.

91. Transcripts from the Chilcott Inquiry or the Iraq Inquiry conducted in order to establish what are described as the facts surrounding the British government's decisions and actions in the Iraq War, are available at http://www.iraqinquiry.org.uk /transcripts.aspx, accessed November 2011. Until the final report of the Iraq Inquiry is completed and made public, it is likely that the transcripts will remain the sole public record.

92. Accenture, *Values, Driven, Leadership: The History of Accenture* (New York: Accenture, 2005).

93. Nigel Thrift, "Remembering the Technological Unconscious by Foregrounding Knowledges of Position," *Environment and Planning D: Society and Space* 22 (2004): 175–90.

94. Jane Bennett, *Vibrant Matter: A Political Ecology of Things* (Durham, NC: Duke University Press, 2010).

95. Gilles Deleuze, *Foucault* (Minneapolis: University of Minnesota, 1988), 92.

Chapter 1: On Authority

1. Giles Foden, *Turbulence: A Novel of the Atmosphere* (London: Faber and Faber, 2009), 287.

2. Foden, *Turbulence*, 209.

3. Ian Hacking, *The Taming of Chance* (Cambridge: Cambridge University Press, 1990).

4. Lorraine Daston, *Classical Probability in the Enlightenment* (Princeton, NJ: Princeton University Press, 1995).

5. Stephen Collier, "Enacting Catastrophe: Preparedness, Insurance, Budgetary Rationalization," *Economy and Society* 37, no. 2 (2008): 224–50.

6. Nikolas Rose, "Governing by Numbers: Figuring out Democracy," *Accounting, Organizations and Society* 16, no. 7 (1991): 673–92.

7. Giorgio Agamben, "Security and Terror," *Theory and Event* 5, no. 4 (2002), 1.

8. Foden, *Turbulence*, 210.

9. Giorgio Agamben, *State of Exception* (Chicago: University of Chicago, 2005), 2.

10. Walter Benjamin, "On the Concept of History," *Walter Benjamin: Selected Writ-*

ings, vol. 4, ed. H. Eiland and M. Jennings (Cambridge, MA: Harvard University Press, 1996), 257.

11. Agamben, *State of Exception*, 7.

12. Agamben, *State of Exception*, 22.

13. Agamben, *State of Exception*, 22.

14. Hacking, *The Taming of Chance*, 1; Ian Hackinig, "Making Up People," *Reconstructing Individualism*, ed. T. Heller (Palo Alto, CA: Stanford University Press, 1986).

15. Jacques Derrida, "Force of Law: The Mystical Foundations of Authority," in *Deconstruction and the Possibility of Justice*, ed. D. Cornell, M. Rosenfeld, and D. G. Carlson (London: Routledge, 1992), 107.

16. E. L. Hargreaves and M. Gowing, *Civil Industry and Trade* (London: HM Stationers Office, 1952), 14.

17. Hargreaves and Gowing, *Civil Industry and Trade*, 4.

18. Miller, "The Margins of Accounting," in *The Laws of the Markets*, ed. Michel Calloon (Oxford: Blackwell, 1998), 175.

19. Ina Zweiniger-Bargielowska, *Austerity in Britain: Rationing, Controls, and Consumption, 1939–1955* (Oxford: Oxford University Press, 2000).

20. Cabinet Office, "Economic Warfare," National Archives, UK, catalogue number cab68/7/23, 1941, 4.

21. Board of Trade, "Supply and Production," National Archives, UK, catalogue number cab/68/5/14, 1940, 53.

22. Memoranda of the War Office, accessed at the National Archives of Kew, London, UK.

23. Ian Hacking, *The Emergence of Probability* (Cambridge: Cambridge University Press, 1975); G. Bowker and S. L. Star, *Sorting Things Out: Classification and Its Consequences* (Cambridge, MA: MIT Press, 1999).

24. Benedict Anderson, *Imagined Communities: Reflections on the Origin and Spread of Nationalism* (London: Verso, 1991); Hacking, *The Taming of Chance*, 18.

25. Cabinet Office, "Control of Imports and Consumption," National Archives, UK, catalogue number cab67/4/10, 1940.

26. Paul Starr, "The Sociology of Official Statistics," in *The Politics of Numbers*, ed. W. Alonso and P. Starr (New York: Russell Sage Foundation, 1987), 7–60.

27. Hacking, *The Taming of Chance*, 17.

28. Arjun Appadurai, *Modernity at Large: Cultural Dimensions of Globalization* (Minneapolis: University of Minnesota Press, 1996).

29. Edgar Jones, *True and Fair: A History of Price Waterhouse* (London: Hamish Hamilton, 1995), 12; emphasis added.

30. Hargreaves and Gowing, *Civil Industry and Trade*, 110.

31. Oral Histories archive, Imperial War Museum, London, UK.

32. Michel Foucault, *Security, Territory, Population: Lectures at the Collège de France, 1977–1978* (Basingstoke: Macmillan, 2007), 33.

33. Cabinet Office, "Economic Warfare," 6.

34. Michel Foucault, *The Birth of Biopolitics: Lectures at the Collège de France, 1978–1979* (Basingstoke: Macmillan, 2008), 281–85.

35. *The Accountant*, vol. LI, issue 2076 (1914): 306–7.

36. *The Accountant*, vol. LIV, issue 2163 (1916): 583.

37. Anne Loft, "Accountancy and the First World War," in *Accounting as Social and Institutional Practice*, ed. A. G. Hopwood and P. Miller (Cambridge: Cambridge University Press, 1994), 116.

38. Hacking, *The Taming of Chance*, 3.

39. Daston, *Classical Probability in the Enlightenment*; Donald MacKenzie, *Statistics in Britain, 1835-1930: The Social Construction of Scientific Knowledge* (Oxford: Oxford University Press, 1981).

40. Theodore Porter, "Making Things Quantitative," in *Accounting and Science: Natural Inquiry and Commercial Reason*, ed. Michael Power (Cambridge: Cambridge University Press, 1994), 36.

41. Jones, *True and Fair*, 191.

42. R. Agrawal, T. Imielinski, and A. Swami, "Mining Association Rules between Sets of Items in Large Databases," SIGMOD Proceedings (1993): 207.

43. Agrawal, Imielinski, and Swami, "Mining Association Rules," 207.

44. Agrawal, Imielinski, and Swami, "Mining Association Rules," 208.

45. Agrawal, Imielinski, and Swami, "Mining Association Rules," 207.

46. See Sally Dibb and Maureen Meadows, "Relationship Marketing and CRM: A Financial Services Case Study," *Journal of Strategic Marketing* 12, no. 2 (2004): 111–25.

47. J. Kestelyn, "For Want of a Nail," *Intelligent Enterprise* 5, no. 7 (2002): 8.

48. U.S. House of Representatives, "Helping Federal Agencies Meet their Homeland Security Missions: How Private Sector Solutions Can Be Applied to Public Sector Problems," Subcommittee on Technology and procurement, February 26, 2002, Washington, DC.

49. Agrawal, "Data Mining: Potentials and Challenges," in BMSA, *The Mathematical Sciences' Role in Homeland Security: Proceedings of a Workshop*, Washington, DC: National Research Council, 2004, 26–27.

50. BMSA, *The Mathematical Sciences' Role in Homeland Security*, 89.

51. BMSA, *The Mathematical Sciences' Role in Homeland Security*, 66.

52. BMSA, *The Mathematical Sciences' Role in Homeland Security*, 82.

53. U.S. Department of Justice, "Hearing on the Financial War on Terrorism and the Administration's Implementation of the Anti-Money-Laundering Provisions of the USA Patriot Act," US Senate Committee on Banking, Housing, and Urban Affairs, 2002, Washington, DC.

54. Derrida, "Force of Law," 231.

55. Foden, *Turbulence*, 231.

56. Daston, *Classical Probability in the Enlightenment*; Gigerenzer, Swijtink, Porter, Beatty, and Krüger, *The Empire of Chance*.

57. G. Gigerenzer, Z. Swijtink, T. Porter, L. Daston, J. Beatty, and L. Krüger, *The Empire of Chance: How Probability Changed Science and Everyday Life* (Cambridge: Cambridge University Press, 1989), 264.

58. Gigerenzer, Swijtink, Porter, Daston, Beatty, and Krüger, *The Empire of Chance*, 237.

59. Agamben, *State of Exception*, 38.

60. Agamben, *State of Exception*, 36.

61. William Connolly, *Pluralism* (Durham, NC: Duke University Press, 2005), 139.

62. Walker, "Sovereignties, Exceptions, Worlds," in *Sovereign Lives: Power in Global Politics*, ed. J. Edkins, V. Pin-Fat, and M. J. Shapiro (New York: Routledge, 2004), 246.

63. Nikolas Rose and Marianna Valverde, "Governed by Law?," *Social and Legal Studies* 7 (1998): 550.

64. Hargreaves and Gowing, *Civil Industry and Trade*, 111.

65. Hargreaves and Gowing, *Civil Industry and Trade*, 328.

66. Crary, *Techniques of the Observer: On Vision and Modernity in the Nineteenth Century* (Cambridge, MA: MIT Press, 1990); Lorraine Daston and Peter Galison, "The Image of Objectivity," *Representations* 40 (1992): 81–128.

67. Cabinet Office, "Economic Warfare."

68. Ian Hacking, "Biopower and the Avalanche of Printed Numbers," *Humanities in Society* 5 (1982): 282.

69. Hacking, *The Taming of Chance*, 1.

70. Adolphe Quetelet cited in Theodore Porter, "Making Things Quantitative," 47.

71. Daston, *Classical Probability in the Enlightenment*, 382.

72. Adolphe Quetelet, *Recherches sur la Loi de la Croissance de l'Homme* (Brussels: Huyez, 1831), 21.

73. Hacking, *The Taming of Chance*, 110.

74. Stigler, "Francis Galton's Account of the Invention of Correlation," *Statistical Science* 4, no. 2 (1986): 73–79.

75. Francis Galton cited in Theodore Porter, "Making Things Quantitative," 47.

76. Matt Metsuda, *The Memory of the Modern* (New York: Oxford University Press, 1996).

77. Michel Foucault, *Society Must Be Defended: Lectures of the Collège de France, 1975–1976* (London: Penguin, 2003), 25.

78. Foucault, *Society Must Be Defended*, 19.

79. Foucault, *Society Must Be Defended*, 17.

80. Agrawal, Imielinski, and Swami, "Mining Association Rules," 208.

81. J. R. Quinlan, "Induction of Decision Trees," *Machine Learning* 1 (1986): 81–106.

82. Quinlan, "Induction of Decision Trees," 82.

83. Agrawal, "Data Mining: Potentials and Challenges," in BMSA, *The Mathematical Sciences' Role in Homeland Security*, 67.

84. IDC, "Identity Management's Role in an Application Centric Security Model," White Paper, Framington, MA: IDC, 11.

85. IDC, "Identity Management's Role in an Application Centric Security Model," 10.

86. Agamben, *State of Exception*, 5–6.

87. Agamben, *State of Exception*, 3.

88. Foucault, *Society Must Be Defended*, 48.

89. Foucault, *Society Must Be Defended*, 46.

90. Agrawal, "Data Mining: Potentials and Challenges," in BMSA, *The Mathematical Sciences' Role in Homeland Security*, 80.

91. Foden, *Turbulence*, 317.

Chapter 2: On Risk

1. Thomas Pynchon, *Gravity's Rainbow* (London: Jonathan Cape, 1973), 65.

2. Pynchon, *Gravity's Rainbow*, 22.

3. Pynchon, *Gravity's Rainbow*, 57.

4. Interview with security analytics specialists, London, May 2009.

5. Department of Homeland Security, *Survey of DHS Data Mining Activities* (Washington, DC: Office of the Iinspector General, 2006).

6. 9/11 Commission, *The 9/11 Commission Report: Final Report of the National Commission on the Terrorist Attacks upon the United States* (New York: W. W. Norton, 2004), 84.

7. Transcripts from the Chilcott Inquiry or the Iraq Inquiry, conducted in order to establish what are described as the facts surrounding the British government's decisions and actions in the Iraq War, are available at http://www.iraqinquiry.org.uk/transcripts .aspx, accessed November 2011. Until the final report of the Iraq Inquiry is completed and made public, it is likely that the transcripts will remain the sole public record.

8. François Ewald, "The Return of Descartes' Malicious Demon: An Outline of a Philosophy of Precaution," ed. Tom Baker and Jonathan Simon (Chicago: University of Chicago Press, 2002), 296.

9. Ewald, "The Return of Descartes' Malicious Demon," 289.

10. Former UK prime minister's testimony before the Iraq Inquiry is available at http://www.iraqinquiry.org.uk/transcripts.aspx, accessed November 2011.

11. Pynchon, *Gravity's Rainbow*, 167.

12. The lively capacities of lines of code, biometric identifiers, and other security devices that I note here are akin to the vivacious things in Jane Bennett's inspiring work on the vitality of things in a world beyond human intentionality and design. See chapter 5 for a more through engagement with Bennett's *The Enchantment of Modern Life* (Princeton, NJ: Princeton University Press, 2001) and *Vibrant Matter: A Political Ecology of Things* (Durham, NC: Duke University Press, 2010).

13. Louise Amoore and Marieke de Goede, "Transactions after 9/11: The Banal Face of the Preemptive Strike," *Transactions of the Institute of British Geographers* 33, no. 2 (2008): 173–85. The rise of more speculative forms of science is beautifully illustrated by Lorraine Daston and Peter Galison in their book *Objectivity* (New York: Zone Books, 2007), a seminal study of intuitive, visual, and haptic forms of knowledge and scientific imaging. Stuart Lane and Sarah Whatmore's "Virtual Engineering: Computer Simulation Modelling for Flood Risk Management in England" (*Science Studies* 24, no. 2 (2011): 3–22) shows some of the novel forms of abstraction at work in the visualization of flood maps.

14. There are substantial literatures on how systems of numbers were deployed to govern populations from the nineteenth century, see for example Rose, "Governing by Numbers: Figuring out Democracy," *Accounting, Organizations and Society* 16, no. 7 (1991): 673–92. In his "Making up People" (*Reconstructing Individualism*, ed. T. Heller [Palo Alto, CA: Stanford University Press, 1986]) what Ian Hacking has called "the making up of a population" via "the enumeration of people and their habits" witnessed the proliferation of disciplinary data collection in the forms of survey and census to identify, register, map, order, and administrate. It is in relation to these specific forms

of data abstraction that modern concepts of rights, liberties, and protection have formed, for example, rights to privacy, data protection, and freedom of information.

15. Foucault, *Security, Territory, Population: Lectures at the Collège de France, 1975–1976* (Basingstoke: Macmillan, 2007), 8.

16. R. Bryan and M. Rafferty, *Capitalism with Derivatives* (Basingstoke: Macmillan, 2006), 44.

17. Duncan Wigan, "Financialisation and Derivatives: Constructing an Artifice of Indifference," *Competition and Change* 13, no. 2 (2009): 159.

18. Langley, *The Everyday Life of Global Finance: Saving and Borrowing in Anglo-America* (Oxford: Oxford University Press, 2008).

19. Ewald, "The Return of Descartes' Malicious Demon," 278.

20. James Der Derian, *Virtuous War* (New York: Routledge, 2002); Rancy Martin, *An Empire of Indifference: American War and the Financial Logic of Risk Management* (Durham, NC: Duke University Press, 2007).

21. Adrian MacKenzie, "Protocols and the Irreducible Traces of Embodiment: The Viterbi Algorithm and the Mosaic of Machine Time," *24/7: Time and Temporality in the Network Society*, ed. Hassan and Purser (Palo Alto, CA: Stanford University Press, 2007), 97.

22. Brian Massumi, "The Future Birth of the Affective Fact," Conference Proceedings, Genealogies of Biopolitics, 2005, http://browse.reticular.info/text/collected /massumi.pdf, 7–8.

23. Ulrich Beck, *World Risk Society* (Oxford: Wiley-Blackwell, 1999), 4.

24. Richard Ericson and Aaron Doyle, "Catastrophe Risk, Insurance and Terrorism," *Economy and Society* 33, no. 2 (2004): 141.

25. Ron Suskind, *The One Percent Doctrine: Deep inside America's Pursuit of Its Enemies since 9/11* (New York: Simon and Schuster, 2006), 14.

26. See Peter Bernstein, *Against the Gods: The Remarkable Story of Risk* (New York: John Wiley, 1998); Pat O'Malley, *Risk, Uncertainty and Government* (London: Cavendish Press, 2004).

27. G. Bowker and S. L. Star, *Sorting Things Out: Classification and Its Consequences* (Cambridge, MA: MIT Press, 1999).

28. Anne Friedberg, *The Virtual Window: From Alberti to Microsoft* (Cambridge, MA: MIT Press, 2007), 92.

29. Interview with IT consultants supplying data analytics to border control agencies, Brussels, August 2009.

30. Randy Martin, *An Empire of Indifference*, 31.

31. Department of Homeland Security, *Survey of DHS Data Mining Activities*, 10.

32. Donald MacKenzie, *Material Markets: How Economic Agents Are Constructed* (Oxford: Oxford University Press, 2009), 14.

33. Alain Badiou, *Being and Event* (London: Continuum, 2005), 17.

34. Badiou, *Being and Event*, 178.

35. Michel Foucault, *Society Must Be Defended: Lectures of the Collège de France, 1973–1976* (London: Penguin, 2003), 247.

36. Stephen Collier reads Foucault's analytic of biopower in *History of Sexuality* (New

York: Pantheon Books, 1978–86) and *Society Must Be Defended* as early forms that are elaborated and more nuanced in *Security, Territory, Population* and the *Birth of Biopolitics: Lectures at the Collège de France, 1978–1979* (Basingstoke: Macmillan). Indeed, both Gilles Deleuze in *Foucault* (Minneapolis: University of Minnesota Press, 1988) and Giorgio Agamben in *Potentialities: Collected Essays in Philosophy* (Palo Alto, CA: Stanford University Press, 1999, 221) signal a "crisis in Foucault's work" after the first volume of *The History of Sexuality*, a crisis centering on the question of life within "the field of biopolitics."

37. Foucault, *Security, Territory, Population*, 107.

38. Foucault, *Security, Territory, Population*, 108.

39. Foucault, *Society Must Be Defended*, 244.

40. Foucault, *Security, Territory, Population*, 61.

41. Foucault, *Security, Territory, Population*, 57–63.

42. Interview with UK e-Borders officials, London, Heathrow, March 2009. The iterative process of refining rules by questions and answers in "real-time" analysis refers to the process of piloting the e-Borders concept on designated flight routes in Project Semaphore, delivered by IBM.

43. Massumi, "National Enterprise Emergency: Steps Towards an Ecology of Powers," *Theory, Culture and Society* 26, no. 6 (2009): 155.

44. Interview with European commissioners on use of passenger information units, Brussels, July 2009.

45. Isabelle Stengers, *The Invention of Modern Science* (Minneapolis: University of Minnesota Press, 2000).

46. Daston, *Classical Probability in the Enlightenment* (Princeton, NJ: Priniceton University Press, 1995), 8.

47. Interview with border security software designers, London, August 2009.

48. In May 2006 the European Court of Justice ruled that the EU–U.S. agreement on the sharing of passenger name record (PNR) data breached European privacy laws. The PNR agreement of 2004 required European carriers to submit thirty-four items of data on each passenger within fifteen minutes of departure for the United States. The data fields include credit card numbers, in-flight meal choices, and past patterns of travel (see E. Guild and E. Brouwer, "The Political Life of Data: The ECJ Decision on the PNR Agreement between the EU and the US," *CEPS Policy Brief* 109, 2006, http://www.libertysecurity). In June 2006 it was also revealed that the Brussels-based financial clearing house the Society for Worldwide Interbank Financial Telecommunication (SWIFT) had routinely extradited citizens' financial data, such as credit card transactions and wire transfers, to the U.S. security authorities. In June 2012 a revised EU–U.S. PNR agreement was agreed upon by the European Parliament, though debates surrounding its legality and the onward analysis of data items continue. See chapter 3 for further analysis of PNR.

49. J. Arnoldi, "Derivatives: Virtual Values and Real Risks," *Theory, Culture and Society* 21, no. 6 (2004): 23; D. MacKenzie, *Material Markets*, 80.

50. Brian Massumi, *Parables for the Virtual: Movement, Affect, Sensation* (Durham, NC: Duke University Press, 2002), 137.

51. Massumi, *Parables for the Virtual*, 138.

52. Gilles Deleuze and Félix Guattari, *A Thousand Plateaus* (London: Continuum, 1987), 361.

53. Karin Knorr Cetina and Alex Preda, eds. *The Sociology of Financial Markets* (New York: Oxford University Press, 2006); Louise Amoore, "Vigilant Visualities: The Watchful Politics of the War on Terror," *Security Dialogue* 38, no. 2 (2007) 215–32; Lane and Whatmore, "Virtual Engineering."

54. W. J. T. Mitchell, "There Are No Visual Media," *Journal of Visual Culture* 4, no. 2 (2005): 265; Mieke Bal, "Visual Essentialism and the Object of Visual Culture," *Journal of Visual Culture* 2, no. 1 (2003): 13.

55. Interview with security software consultant, London, September 2009.

56. Jonathan Crary, *Suspensions of Perception: Attention, Spectacle, and Modern Culture* (Cambridge, MA: MIT Press, 1999), 74.

57. Barbara Maria Stafford, *Echo Objects: The Cognitive Work of Images* (Chicago: University of Chicago Press, 2009), 289.

58. Kaja Silverman, *The Threshold of the Visible World* (New York: Routledge, 1996).

59. Louise Amoore and Alexandra Hall, "Taking People Apart: Digitized Dissections and the Body at the Border," *Environment and Planning D: Society and Space* 27, no. 3 (2009): 450.

60. Paul Langley, "Debt, Discipline and Government: Foreclosure and Forbearance in the Sub-Prime Mortgage Crisis," *Environment and Planning A* 41, no. 6 (2009): 1404–19.

61. Shane Scott, "Lapses Allowed Suspect to Board Plane," *New York Times*, May 4, 2010.

62. 9/11 Commission, *The 9/11 Commission Report*; 7 July Review Committee, "Report of the 7 July Review Committee: Volume 3." London Assembly, 2006. http://www.london.gov.uk/mayor-assembly/london-assembly/publications/report -7-july-review-committee.

63. Tom Baker and Jonathan Simon, *Embracing Risk: The Changing Culture of Insurance and Responsibility* (Chicago: University of Chicago Press, 2002), 1–22.

64. Foucault, *Security, Territory, Population*, 45.

65. Foucault, *Security, Territory, Population*, 31, 65.

66. Foucault, *Security, Territory, Population*, 45.

67. Foucault, *Security, Territory, Population*, 65.

68. Tim Cresswell, *On the Move: Mobility in the Modern Western World* (London: Routledge, 2006), 220.

69. Donald Mackenzie, *An Engine, Not a Camera: How Financial Models shape Markets* (Cambridge, MA: MIT Press, 2008), 251.

70. Michael Dillon, "Governing Through Contingency: The Security of Biopolitical Governance," *Political Geography* 26 (2007): 41–47; Michael Dillon and Luis Lobo Guerrero, "Biopolitics of Security in the 21st Century: An Introduction," *Review of International Studies* 34, no. 2 (2008): 265–92; William Walters, "Border/Control," *European Journal of Social Theory* 9, no. 2 (2006): 187–204.

71. Anderson Consulting, *Embrace Risk: Managing Risk to Create Value*. 2002. http://www.andersen.com/website.nsf/co. . ./marketofferingsriskconsulting.

72. Pynchon, *Gravity's Rainbow*, 62.

73. Pynchon, *Gravity's Rainbow*, 63.

74. Nassim Taleb, *The Black Swan: The Impact of the Highly Improbable* (New York: Random House, 2007).

75. Friedrich Kittler, *Literature, Media, Information Systems* (Amsterdam: G and B Arts, 1997).

76. Gilles Deleuze, *Pure Immanence: Essays on a Life* (New York: Zone Books, 2001), 29.

Chapter 3: On the Line

1. Ewen Callaway, "'DNA Mugshots' Narrow Search for Madrid Bombers," *New Scientist*, August 18, 2011, 10.

2. Callaway, "'DNA Mugshots' Narrow Search for Madrid Bombers," 10.

3. John Travis, "Scientists Decry 'Flawed' and 'Horrifying' Nationality Tests," *Science*, September 29, 2009, 14.

4. Leading genetic scientist Jane Evans deploys the "life signatures" of SNPs and isotope analysis in order to infer the origins and migration patterns of animals, birds, and people found in archaeological sites. She has pioneered work on how emergent properties within DNA signatures can be traced to the minerals, water, and climatic conditions of a geographic place. See J. A. Evans, N. Stoodley, and C. A. Chenery, "A Strontium and Oxygen Isotope Assessment of a Possible 4th Century Immigrant Population in a Hampshire Cemetery," *Journal of Archaeological Sciences* 33 (2006): 265–72.

5. From the minutes of a meeting held between the Human Genetics Commission and the UK Border Agency, February 10, 2010, Wellcome Trust, London.

6. Louise Amoore, "Biometric Borders: Governing Mobilities in the War on Terror," *Political Geography* 25, no. 2 (2006): 336–51.

7. Melinda Cooper, *Life as Surplus: Biotechnology and Capitalism in the Neoliberal Era* (Seattle: University of Washington Press, 2008).

8. Matthew Sparke, *In the Space of Theory: Postfoundational Geographies of the Nation-State* (Minneapolis: University of Minnesota Press, 2005), xii.

9. Michel Foucault, *Security, Territory, Population: Lectures at the Collège de France, 1977–1978* (Basingstoke: Macmiillan, 2007), 45.

10. Michel Foucault, *The Birth of Biopolitics: Lectures at the Collège de France, 1978–1979* (Basingstoke: Macmillan, 2008), 259.

11. Michael Dillon, "Correlating Sovereign and Bio Power," in *Sovereign Lives* (New York: Routledge, 2004), 55.

12. Richard Flanagan, *The Unknown Terrorist* (London: Atlantic Books, 2006), 261.

13. Giorgio Agamben, *State of Exception* (Chicago: University of Chicago, 2005), 41–43.

14. The revised proposals for the sharing of passenger name record (PNR) data between Europe and the United States have been met with juridical claims that the security measures breach European laws. The legal advisors to the European Commission have warned that they "have reviewed the draft agreement and consider that there are grave doubts as to its compatibility with fundamental rights. [Their] most serious

concerns are . . . the use of PNR, Article 4(3) 'PNR may also be used to ensure border security in order to identify persons who would be subject to closer questioning or examination.' This clause, which is not linked to the purpose of preventing terror or organized crime, seems to allow the use of PNR also for the purposes of border security, i.e., for customs and immigration offences however minor." In the European Commission Legal Service's "Note on the Draft Agreement on the Use of Passenger Name Records," the juridical problem is centered on the very raison d'être of PNR—its collapsing of distinctions between counterterrorism and border controls.

15. Gilles Deleuze, "Postscript on the Societies of Control," *October* 59 (1992): 5.

16. The Special Immigration Appeals Commission (SIAC) appoints special advocates to represent the appellant in the secret closed sessions. Senior barristers with a high level of security clearance, the special advocates, are not permitted to confer or discuss with the appellant or the legal team any of the material that is presented in the closed session.

17. Interview with senior barrister and former SIAC special advocate, February 2011.

18. See Marieke de Goede's brilliantly observed *Speculative Security: The Politics of Pursuing Terrorist Monies* (Minneapolis: University of Minnesota, 2012).

19. U.S. Senate Committee, "Ten Years after 9/11: Is Intelligence Reform Working?" (Washington, DC: U.S. Senate Committee on Homeland Security and Governmental Affairs, 2011), 17.

20. U.S. Senate Committee, "Ten Years after 9/11," 16.

21. Michael Chertoff, "A Tool We Need to Stop the Next Airliner Plot," *Washington Post*, 29 August 2006, A15.

22. Michael Chertoff, "Speech Delivered to the Committee on Justice, Civil Liberties and Home Affairs," European Parliament, Strasbourg, 15 May 2007, http://useu .usmission.gov/may1407_chertoff_ep.html.

23. Eric Lichtblau and James Risen, "Bank Data Is Sifted by U.S. in Secret Move to Block Terror," *New York Times*, 22 June 2006.

24. Juan Carlos Zarate, "Bankrupting Terrorists," *E-Journal USA, The Gloval War on Terrorist Finance.* September 14, 2004; de Goede, *Speculative Security*.

25. Though the European Parliament succeeded in having the number of PNR data fields transferred to the United States reduced from forty to nineteen, the director of the company that handles the departure control data reported in an interview that the available PNR data fields exceed eighty. In a sense this merely illustrates the point that, once the data cease to be linked in a one-to-one match with individuals as such, the reduction of the number of data elements serves no juridically or politically protective purpose. At the time of writing in 2011, the EU–U.S. PNR agreement includes data types such as "ticketing information," "historical patterns of one-way tickets," "all available payment/billing information," "available frequent flier and benefits information," and "other names linked to the PNR." The PNR is "pushed" to DHS ninety-six hours before a flight departs, when it is then "processed" for the purposes of "preventing, detecting, investigating, and prosecuting." See European Commission, "Draft Agreement between the USA and EU on the Use and Transfer of Passenger Name Record Data," May 20, 2011, Brussells COM 17434.

26. Cooper, *Life as Surplus*, 79.

27. U.S. Attorney General, "Review of Passenger Name Records Data" (Washington, DC: Office of the Attorney General, 2010).

28. See Alexandra Hall and John Mendel's "Threatprints, Threads and Triggers: Risk Imaginaries in the War on Terror" (*Journal of Cultural Economy* 55, no. 1 [2012]: 9–27), an account of the processes by which a series of "touchpoints" and "travel cycles" actively reinscribe the UK border.

29. Council of the European Union, "Real Time Risk Assessment," *Papers from the EU-US Summit on Data Sharing* (Brussells: November 2011), 16–17.

30. Interview conducted in March 2010.

31. William Walters, "Border/Control," *European Journal of Social Theory* 9, no. 2 (2006): 187-204.

32. European Commission, "Draft Agreement Between the USA and EU on the Use and Transfer of Passenger Name Record Data," 11.

33. European Commission, "Draft Agreement Between the USA and EU on the Use and Transfer of Passenger Name Record Data,"12.

34. U.S. Senate Committee, "Ten Years after 9/11," 6.

35. Deleuze, "Postscript on the Societies of Control," 5.

36. Foucault, *The Birth of Biopolitics*, 259.

37. Deleuze, "Postscript on the Societies of Control," 4.

38. Najibullah Zazi, an Afghan American, was convicted of the plot to bomb trains on the New York subway in 2009. His past pattern of travel to Pakistan was an apparent factor in his coming to attention. In the case of Umar Farouk Abdulmutallab, convicted of the attempt to detonate explosives on board a Detroit-bound airliner, he was permitted to board the flight despite being on a terrorism watch list. Again, it is his past patterns of travel, particularly to Yemen, that have subsequently become the indicators for new risk measures. Similarly, the so-called Times Square bomber Faisal Shahzad boarded an Emirates flight bound for Pakistan despite his name being on a no-fly list. In his subsequent trial, it is his past patterns of travel and association that have been presented as incipient threat. The three names of Zazi, Abdulmutallab, and Shahzad feature in U.S. Senate Committee hearings on the case for acting on the basis of incomplete and partial security data; see U.S. Senate Committee "Ten Years after 9/11."

39. Deleuze, "Postscript on the Societies of Control," 3.

40. Deleuze, "Postscript on the Societies of Control," 1.

41. DeLanda, *Intensive Science and Virtual Philosophy*, 85.

42. William Connolly, *A World of Becoming* (Durham, NC: Duke University Press, 2011), 71, 135.

43. Gilles Deleuze and Félix Guattari, *A Thousand Plateaus* (London: Continuum, 1987), 223.

44. A copy of the letter was supplied during the course of a series of interviews I conducted with members of the European Parliament's Committee on Civil Liberties, Justice and Home Affairs.

45. Chertoff, "Speech Delivered to the Committee on Justice, Civil Liberties and Home Affairs."

46. In 2011 the estimated biometric gathering in U.S. military theaters extended to the digital fingerprint, facial imaging, and iris scanning of 1.5 million Afghans and 2.2 million Iraqis, or one in every fourteen citizens. See Shanker, "To Track Militants, U.S. Has System that Never Forgets a Face."

47. Interview with software designer of system integrating biometrics with risk-based data, Paris, March 2010.

48. Matthew Sparke, "A Neoliberal Nexus: Economy, Security, and the Biopolitics of Citizenship on the Border," *Political Geography* 25 (2006): 151–80; Stephen Graham, "Software Sorted Geographies," *Progress in Human Geography* 29 (2005): 562–80.

49. Giorgio Agamben, "No to Biopolitical Tattooing," *Le Monde*, January 10, 2004.

50. Gilles Deleuze, *Difference and Repetition* (London: Continuum, 2004), 256.

51. Irma Van der Ploeg, "Biometrics and the Body as Information: Normative Issues of the Socio-Technical Coding of the Body," *Surveillance as Social Sorting*, ed. David Lyon (London: Routledge, 2003), 67, 70.

52. Francis Galton, "Composite Portraits," *Journal of the Anthropological Institute of Great Britain and Ireland* 8 (1878): 135.

53. Lorraine Daston and Peter Galison, "The Image of Objectivity," *Representations* 40 (1992): 103.

54. Galton, "Composite Portraits," 135.

55. Lorraine Daston and Peter Galison, *Objectivity* (New York: Zone Books, 2007), 43.

56. Jonathan Crary, *Suspensions of Perception: Attention, Spectacle, and Modern Culture* (Cambridge, MA: MIT Press, 1999), 142.

57. Gilles Deleuze and Félix Guattari, *Anti-Oedipus: Capitalism and Schizophrenia* (London: Continuum, 2004), 15–16.

58. The whole body scanner or Backscatter X-ray utilizes Compton scattering, where the momentum and wavelength of X-rays change when coming into contact with matter, with lower energy rays recoiling from a surface or scatter point. Named for the scientist Arthur Compton (who won a Nobel Prize in 1927 for his achievements), Compton scattering was a key milestone in twentieth-century physics, helping to establish the particle nature of electromagnetic radiation. In the Backscatter X-ray, the low-energy, excess "scattered" radiation is harnessed to produce an image of a person on a screen. In 2005 the UK Home Office and the U.S. Transportation Security Administration began trials of new X-ray devices for the screening of bodies at the border.

59. Rapiscan Systems, "Rapiscan Secure 100 Datasheet," 2006, http://www.rapiscansystems.com/datasheets/Rapiscan Secure1000 Screen.pdf.

60. Rapiscan Systems, "Rapiscan Secure 100 Datasheet."

61. Barbara Maria Stafford, *Body Criticism: Imaging the Unseen in Enlightenment Art and Medicine* (Cambridge, MA: MIT Press, 1993), 17.

62. Jose Van Dijk, *The Transparent Body: A Cultural Analysis of Medical Imaging* (Seattle: University of Washington Press, 2005), 5.

63. Crary, *Suspensions of Perception*.

64. Chertoff, "Speech to the Johns Hopkins University Paul H. Nitze School of Advanced International Studies," May 3, 2007.

65. Jacques Rancière, *The Politics of Aesthetics: The Distribution of the Sensible* (New York: Continuum, 2004).

66. Transcripts of the SIAC judgments can be found at http://www.justice.gov.uk/tribunals/special-immigration-appeals-commission/decisions, accessed July 2012. See document code SC/101/2011 for the extracts cited here.

67. Brian Barder, "On SIAC: The Special Immigration Appeals Commission," *London Review of Books* 26, no. 6 (2004): 41.

68. Joel Snyder, "Visualization and Visibility," *Picturing Science, Producing Art*, ed. Caroline Jones and Peter Galison (London: Routledge, 1998), 48.

69. Flanagan, *The Unknown Terrorist*, 309.

Chapter 4: On Location

1. In 2004 the global consultants Accenture were awarded the United States Visitor and Immigration Status Indicator Technology (US-VISIT) contract. The contract has a minimum value of $10 million and maximum value of $10 billion, as set by the Department for Homeland Security, see Eric Lichtblau and John Markoff, "Accenture Is Awarded US Contract for Borders," *New York Times*, June 2, 2004. Raytheon is among the subcontractors for the project.

2. Jane Bennett, *The Enchantment of Modern Life* (Princeton, NJ: Princeton University Press, 2001), 15.

3. Bennett, *The Enchantment of Modern Life*, 171.

4. Bennett, *The Enchantment of Modern Life*, 131.

5. Dana Cuff, "Immanent Domain: Pervasive Computing and the Public Realm," *Journal of Architectural Education* 57, no. 1 (2003), 43.

6. Gilles Deleuze and Félix Guattari, *A Thousand Plateaus* (London: Continuum, 1987), 524.

7. Thrift, "Remembering the Technological Unconscious by Foregrounding Knowledges of Position," 176.

8. Deleuze and Guattari, *A Thousand Plateaus*, 529.

9. Deleuze and Guattari, *A Thousand Plateaus*, 529.

10. Nigel Thrift, "Remembering the Technological Unconscious by Foregrounding Knowledges of Position," *Environment and Planning D: Society and Space* 22 (2004): 181; see also Nigel Thrift and Paul Glennie, "Reworking E. P. Thompson's Time, Work-Discipline and Industrial Capitalism," *Time and Society* 5, no. 3 (1996): 275–99.

11. The Hollerith machine was first used in the U.S. Census of 1890. The IBM Hollerith machines were used in Nazi Germany to identify Jews, to locate names and places, and to track the transportation of people to the concentration camps; see Edwin Black's, *IBM and the Holocaust: The Strategic Alliance between Nazi Germany and America's Most Powerful Corporation* (Washington, DC: Dialog Press, 2001). In the 1950s the punch card records were used once more in relation to governing war, this time by the Red Cross in the search for the missing and the identification of those murdered.

12. Deleuze and Guattari, *A Thousand Plateaus*, 529.

13. Ian Hacking, *The Taming of Chance* (Cambridge: Cambridge University Press, 1990), 53.

14. Deleuze and Guattari, *A Thousand Plateaus*, 524.

15. Reinhold Martin, *The Organizational Complex: Architecture, Media and Corporate Space* (Cambridge, MA: MIT Press, 2003), 158.

16. Cited in Martin, *The Organizational Complex*, 159.

17. Jerry Kang and Dana Cuff, "Pervasive Computing: Embedding the Public Sphere," *Public Law Research*, Paper Series nos. 04–23 (Los Angeles: University of California, 2005), 94.

18. Kang and Cuff, "Pervasive Computing," 94.

19. Thrift, "Remembering the Technological Unconscious by Foregrounding Knowledges of Position," 183.

20. Joshua R. Smith et al., "RFID-based Techniques for Human Activity Detection," *Communications of the ACM* 48, no. 9 (September 2005): 39.

21. Deleuze and Guattari, *A Thousand Plateaus*, 527.

22. Deleuze and Guattari, *A Thousand Plateaus*, 524.

23. Deleuze and Guattari, *A Thousand Plateaus*, 529.

24. H. Stockman, "Communicating by Means of Reflected Power," *Proceedings of the Institute of Radio Engineers* (October 1948): 1196–1204.

25. U.S. House of Representatives, "Testimony of Mr. William Galione of Philips Semiconductors," Subcommittee Hearing on RFID—What the future Holds for Security, Commerce and the Consumer, July 14, 2004, Washington, DC, 6.

26. OECD, *Proceedings of the OECD Foresight Forum on Radio Frequency Identification* (Paris: OECD, 2005), 17. http://www.oecd.org/sti/ieconomy/36069207.pdf.

27. OECD, *Proceedings of the OECD Foresight Forum on Radio Frequency Identification*, 18.

28. Deleuze and Guattari, *A Thousand Plateaus*, 525.

29. "New RFID Tags Could Mean the End of Bar Codes," *Wired*, March 26, 2010, 16.

30. Deleuze and Guattari, *A Thousand Plateaus*, 524.

31. Peter Weiss, "Beyond Bar Codes: Tuning Up Plastic Radio Labels," *Science News* 169, no. 6 (2006): 83.

32. Jerry Kang, "Information Privacy in Cyberspace Transactions," Stanford Law Review 1193 (1998): 107.

33. Michel Foucault, *Security, Territory, Population: Lectures at the Collège de France, 1977-1978*, trans. G. Burchell (Basingstoke: Macmillan, 2007), 45–49.

34. Deleuze and Guattari, *A Thousand Plateaus*, 531.

35. Foucault, *Security, Territory, Population*, 48.

36. Foucault, *Security, Territory, Population*, 49.

37. Frank Knight, *Risk, Uncertainty and Profit* (Boston: Hart, Schaffner and Marx, 1921), 311.

38. David Campbell, *Writing Security: United States' Foreign Policy and the Politics of Identity* (Minneapolis: University of Minnesota, 1998), 12.

39. Foucault, *Security, Territory, Population*, 21.

40. Foucault, *Security, Territory, Population*, 21.

41. Foucault, *Security, Territory, Population*, 23.

42. William Connolly, *Pluralism* (Durham, NC: Duke University Press, 2005), 148.

43. See Deborah Cowen, "A Geography of Logistics: Market Authority and the Security of Supply Chains," *Annals of the Association of American Geographers* 100, no. 3 (2010): 600–620.

44. John Vine, the UK's independent chief inspector of the Border Agency, reported to the British Parliament that risk-based border checks designed to keep people moving were leading to lapses in the sovereign capacity to secure the border. See Independent Chief Inspector of the UK Border Agency, "An Investigation into Border Security Checks" (London: HMSO, 2012).

45. Michel Foucault, *The Birth of Biopolitics: Lectures at the Collège de France, 1978-1979*. Trans. G. Burchell (Basingstoke: Macmillan, 2008), 19–20.

46. Foucault, *The Birth of Biopolitics*, 24.

47. Bruce Eckfeldt, "What does RFID Do for the Consumer?" *Communications of the ACM* 48, no. 9 (2005): 77–79.

48. Oliver Günther and Sarah Spiekerman, "RFID and the Perception of Control: The Consumer's View." *Communications of the ACM* 48, no. 9 (2005): 73–76.

49. Jordan Crandall, "Envisioning the Homefront: Militarization, Tracking and Security Culture," *Journal of Visual Culture* 4, no. 1 (2006): 13.

50. Foucault, *Security, Territory, Population*, 21.

51. Michael J. Shapiro, "Every Move You Make: Bodies, Surveillance, and Media," *Social Text* 23, no. 2 (2005): 30.

52. Barnaby Feder, "Billboards That Know You by Name," *New York Times*, January 29, 2007.

53. Foucault, *The Birth of Biopolitics*, 67.

54. Mark Hansen, *Bodies in Code: Interfaces with Digital Media* (New York: Routledge, 2006).

55. A team of researchers from Radboud University in the Netherlands hacked the details of Oyster card identifiers on the London Underground, demonstrating the ease with which MIFARE systems could be infiltrated. They then built a counterfeit card with hacked data and traveled on the Underground system in order to vividly illustrate the capacity for data to travel beyond its design.

56. Interview with Transport for London, July 2009.

57. Eckfeldt, "What Does RFID Do for the Consumer?," 90.

58. See David Lyon, *Surveillance after September 11* (Cambridge: Polity, 2003); Richard Ericson, *Crime in an Insecure World* (Cambridge: Polity, 2007).

59. Foucault, *The Birth of Biopolitics*, 73.

60. Foucault, *The Birth of Biopolitics*, 66.

61. Matthew Sparke, *In the Space of Theory: Postfoundational Geographies of the Nation-State* (Minneapolis: University of Minnesota Press, 2005), 102.

62. Crandall, "Envisioning the Homefront," 12.

63. David Basulto, "US Embassy in London," *Architecture Daily*, February 24, 2010.

64. Will Hunter, "An Interview with Kieran Timberlake." *Architectural Review*, June 1, 2010.

65. Deleuze and Guattari, *A Thousand Plateaus*, 546.

66. Richard Norton-Taylor, "High-Flying Lifestyle of the CIA's Rendition Men." *vc*, October 26, 2006.

Chapter 5: On Aesthetics

1. Barack Obama, *United States National Security Strategy*, Washington, DC, 18. www.whitehouse.gov/sites/default/files/rss_viewer/national-security-strategy-pdf.

2. Martin Heidegger, "Das Ding," *Vorträge und Aufsätze* (Pfullingen, Germany: Neske, 1954).

3. Jane Bennett, *Vibrant Matter: A Political Ecology of Things* (Durham, NC: Duke University Press, 2010), xvi, 6.

4. William Hogarth, *The Analysis of Beauty: Written with a View of Fixing the Fluctuating Ideas of Taste* (London: W. Strahan, 1753), xvi.

5. Hogarth, *The Analysis of Beauty*, 8.

6. Heisenberg, "Über den Anschaulichen Inhalt der Quantentheoretischen Kinematik und Mechanik," *Zeitschrift für Physik* 43 (1927): 172–98; John Bell, "On the Einstein Podolsky Rosen Paradox," *Physics* 1 (1964): 195–200; John Bell, "Bertlmann's Socks and the Nature of Reality," *Journal de Physique* 2, no. 3 (1981): 41–61.

7. Alfred North Whitehead, *Science and the Modern World* (New York: Simon and Schuster, 1967), 6.

8. Tom Black, CEO of Detica Group, delivered a keynote speech, "The Information Revolution and Its Impact on Homeland Security" to the UK's annual Homeland and Border Security procurement event, London, July 3, 2008.

9. Black, "The Information Revolution and Its Impact on Homeland Security."

10. Valdis E. Krebs, "Uncloaking Terrorist Networks," *First Monday* 7, no. 4 (April 2002).

11. Michel Foucault, *Security, Territory, Population: Lectures at the Collège de France, 1977–1978*, trans. G. Burchell (Basingstoke: Macmillan, 2007), 65.

12. In the weeks following the terror attacks of September 11, for example, mathematicians working on the network links between the hijackers reported that the spatial form of the connections had resembled a serpent.

13. Gilles Deleuze and Félix Guattari, *A Thousand Plateaus* (London: Continuum, 1987), 284.

14. F. Ogée and O. Meslay, "Introduction," in *Hogarth*, by M. Hallett and C. Riddings (London: Tate Publishing, 2006), 23.

15. Hogarth, *The Analysis of Beauty*, 2.

16. Hogarth, *The Analysis of Beauty* 48–49.

17. J. Bender, "Matters of Fact: Virtual Witnessing and the Public in Hogarth," in *Hogarth: Representing Nature's Machines*, ed. D. Bindman, F. Ogée, and H. Wagner (Manchester, UK: Manchester University Press, 2001), 50.

18. Mark Hallett and Christine Riding, *Hogarth* (London: Tate Publishing, 2006).

19. Hogarth, *The Analysis of Beauty*, 6.

20. Hogarth, *The Analysis of Beauty*, 8.

21. Hogarth, *The Analysis of Beauty*, 46.

22. Hogarth, *The Analysis of Beauty*, 10.

23. Hogarth, *The Analysis of Beauty*, 19.

24. Theodore Porter, "Making Things Quantitative," in *Accounting and Science: Natural Inquiry and Commercial Reason*, ed. Michael Power (Cambridge: Cambridge University Press, 1994), 47.

25. G. Gigerenzer, Z. Swijtink, T. Porter, L. Daston, J. Beatty, and L. Krüger, *The Empire of Chance: How Probability Changed Science and Everyday Life* (Cambridge: Cambridge University Press, 1989).

26. Ian Hacking, *The Taming of Chance* (Cambridge: Cambridge University Press, 1990), 110.

27. Michel Foucault, *Society Must Be Defended: Lectures at the Collége de France, 1975–1976* (London: Penguin, 2003), 243.

28. Nassim Taleb, *The Black Swan: The Impact of the Highly Improbably* (New York: Random House, 2007), 232.

29. Hogarth, *The Analysis of Beauty*, 20.

30. Hogarth, *The Analysis of Beauty*, 9.

31. Taleb, *The Black Swan*.

32. Mark Hallett, "The View across the City: William Hogarth and the Visual Culture of Eighteenth-Century London," in *Hogarth: Representing Nature's Machines*, ed. D. Bindman, F. Ogée, and H. Wagner (Manchester, UK: Manchester University Press, 2001), 161.

33. Hogarth, *The Analysis of Beauty*, 27.

34. Hogarth, *The Analysis of Beauty*, 25.

35. Home Office, "INSTINCT," 2009. http://security.homeoffice.gov.uk/science-innovation/instinct/.

36. Louise Amoore, "Vigilant Visualities: The Watchful Politics of the War on Terror," *Security Dialogue* 38, no. 2 (2007): 215–32.

37. Lorraine Daston, ed., *Things That Talk: Object Lessons from Art and Science* (Minneapolis: University of Minnesota, 2008), 13.

38. Bennett, *Vibrant Matter*, 4.

39. Interview, Paris, May 2009.

40. Daston, *Things That Talk*, 11.

41. Lorraine Daston, "The Glass Flowers," in *Things That Talk: Object Lessons from Art and Science* (Minneapolis: University of Minnesota, 2008), 228.

42. Daston, *Things That Talk*, 20.

43. Daston, "The Glass Flowers," 228.

44. I have drawn considerable inspiration from Jane Bennett's spellbinding discussions of practices of "hoarding" in the context of finding ways to attend to that which exceeds purposive or instrumental use of an object. In her "Powers of the Hoard: Notes on Material Agency" (paper presented to the Political Life of Things conference, Imperial War Museum, London, December 3, 2010), she proposes a spectrum of relationships, from the "owner" of things (where the human subject is foregrounded and apparently in control of things) to the "hoarder" of things (where the things themselves are foregrounded and, citing Walter Benjamin, "things are freed from the burden of

being useful"). A similar spectrum might be said to apply to the "collection" of data in the disciplinary sense at one extreme and the "gathering" or self-gathering properties of social network data at another.

45. Heidegger, "Das Ding."

46. Martin Heidegger, "Bauen, Wohnen, Denken," *Vorträge und Aufsätze* (Pfullingen, Germany: Neske, 1954), 144.

47. Heidegger, "Bauen, Wohnen, Denken," 144.

48. Bennett, *Vibrant Matter*, 61; see also Perniola, *The Sex Appeal of the Inorganic*.

49. Martin Heidegger, *Being and Time* (Oxford: Wiley-Blackwell, 1978), 68. When things are understood to have "failed," they talk in quite specific ways about the assemblage of which they were once a part. Their representation as safe "objects" is fleetingly curled at the edges so that we can see their thingness in partial view. As Jane Bennett has written in her "The Agency of Assemblages and the North American Blackout" (*Public Culture* 17, no. 3 [2005]: 445–65), the assemblage of human and nonhuman entities that contributed to the cascade effect included "electricity, with its internal differentiation into 'active' and 'reactive' power; the power plants, which are understaffed by humans but overprotective in their mechanisms; the wires of transmission lines, which tolerate only so much heat before they refuse to transmit the electron flow; the brush fire in Ohio underneath a transmission line; FirstEnergy and other energy-trading corporations, who, by legal and illegal means, had been milking the grid without maintaining its infrastructure; consumers, whose demand for electricity is encouraged to grow without concern for consequences; and the Federal Energy Regulatory Commission, whose Energy Policy Act of 1992 deregulated the grid, separated the generation of electricity from its transmission and distribution, and advanced the privatization of electricity" (449). Bruce Braun's "Hurricane Katrina and Abandoned Being" (*Environment and Planning D: Society and Space* 23 [2005]: 802–8) similarly emphasizes the capacity of things that "fail" to speak to the world.

50. See, for example, Michael J. Shapiro, *The Time of the City: Politics, Philosophy and Genre* (London: Routledge, 2010); William Connolly, *A World of Becoming* (Durham, NC: Duke University Press, 2011); Bruno Latour, "On Actor-Network Theory: A Few Clarifications," *Soziale Welt* 47, no. 4 (1996): 369–80; Bruno Latour, *Reassembling the Social: An Introduction to Actor-Network Theory* (Oxford: Oxford University Press, 2005); G. Harman, *Tool Being: Heidegger and the Metaphysics of Objects* (Chicago: Open Court, 2002); Quentin Meillassoux, *After Finitude: An Essay on the Necessity of Contingency* (New York: Continuum, 2008).

51. Giorgio Agamben, *Potentialities: Collected Essays in Philosophy* (Palo Alto, CA: Stanford University Press, 1999), 229.

52. Michel Foucault, "Life: Experience and Science," *The Essential Foucault: 1954–1984*, ed. Paul Rabinow and Nikolas Rose (New York: New Press, 1994), 15.

53. Foucault, "Life: Experience and Science," 19.

54. Gilles Deleuze, *Foucault* (Minneapolis: University of Minnesota, 1988), 79.

55. See Michael Dillon, "Governing through Contingency: The Security of Biopolitical Governance," *Political Geography* 26 (2007): 41–47; M. DeLanda, *Intensive Science and Virtual Philosophy* (London: Continuum, 2002); Brian Massumi, *Parables for the*

Virtual: Movement, Affect, Sensation (Durham, NC: Duke University Press, 2002); Stephen Collier, "Enacting Catastrophe: Preparedness, Insurance, Budgetary Rationalization," *Economy and Society* 37, no. 2 (2008): 224–50; Melinda Cooper, *Life as Surplus: Biotechnology and Capitalism in the Neoliberal Era* (Seattle: University of Washington Press, 2008).

56. Cooper, *Life as Surplus*, 33, 79.

57. M. DeLanda, "Emergence, Causality, and Realism," in The Speculative Turn: Continental Materialism and Realism, ed. L. Bryant, N. Srnick, and G. Harman (Melbourne: re.press, 2011), 384.

58. Louisa Gilder, *The Age of Entanglement: When Quantum Physics Was Reborn* (New York: Random House, 2008), 3.

59. Whitehead, *Science and the Modern World*, 35.

60. Whitehead, *Science and the Modern World*, 135, 139.

61. Bell, "Bertlmann's Socks and the Nature of Reality," 41.

62. Bell, "Bertlmann's Socks and the Nature of Reality," 42.

63. Peter Galison, "Quantum Histories," in *Science and Society: The History of Modern Physical Science in the 20th Century*, vol.4, ed. P. Galison, M. Gordon, and D. Kaiser (New York: Routledge, 2001), 56.

64. Gilder, *The Age of Entanglement*, 6.

65. Foucault, *Security, Territory, Population*, 20.

66. Quentin Meillassoux, "The Contingency of the Laws of Nature," *Environment and Planning D: Society and Space* 30, no. 2 (2012): 323.

67. Isabelle Stengers, "Wondering about Materialism," in *The Speculative Turn: Continiental Materialism and Realism*, ed. L. Bryant, N. Srnick, and G. Harman, 371.

Chapter 6: On a Potential Politics

1. Michel Foucault, "The Masked Philosopher," *The Essential Foucault: 1954–1984*, ed. P. Rabinow and N. Rose (New York: New Press, 1994), 174.

2. Foucault, "The Masked Philosopher," 176.

3. Michel Foucault, "What Is an Author?," *The Essential Foucault: 1954-1984*, ed. P. Rabinow and N. Rose (New york: New Press, 1994), 391.

4. Gilles Deleuze, *Pure Immanence: Essays on a Life* (New York: Zone Books, 2001), 21.

5. Deleuze, *Pure Immanence*, 30.

6. Michel Foucault, *The Birth of Biopolitics: Lectures at the Collège de France, 1978–1979*, trans. G. Burchell (Basingstoke: Macmillan, 2008), 36.

7. Deleuze, *Pure Immanence*, 28; Giorgio Agamben, *Potentialities: Collected Essays in Philosophy* (Palo Alto: CA: Stanford University Press, 1999), 254.

8. Jennifer Egan, *A Visit from the Goon Squad* (New York: Knopf, 2010).

9. Egan, *A Visit from the Goon Squad*, 23.

10. Brian Massumi, *Parables for the Virtual: Movement, Affect, Sensation* (Durham, NC: Duke University Press, 2002), 137.

11. Massumi, *Parables for the Virtual*, 138.

12. Massumi, *Parables for the Virtual*, 142.

13. Massumi, *Parables for the Virtual*, 139.

14. Massumi, *Parables for the Virtual*, 138.

15. Massumi, *Parables for the Virtual*, 142.

16. Interview with software engineer, London, March 2011.

17. Jacques Derrida, *The Gift of Death* (Chicago: University of Chicago Press, 1995), 24.

18. Interview with UK e-Borders managers, London, March 2009.

19. Gilles Deleuze, *Essays Critical and Clinical*, trans. Daniel W. Smith (Minneapolis: University of Minnesota Press, 1997), 134–35.

20. Jacques Derrida, "Nietzsche and the Machine," *Journal of Nietzsche Studies* 7 (1994): 60.

21. Joseph O'Neill, *Netherland* (London: HarperCollins, 2008), 85.

22. O'Neill, *Netherland*, 86.

23. HM Coroner, "Coroner's Inquests into the London Bombings of 7 July 2005," 45§13. http://7julykinquests.independent.gov.uk/hearing_transcripts/.

24. HM Coroner, "Coroner's Inquests into the London Bombings of 7 July 2005," 36§5.

25. Deleuze, *Pure Immanence*, 25.

26. Deleuze, *Pure Immanence*, 28.

27. Thomas Keenan and Eyal Weizman, *Mengele's Skull: The Advent of Forensic Aesthetics* (New York: Sternberg Press, 2012).

28. Egan, *A Visit from the Goon Squad*, 61–62.

29. Deleuze, *Pure Immanence*, 29.

30. Interview with Meghan Trainor, Barcelona, October 2008.

31. Michel Foucault, *Ethics: Subjectivity and Truth* (New York: New Press, 1997), 287.

32. Foucault, *Ethics: Subjectivity and Truth*.

33. Jane Bennett, *The Enchantment of Modern Life* (Princeton, NJ: Princeton University Press, 31.

34. Bennett, *The Enchantment of Modern Life*, 4.

35. Thomas Keenan, *Fables of Responsibility* (Palo Alto, CA: Stanford University Press, 1997), 1.

36. Keenan, *Fables of Responsibility*, 134.

37. Keenan, *Fables of Responsibility*, 11.

38. Jonathan Crary, "Foreword," in *Installation Art in the New Millennium: The Empire of the Senses*, ed. N. De Oliveira, N. Oxley, and M. Perry (London: Thames and Hudson, 2003), 7.

39. Edward Said, *On Late Style: Music and literature Against the Grain* (London: Bloomsbury, 2007), 53.

40. Derrida, *The Gift of Death*, 26.

41. O'Neill, *Netherland*, 21.

42. O'Neill, *Netherland*, 96.

43. Walter Benjamin, *Illuminations*, trans. Harry Zohn (New York: Schocken Books, 1986), 150.

44. Egan, *A Visit From the Goon Squad*, 180.

45. Benjamin, *Illuminations*, 237.

46. Egan, *A Visit from the Goon Squad*, 99.

47. Deleuze, *Pure Immanence*, 27–28.

48. In order to exemplify a singular life without individuality, Deleuze offers the gestures of small children—smiles, funny faces—as singularities without subjective qualities. Such gestures are "virtual" in the sense that they are not fully actualized, containing only their potential, in the process of actualization (*Pure Immanence*, 30).

49. William Connolly, *A World of Becoming* (Durham, NC: Duke University Press, 2011), 158

50. Connolly, *A World of Becoming*, 158.

51. Agamben, *Potentialities*, 255.

52. Deleuze, *Essays Critical and Clinical*, 74.

53. Derrida, *The Gift of Death*, 75.

54. Egan, *A Visit from the Goon Squad*, 327.

55. Egan, *A Visit from the Goon Squad*, 33.

Bibliography

Accenture. *Values, Driven, Leadership: The History of Accenture*. New York: Accenture, 2005.

Adam, Barbara, and Joost van Loon. "Introduction: Repositioning Risk." In *The Risk Society and Beyond: Critical Issues for Social Theory*, edited by Barbara Adam and Joost van Loon, 1–32. London: Sage, 2000.

Agamben, Giorgio. *The Coming Community*. Minneapolis: University of Minnesota Press, 1990.

———. *Homo Sacer: Sovereign Power and Bare Life*. Palo Alto, CA: Stanford University Press, 1998.

———. "No to Biopolitical Tattooing." *Le Monde*, January 10, 2004.

———. *Potentialities: Collected Essays in Philosophy*. Palo Alto, CA: Stanford University Press, 1999.

———. "Security and Terror." *Theory and Event* 5, no. 4 (2002).

———. *State of Exception*. Chicago: University of Chicago Press, 2005.

Agrawal, Rakesh. *Privacy Preserving Data Mining*. Almaden: IBM, 2002.

Agrawal, R., T. Imielinski, and A. Swami. "Mining Association Rules between Sets of Items in Large Databases." *SIGMOD Proceedings* (1993): 207–17.

Aitken, Rob. "Capital at Its Fringes." *New Political Economy* 11, no. 4 (2006): 479–98.

Amoore, Louise. "Biometric Borders: Governing Mobilities in the War on Terror." *Political Geography* 25, no. 2 (2006): 336–51.

———. "Risk, Reward and Discipline at Work." *Economy and Society* 33, no. 2 (2004): 174–96.

———. "Vigilant Visualities: The Watchful Politics of the War on Terror." *Security Dialogue* 38, no. 2 (2007): 215–32.

Amoore, Louise, and Marieke de Goede. "Governance, Risk and Dataveillance in the War on Terror." *Crime, Law and Social Change* 43, no. 2 (2005): 149–73.

———. "Transactions after 9/11: The Banal Face of the Preemptive Strike." *Transactions of the Institute of British Geographers* 33, no. 2 (2008): 173–85.

———, ed. *Risk and the War on Terror*. London: Routledge, 2008.

Amoore, Louise, and Alexandra Hall. "Taking People Apart: Digitized Dissections and the Body at the Border." *Environment and Planning D: Society and Space* 27, no. 3 (2009): 444–64.

Anderson, Benedict. *Imagined Communities: Reflections on the Origin and Spread of Nationalism*. London: Verso, 1991.

Andersen Consulting. *Embrace Risk: Managing Risk to Create Value*, 2002. Available at http://www.andersen.com/website.nsf/co . . . /marketofferingsriskconsulting. Accessed May 2004.

Appadurai, Arjun. *Modernity at Large: Cultural Dimensions of Globalization*. Minneapolis: University of Minnesota Press, 1996.

Arnoldi, J. "Derivatives: Virtual Values and Real Risks." *Theory, Culture and Society* 21, no. 6 (2004): 23–24.

Badiou, Alain. *Being and Event*. London: Continuum, 2005.

Baker, Tom, and Jonathan Simon. "Embracing Risk." In *Embracing Risk: The Changing Culture of Insurance and Responsibility*, edited by Tom Baker and Jonathan Simon, 1–22. Chicago: University of Chicago Press, 2002.

Bal, Mieke. "Visual Essentialism and the Object of Visual Culture." *Journal of Visual Culture* 2, no. 1 (2003): 5–32.

Barder, Brian. "On SIAC: The Special Immigration Appeals Commission." *London Review of Books* 26, no. 6 (2004): 40–41.

Basulto, David. "US Embassy in London." *Architecture Daily*, February 24, 2010. www.archdaily.com/50922/us-embassy-in-london-kieran-timberlake/.

Beck, Ulrich. *Risk Society: Towards a New Modernity*. London: Sage, 1992.

———. "The Terrorist Threat: World Risk Society Revisited." *Theory, Culture and Society* 19, vol. 4 (2000): 39–55.

———. *World Risk Society*. Oxford: Wiley-Blackwell, 1999.

Bell, John. "Bertlmann's Socks and the Nature of Reality." *Journal de Physique* 2, no. 3 (1981): 41–61.

———. "On the Einstein Podolsky Rosen Paradox." *Physics* 1 (1964): 195–200.

Bender, J. "Matters of Fact: Virtual Witnessing and the Public in Hogarth." In *Hogarth: Representing Nature's Machines*, edited by D. Bindman, F. Ogée, and H. Wagner, 49–69. Manchester, UK: Manchester University Press, 2001.

Benjamin, Walter. *Illuminations*. Translated by Harry Zohn. New York: Schocken Books, 1986.

———. "On the Concept of History." Translated by Harry Zohn. *Walter Benjamin: Selected Writings*, volume 4, edited by H. Eiland and M. Jennings. Cambridge, MA: Harvard University Press, 1996.

Bennett, Jane. "The Agency of Assemblages and the North American Blackout." *Public Culture* 17, no. 3 (2005): 445–65.

———. *The Enchantment of Modern Life*. Princeton, NJ: Princeton University Press, 2001.

———. "Powers of the Hoard: Notes on Material Agency." Paper presented to the Political Life of Things conference, Imperial War Museum, London, December 3, 2010.

———. *Vibrant Matter: A Political Ecology of Things*. Durham, NC: Duke University Press, 2010.

Bernstein, Peter. *Against the Gods: The Remarkable Story of Risk*. New York: John Wiley, 1998.

Best, Jacqueline. *The Limits of Transparency: Ambiguity and the History of International Governance*. Ithaca, NY: Cornell University Press, 2005.

Bigo, Didier. "The Möbius Ribbon of Internal and External Security(ies)." In *Identities, Borders, Orders: Rethinking International Relations Theory*, edited by M. Albert, D. Jacobson, and Y. Lapid, 91–116. Minneapolis: University of Minnesota Press, 2001.

———. "Security and Immigration: Toward a Critique of the Governmentality of Unease." *Alternatives* 27 (2002): 63–92.

Black, Edwin. *IBM and the Holocaust: The Strategic Alliance between Nazi Germany and America's Most Powerful Corporation*. Washington, DC: Dialog Press, 2001.

Black, Tom. "The Information Revolution and its Impact on Homeland Security." Keynote speech delivered to Homeland and Border Security procurement event, London, July 3, 2008.

Blyth, Mark. *Great Transformations: Economic Ideas and Institutional Change in the Twentieth Century*. Cambridge: Cambridge University Press, 2002.

BMSA. *The Mathematical Sciences' Role in Homeland Security: Proceedings of a Workshop*. Washington, DC: National Research Council, 2004.

Board of Trade. "Supply and Production." National Archives, UK, catalogue number cab/68/5/14, 1940.

Bowker, G., and S. L. Star. *Sorting Things Out: Classification and Its Consequences*. Cambridge, MA: MIT Press, 1999.

Braun, Bruce. "Hurricane Katrina and Abandoned Being." *Environment and Planning D: Society and Space* 23 (2005): 802–8.

Bryan, R., and M. Rafferty. *Capitalism with Derivatives*. Basingstoke: Macmillan, 2006.

Burriello, G. "RFID: Tagging the World." *Communications of the ACM* 48 (2005): 34–37.

Butler, Judith. *Bodies That Matter: On the Discursive Limits of Sex*. New York: Routledge, 1993.

———. *Frames of War: When Is Life Grievable?* London: Verso, 2009.

———. *Gender Trouble: Feminism and the Subversion of Identity*. New York: Routledge, 1990.

———. *Precarious Life: The Powers of Mourning and Violence*. London: Verso, 2004.

Cabinet Office, "Control of Imports—Consumption." National Archives, UK, catalogue number cab67/4/10, 1940.

———. "Economic Warfare." National Archives, UK, catalogue number cab68/7/23, 1941.

Callaway, Ewen. "'DNA Mugshots' Narrow Search for Madrid Bombers." *New Scientist*, August 18, 2011.

Campbell, David. *Writing Security: United States' Foreign Policy and the Politics of Identity*. Minneapolis: University of Minnesota Press, 1998.

Chertoff, Michael. "Speech Delivered to the Committee on Justice, Civil Liberties and Home Affairs." European Parliament, Strasbourg, May 15, 2007, accessed April 2013, http://useu.usmission.gov/may1407_chertoff_ep.html.

———. "Speech to the Johns Hopkins University Paul H. Nitze School of Advanced International Studies." May 3, 2007.

———. "A Tool We Need to Stop the Next Airliner Plot." *Washington Post*, 29 August 2006: A15.

Collier, Stephen. "Enacting Catastrophe: Preparedness, Insurance, Budgetary Rationalization." *Economy and Society* 37, no. 2 (2008): 224–50.

———. "Topologies of Power: Foucault's Analysis of Political Power Beyond Governmentality." *Theory, Culture and Society* 26, no. 6 (2009): 78–108.

Connolly, William. *Capitalism and Christianity, American Style*. Durham, NC: Duke University Press, 2008.

———. "The Complexity of Sovereignty." In *Sovereign Lives: Power in Global Politics*, edited by Jenny Edkins, Veronique Pin-Fat, and Michael Shapiro, 23–40. London: Routledge, 2004.

———. *Pluralism*. Durham, NC: Duke University Press, 2005.

———. *A World of Becoming*. Durham, NC: Duke University Press, 2011.

Cooper, Melinda. *Life as Surplus: Biotechnology and Capitalism in the Neoliberal Era*. Seattle: University of Washington Press, 2008.

Council of the European Union. "Real Time Risk Assessment." *Papers from the EU-US Summit on Data Sharing*. Brussels, November 2011.

Cowen, Deborah. "A Geography of Logistics: Market Authority and the Security of Supply Chains." *Annals of the Association of American Geographers* 100, no. 3 (2010): 600–20.

Crandall, Jordan. "Envisioning the Homefront: Militarization, Tracking and Security Culture." *Journal of Visual Culture* 4, no. 1 (2006): 17–38.

Crary, Jonathan. "Foreword." In *Installation Art in the New Millennium: The Empire of the Senses*, edited by Nicolas De Oliveira, Nicola Oxley, and Michael Perry, 1–18. London: Thames and Hudson, 2003.

———. *Suspensions of Perception: Attention, Spectacle, and Modern Culture*. Cambridge, MA: MIT Press, 1999.

———. *Techniques of the Observer: On Vision and Modernity in the Nineteenth Century*. Cambridge, MA: MIT Press, 1990.

Cresswell, Tim. *On the Move: Mobility in the Modern Western World*. London: Routledge, 2006.

Cuff, Dana. "Immanent Domain: Pervasive Computing and the Public Realm." *Journal of Architectural Education* 57, no. 1 (2003): 43–49.

Daston, Lorraine. *Classical Probability in the Enlightenment*. Princeton, NJ: Princeton University Press, 1995.

———. "The Glass Flowers." In *Things That Talk: Object Lessons from Art and Science*, edited by Lorraine Daston, 223–56. Minneapolis: University of Minnesota Press.

———, ed. *Things That Talk: Object Lessons from Art and Science*. Minneapolis: University of Minnesota Press, 2008.

Daston, Lorraine, and Peter Galison. "The Image of Objectivity." *Representations* 40 (1992): 81–128.

———. *Objectivity*. New York: Zone Books, 2007.

Day, Gary. "A Brief History of How Culture and Commerce were Really Made for Each Other." *Critical Quarterly* 44, no. 3 (2002): 37–44.

Dean, Mitchell. *Governmentality: Power and Rule in Modern Society.* London: Sage, 1999.

de Goede, Marieke. "Beyond Economism in International Political Economy, *Review of International Studies* 29 (2003): 79–97.

———. "Hawala Discourses and the War on Terrorist Finance." *Environment and Planning D: Society and Space* 21, no. 5 (2003): 513–32.

———. "Repoliticising Financial Risk." *Economy and Society* 33, no. 2 (2004): 197–217.

———. *Speculative Security: The Politics of Pursuing Terrorist Monies.* Minneapolis: University of Minnesota Press, 2012.

DeLanda, M. "Emergence, Causality, and Realism." In *The Speculative Turn: Continental Materialism and Realism*, edited by Levi Bryant, Nick Srnick, and Graham Harman, 381–92. Melbourne: re.press, 2011.

———. *Intensive Science and Virtual Philosophy.* London: Continuum, 2002.

Deleuze, Gilles. *Difference and Repetition.* London: Continuum, 2004.

———. *Essays Critical and Clinical.* Translated by Daniel W. Smith. Minneapolis: University of Minnesota Press, 1997.

———. *Foucault.* Minneapolis: University of Minnesota Press, 1988.

———. "Postscript on the Societies of Control." *October* 59 (1992): 3–7.

———. *Pure Immanence: Essays on a Life.* New York: Zone Books, 2001.

Deleuze, Gilles, and Félix Guattari. *Anti-Oedipus: Capitalism and Schizophrenia.* London: Continuum, 2004.

———. *A Thousand Plateaus.* London: Continuum, 1987.

Department of Homeland Security. *Survey of DHS Data Mining Activities.* Washington, DC: Office of the Inspector General, 2006.

———. "Transcript of Secretary of Homeland Security Tom Ridge at the Center for Transatlantic Relations at Johns Hopkins University," September 13, 2004. https://www.hsdl.org/?view&did=475404.

———. "US-VISIT Begins Testing RFID Technology to Improve Border Security and Travel." Press release. August 8, 2005.

Der Derian, James. *Virtuous War.* New York: Routledge, 2002.

Derrida, Jacques. "Force of Law: the Mystical Foundations of Authority." In *Deconstruction and the Possibility of Justice*, edited by D. Cornell, M. Rosenfeld, and D. G. Carlson, 3–67. London: Routledge, 1992.

———. *The Gift of Death.* Chicago: University of Chicago Press, 1995.

Derrida, Jacques, in conversation with Richard Beardsworth. "Nietzsche and the Machine." *Journal of Nietzsche Studies* 7 (1994): 7–65.

Dibb, Sally, and Maureen Meadows. "Relationship Marketing and CRM: A Financial Services Case Study." *Journal of Strategic Marketing* 12, no. 2 (2004): 111–25.

Diken, Bülent, and Carsten Bagge Laustsen. *The Culture of Exception: Sociology Facing the Camp.* London: Routledge, 2005.

Dillon, Michael. "Correlating Sovereign and Bio Power." In *Sovereign Lives*, edited by Jenny Edkins, Veronique Pin-Fat, and Michael Shapiro, 41–60. New York: Routledge, 2004.

———. "Governing through Contingency: The Security of Biopolitical Governance." *Political Geography* 26 (2007): 41–47.

Dillon, Michael, and Luis Lobo Guerrero. "Biopolitics of Security in the 21st Century: An Introduction." *Review of International Studies* 34, no. 2 (2008): 265–92.

Dillon, Michael, and Julian Reid. *The Liberal Way of War: Killing to Make Life Live*. London: Routledge, 2009.

Eckfeldt, Bruce. "What Does RFID Do for the Consumer?" *Communications of the ACM* 48, no. 9 (2005): 77–79.

Edkins, Jenny. *Poststructuralism and International Relations: Bringing the Political Back In*. Boulder, CO: Lynne Rienner, 1999.

———. "Whatever Politics." In *Agamben: Sovereignty and Life*, edited by M. Calarco and S. Decordi, 70–91. Palo Alto, CA: Stanford University Press, 2007.

Edkins, Jenny, and Veronique Pin-Fat. "Introduction: Life, Power, Resistance." In *Sovereign Lives*, edited by Jenny Edkins, Veronique Pin-Fat, and Michael J. Shapiro, 1–22. London: Routledge, 2004.

Edkins, Jenny, Veronique Pin-Fat, and Michael Shapiro, ed. *Sovereign Lives*. London: Routledge, 2004.

Egan, Jennifer. *A Visit from the Goon Squad*. New York: Knopf, 2010.

Ericson, Richard. *Crime in an Insecure World*. Cambridge: Polity, 2007.

Ericson, Richard, and Aaron Doyle. "Catastrophe Risk, Insurance and Terrorism." *Economy and Society* 33, no. 2 (2004): 135–73.

European Commission. "Draft Agreement between the USA and EU on the Use and Transfer of Passenger Name Record Data to the US Department of Homeland Security," May 20, 2011. Brussels COM 17434.

European Commission Legal Service. "Note on the Draft Agreement on the Use of PNR," Brussels, May 10, 2011. SJF 603425.

Evans, J. A., N. Stoodley, and C. A. Chenery. "A Strontium and Oxygen Isotope Assessment of a Possible 4th Century Immigrant Population in a Hampshire Cemetery." *Journal of Archaeological Sciences* 33 (2006): 265–72.

Ewald, François. "Insurance and Risk." In *The Foucault Effect: Studies in Governmentality*, edited by G. Burchell, C. Gordan, and P. Miller, 138–61. Chicago: University of Chicago Press, 1991.

———. "The Return of Descartes' Malicious Demon: An Outline of a Philosophy of Precaution." In *Embracing Risk: The Changing Culture of Insurance and Responsibility*, edited by Tom Baker and Jonathan Simon, 273–301. Chicago: University of Chicago Press, 2002.

Feder, Barnaby. "Billboards That Know You by Name." *New York Times*, January 29, 2007.

Flanagan, Richard. *The Unknown Terrorist*. London: Atlantic Books, 2006.

Foden, Giles. *Turbulence: A Novel of the Atmosphere*. London: Faber and Faber, 2009.

Folse, Henry J. *The Philosophy of Niels Bohr: The Framework of Complementarity*. Amsterdam: North Holland, 1985.

Foucault, Michel. *The Birth of Biopolitics: Lectures at the Collège de France, 1978–1979*. Translated by G. Burchell. Basingstoke: Macmillan, 2008.

———. *Discipline and Punish: The Birth of the Prison*. London: Penguin Books, 1977.

———. *Ethics, Subjectivity and Truth*. New York: New Press, 1997.

———. "Governmentality." *The Foucault Effect: Studies in Governmentality,* edited by Graham Burchell, Colin Gordon, and Peter Miller, 87–104. Chicago: Chicago University Press, 1991.

———. *The History of Sexuality.* Translated by Robert Hurley. New York: Pantheon Books, 1978–86.

———. "Life: Experience and Science." *The Essential Foucault: 1954–1984,* edited by Paul Rabinow and Nikolas Rose, 6–17. New York: New Press, 1994.

———. "The Masked Philosopher." *The Essential Foucault: 1954–1984,* edited by Paul Rabinow and Nikolas Rose, 174–79. New York: New Press, 1994.

———. "Questions of Method." *The Foucault Effect: Studies in Governmentality,* edited by Graham Burchell, Colin Gordon, and Peter Miller, 73–86. Chicago: University of Chicago Press, 1991.

———. *Security, Territory, Population: Lectures at the Collège de France, 1977–1978.* Translated by G. Burchell. Basingstoke: Macmillan, 2007.

———. *Society Must Be Defended: Lectures at the Collège de France, 1975–1976.* London: Penguin, 2003.

———. "What Is an Author?" *The Essential Foucault: 1954–1984,* edited by Paul Rabinow and Nikolas Rose, 377–91. New York: New Press, 1994.

Friedberg, Anne. *The Virtual Window: From Alberti to Microsoft,* Cambridge, MA: MIT Press, 2007.

Galison, Peter. "Quantum Histories." In *Science and Society: The History of Modern Physical Science in the 20th Century Volume IV,* edited by P. Galison, M. Gordon, and D. Kaiser, 376–92. New York: Routledge.

Galton, Francis. "Composite Portraits." *Journal of the Anthropological Institute of Great Britain and Ireland* 8 (1878): 132–42.

Gibson-Graham, J. K. *A Postcapitalist Politics.* Minneapolis: University of Minnesota Press, 2006.

Gigerenzer, G., Z. Swijtink, T. Porter, L. Daston, J. Beatty, and L. Krüger. *The Empire of Chance: How Probability Changed Science and Everyday Life.* Cambridge: Cambridge University Press, 1989.

Gilder, Louisa. *The Age of Entanglement: When Quantum Physics Was Reborn.* New York: Random House, 2008.

Graham, Stephen. "Software-Sorted Geographies." *Progress in Human Geography* 29 (2005): 562–80.

Gregory, Derek. *The Colonial Present.* Oxford: Blackwell, 2004.

Grossman, Lisa. "New RFID Tags Could Mean the End of Bar Codes." Wired.com, March 26, 2010.

Guild, E., and E. Brouwer. "The Political Life of Data: The ECJ Decision on the PNR Agreement between the EU and the US." *CEPS Policy Brief* 109, 2006. http://www.libertysecurity.

Günther, Oliver, and Sarah Spiekerman. "RFID and the Perception of Control: The Consumer's View." *Communications of the ACM* 48, no. 9 (2005): 73–76.

Hacking, Ian. "Biopower and the Avalanche of Printed Numbers." *Humanities in Society* 5 (1982): 279–95.

———. *The Emergence of Probability*. Cambridge: Cambridge University Press, 1975.

———. "Making Up People." *Reconstructing Individualism*, edited by T. Heller. Palo Alto, CA: Stanford University Press, 1986.

———. *The Taming of Chance*. Cambridge: Cambridge University Press, 1990.

Hall, Alexandra, and John Mendel. "Threatprints, Threads and Triggers: Risk Imaginaries in the War on Terror." *Journal of Cultural Economy* 55, no. 1 (2012): 9–27.

Hallett, Mark. "The View across the City: William Hogarth and the Visual Culture of Eighteenth-Century London." In *Hogarth: Representing Nature's Machines*, edited by D. Bindman, F. Ogée, and H. Wagner, 146-61. Manchester, UK: Manchester University Press, 2001.

Hallett, Mark, and Christine Riding. *Hogarth*. London: Tate Publishing, 2006.

Hansen, Mark. *Bodies in Code: Interfaces with Digital Media*. New York: Routledge, 2006.

Hargreaves, E. L., and M. Gowing. *Civil Industry and Trade*. London: HM Stationers Office, 1952.

Harman, G. *Tool Being: Heidegger and the Metaphysics of Objects*. Chicago: Open Court, 2002.

Heidegger, Martin. "Bauen, Wohnen, Denken." *Vorträge und Aufsätze*. Pfullingen, Germany: Neske, 1954.

———. *Being and Time*. Oxford: Wiley-Blackwell, 1978.

———. "Das Ding." *Vorträge und Aufsätze*. Pfullingen: Neske, 1954.

Heisenberg, Werner. "Über den Anschaulichen Inhalt der Quantentheoretischen Kinematik und Mechanik." *Zeitschrift für Physik* 43 (1927): 172–98.

HM Coroner. "Coroner's Inquests into the London Bombings of 7 July 2005." http://7julyinquests.independent.gov.uk/hearing_transcripts/.

HM Government. *A Strong Britain in an Age of Uncertainty: The National Security Strategy* London: HM Government, 2010. http://www.cabinetoffice.gov.uk/resource-library /national-security-strategy-strong-britain-age-uncertainty.

Hogarth, William. *The Analysis of Beauty: Written with a View of Fixing the Fluctuating Ideas of Taste*. London: W. Strahan, 1753.

Home Office. "INSTINCT," 2009. http://security.homeoffice.gov.uk/science-innovation /instinct/. Accessed April 2010.

Hunter, Will. "An Interview with Kieran Timberlake." *Architectural Review*, June 1, 2010. http://www.architectural-review.com/view/london-uk-an-interview-with -kieran-timberlake/8600486.article.

IDC. "Identity Management's Role in an Application Centric Security Model." White Paper. Framingham, UK: IDC.

Independent Chief Inspector of the UK Border Agency. "An Investigation into Border Security Checks." London: HMSO, 2012.

Jones, Edgar. *True and Fair: A History of Price Waterhouse*. London: Hamish Hamilton, 1995.

Kang, Jerry. "Information Privacy in Cyberspace Transactions." *Stanford Law Review* 1193 (1998): 1198–99.

Kang, Jerry, and Dana Cuff. "Pervasive Computing: Embedding the Public Sphere."

Public Law Research, Paper Series nos. 04–23. Los Angeles: University of California, 2005.

Keenan, Thomas. *Fables of Responsibility*. Palo Alto, CA: Stanford University Press, 1997.

Keenan, Thomas, and Eyal Weizman. *Mengele's Skull: The Advent of Forensic Aesthetics*. New York: Sternberg Press, 2012.

Kestelyn, J. "For Want of a Nail." *Intelligent Enterprise* 5, no. 7 (2002): 8.

Kittler, Friedrich. *Literature, Media, Information Systems*, Amsterdam: G and B Arts, 1997.

Knight, Frank. *Risk, Uncertainty and Profit*. Boston: Hart, Schaffner and Marx, 1921.

Knorr Cetina, Karin, and Alex Preda, ed. *The Sociology of Financial Markets*. New York: Oxford University Press, 2006.

Krebs, Valdis E. "Uncloaking Terrorist Networks." *First Monday* 7, no. 4 (April 2002).

Lane, Stuart, and Sarah Whatmore. "Virtual Engineering: Computer Simulation Modelling for Flood Risk Management in England." *Science Studies* 24, no. 2 (2011): 3–22.

Langley, Paul. "Debt, Discipline and Government: Foreclosure and Forbearance in the Sub-Prime Mortgage Crisis." *Environment and Planning A* 41, no. 6, (2009): 1404–19.

———. *The Everyday Life of Global Finance: Saving and Borrowing in Anglo-America*. Oxford: Oxford University Press, 2008.

———. "Sub-prime Mortgage Lending: A Cultural Economy." *Economy and Society* 37, no. 4 (2008): 469–94.

Latour, Bruno. "On Actor-Network Theory: A Few Clarifications." *Soziale Welt* 47, no. 4 (1996): 369–80.

———. *Reassembling the Social: An Introduction to Actor-Network Theory*. Oxford: Oxford University Press, 2005.

Lichtblau, Eric, and John Markoff. "Accenture Is Awarded U.S. Contract for Borders," *New York Times*, June 2, 2004.

Lichtblau, Eric, and James Risen. "Bank Data Is Sifted by U.S. in Secret Move to Block Terror." *New York Times*, June 22, 2006.

Lipton, Eric. "Former Antiterror Officials Find Industry Pays Better." *New York Times*, 18 June 2006.

Loft, Anne. "Accountancy and the First World War." In *Accounting as Social and Institutional Practice*, edited by A. G. Hopwood and P. Miller, 116–61. Cambridge: Cambridge University Press, 1994.

Lyon, David. *Surveillance after September 11*. Cambridge: Polity, 2003.

MacKenzie, Adrian. "Protocols and the Irreducible Traces of Embodiment: The Viterbi Algorithm and the Mosaic of Machine Time." In *24/7: Time and Temporality in the Network Society*, edited by R. Hassan and R. Purser, 89–105. Palo Alto, CA: Stanford University Press, 2007.

MacKenzie, Donald. *An Engine, Not a Camera: How Financial Models Shape Markets*. Cambridge, MA: MIT Press, 2008.

———. *Material Markets: How Economic Agents Are Constructed*. Oxford: Oxford University Press, 2009.

———. *Statistics in Britain, 1835–1930: The Social Construction of Scientific Knowledge*. Oxford: Oxford University Press, 1981.

Martin, Randy. *An Empire of Indifference: American War and the Financial Logic of Risk Management*. Durham, NC: Duke University Press, 2007.

Martin, Reinhold. *The Organizational Complex: Architecture, Media and Corporate Space*. Cambridge, MA: MIT Press, 2003.

Massumi, Brian. "The Future Birth of the Affective Fact." Conference Proceedings, Genealogies of Biopolitics, 2005. http://browse.reticular.info/text/collected/massumi.pdf.

——. "National Enterprise Emergency: Steps Towards an Ecology of Powers." *Theory, Culture and Society* 26, no. 6 (2009): 153–85.

——. *Parables for the Virtual: Movement, Affect, Sensation*. Durham, NC: Duke University Press, 2002.

Mckinsey & Company. *Increasing FDNY's Preparedness*. New York: McKinsey & Company, 2002.

——. *Improving NYPD Emergency Preparedness and Response*. New York: McKinsey & Company, 2002.

——. "Strategy in an Uncertain World." *McKinsey Quarterly*. New York: McKinsey & Company, 2001.

Meillassoux, Quentin. *After Finitude: An Essay on the Necessity of Contingency*. New York: Continuum, 2008.

——. "The Contingency of the Laws of Nature." *Environment and Planning D: Society and Space* 30, no. 2 (2012): 322–34.

——. "Potentiality and Virtuality." In *The Speculative Turn: Continental Materialism and Realism*, edited by Levi Bryant, Nick Srnick, and Graham Harman, 224–36. Melbourne: re.press, 2011.

Metsuda, Matt. *The Memory of the Modern*. New York: Oxford University Press, 1996.

Miller, Peter. "The Margins of Accounting." In *The Laws of the Markets*, edited by Michel Callon, 605–21. Oxford: Blackwell, 1998.

Miller, Peter, and Nikolas Rose. "Governing Economic Life." *Economy and Society* 19, no. 1 (1990): 1–31.

——. *Governing the Present*. Cambridge: Polity, 2008.

Minca, Claudio. "The Return of the Camp." *Progress in Human Geography* 29 (2005): 405–12.

Mitchell, W. J. T. "There Are No Visual Media." *Journal of Visual Culture* 4, no. 2 (2005): 257–66.

9/11 Commission. *The 9/11 Commission Report: Final Report of the National Commission on the Terrorist Attacks upon the United States*. New York: W. W. Norton, 2004.

Norton-Taylor, Richard. "High-Flying Lifestyle of the CIA's Rendition Men." *Guardian*, October 26, 2006.

Obama, Barack. *United States National Security Strategy*, Washington, DC. www.whitehouse.gov/sites/default/files/rss_viewer/national-security-strategy-pdf.

OECD. *Proceedings of the OECD Foresight Forum on Radio Frequency Identification*, Paris, OECD, 2005. http://www.oecd.org/sti/ieconomy/36069207.pdf.

Ogée, F., and O. Meslay. "Introduction." In *Hogarth*, by M. Hallett and C. Riddings, 1–16. London: Tate Publishing, 2006.

Ohkubo, Miyako, Koutarou Suzuki, and Shingo Kinoshita. "RFID Privacy Issues and Technical Challenges." *Communications of the ACM* 48, no. 9 (2005): 66–71.

O'Malley, Pat. *Risk, Uncertainty and Government.* London: Cavendish Press/Glasshouse, 2004.

———. "Uncertain Subjects: Risk, Liberalism and Contract." *Economy and Society* 29 (2000): 460–84

O'Neill, Joseph. *Netherland.* London: HarperCollins, 2008.

Perniola, Mario. *The Sex Appeal of the Inorganic.* New York: Continuum, 2004.

Pinault, Lewis. *Consulting Demons: Inside the Unscrupulous World of Corporate Consulting.* New York: Harper Business, 2001.

Porter, Theodore. "Making Things Quantitative." In *Accounting and Science: Natural Inquiry and Commercial Reason*, edited by Michael Power, 389–407. Cambridge: Cambridge University Press, 1994.

———. "Objectivity as Standardization: The Rhetoric of Impersonality in Measurement, Statistics, and Cost-Benefit Analysis." *Annals of Scholarship* 9 (1992): 19–59.

———. "Quantification and the Accounting Ideal in Science." *Social Studies of Science* 22 (1992): 633–51.

Porter, Tony. "Private Authority, Technical Authority, and the Globalization of Accounting Standards." *Business and Politics* 7, no. 3 (2005): 427–40.

Power, Michael. *The Audit Society: Rituals of Verification.* Oxford: Oxford University Press, 1999.

———. "Introduction: From Science of Accounts to Financial Accounting of Science." In *Accounting and Science: Natural Inquiry and Commercial Reason*, edited by Michael Power, 1–35. Cambridge: Cambridge University Press, 1994.

———. *Organized Uncertainty: Designing a World of Risk Management.* Oxford: Oxford University Press, 2007.

Pynchon, Thomas. *Gravity's Rainbow.* London: Jonathan Cape, 1973.

Quetelet, Adolphe. *Recherches sur la Loi de la Croissance de l'homme*, Brussels: Huyez, 1831.

Quinlan, J. R. "Induction of Decision Trees." *Machine Learning* 1 (1986): 81–106.

Rancière, Jacques. *The Politics of Aesthetics: The Distribution of the Sensible.* New York: Continuum, 2004.

———. "Who Is the Subject of the Rights of Man?" *South Atlantic Quarterly* 103, nos. 2–3 (2004): 297–310.

RAND. *Forging America's New Normalcy: Securing our Homeland, Preserving Our Liberty.* Arlington, VA: Rand Corporation, 2003.

Rapiscan Systems. "Rapiscan Secure 100 Datasheet," 2006. Accessed November 2009. http://www.rapiscansystems.com/datasheets/Rapiscan Secure1000 Screen .pdf.

Robson, K. "Connecting Science to the Economic." In *Accounting and Science: Natural Inquiry and Commercial Reason*, edited by Michael Power, 151–69. Cambridge: Cambridge University Press, 1994.

Rose, Nikolas. "Governing by Numbers: Figuring out Democracy." *Accounting, Organizations and Society* 16, no. 7 (1991): 673–92.

Rose, Nikolas, and Peter Miller. "Political Power beyond the State: Problematics of Government." *British Journal of Sociology* 43, no. 2 (1992): 173–205.

Rose, Nikolas, and Marianna Valverde. "Governed by Law?" *Social and Legal Studies* 7 (1998): 540–62.

Said, Edward. *On Late Style: Music and Literature Against the Grain*. London: Bloomsbury, 2007.

Salter, Mark. "When the Exception Becomes the Rule: Borders, Sovereignty, Citizenship." *Citizenship Studies* 12, no. 4 (2008): 365–80.

Scott, Shane. "Lapses Allowed Suspect to Board Plane." *New York Times*, May 4, 2010.

7 July Review Committee. "Report of the 7 July Review Committee: Volume 3." London Assembly, 2006. http://www.london.gov.uk/mayor-assembly/london-assembly /publications/report-7-july-review-committee.

Shanker, Thom. "To Track Militants, U.S. Has System that Never Forgets a Face." *New York Times*, July 13, 2011.

Shapiro, Michael J. "Every Move You Make: Bodies, Surveillance, and Media." *Social Text* 23, no. 2 (2005): 21–34.

———. *The Time of the City: Politics, Philosophy and Genre*. London: Routledge, 2010.

Silverman, Kaja. *The Threshold of the Visible World*. New York: Routledge, 1996.

Smith, Joshua R., et al. "RFID-based Techniques for Human Activity Detection." *Communications of the ACM* 48, no. 9 (September 2005): 39–44.

Snyder, Joel. "Visualization and Visibility." In *Picturing Science, Producing Art*, edited by Caroline Jones and Peter Galison, 379–97. London: Routledge, 1998.

Sparke, Matthew. "A Neoliberal Nexus: Economy, Security, and the Biopolitics of Citizenship on the Border." *Political Geography* 25 (2006): 151–80.

———. *In the Space of Theory: Postfoundational Geographies of the Nation-State*. Minneapolis: University of Minnesota Press, 2005.

Stafford, Barbara Maria. *Body Criticism: Imaging the Unseen in Enlightenment Art and Medicine*. Cambridge, MA: MIT Press, 1993.

———. *Echo Objects: The Cognitive Work of Images*. Chicago: University of Chicago Press, 2009.

Starr, Paul. "The Sociology of Official Statistics." In *The Politics of Numbers*, edited by W. Alonso and P. Starr, 7–60. New York: Russell Sage Foundation, 1987.

Stengers, Isabelle. *Cosmopolitics I: The Science Wars*. Minneapolis: University of Minnesota Press, 2010.

———. *The Invention of Modern Science*. Minneapolis: University of Minnesota Press, 2000.

———. "Wondering about Materialism." In *The Speculative Turn: Continental Materialism and Realism*, edited by Levi Bryant, Nick Srnick, and Graham Harman, 368–80. Melbourne: re.press.

Stigler, Stephen. "Francis Galton's Account of the Invention of Correlation." *Statistical Science* 4, no. 2 (1986): 73–79.

Stockman, H. "Communicating by Means of Reflected Power." *Proceedings of the Institute of Radio Engineers* (October 1948): 1196–1204.

Suskind, Ron. *The One Percent Doctrine: Deep inside America's Pursuit of Its Enemies since 9/11*. New York: Simon and Schuster, 2006.

Taleb, Nassim. *The Black Swan: The Impact of the Highly Improbable*. New York: Random House, 2007.

Thrift, Nigel. *Knowing Capitalism*. London: Sage, 2005.

———. "Movement-Space: The Changing Domain of Thinking Resulting from the Development of New Kinds of Spatial Awareness." *Economy and Society* 33, no. 4 (2004): 582–604.

———. "Remembering the Technological Unconscious by Foregrounding Knowledges of Position." *Environment and Planning D: Society and Space* 22 (2004): 175–90.

Thrift, Nigel, and Paul Glennie. "Reworking E. P. Thompson's Time, Work-Discipline and Industrial Capitalism." *Time and Society* 5, no. 3 (1996): 275–99.

Travis, John. "Scientists Decry 'Flawed' and 'Horrifying' Nationality Tests." *Science*, September 29, 2009.

UKBA. "Minutes of a Meeting between the Human Genetics Commission and the UK Border Agency," February 10, 2010. London: Wellcome Trust, 2010.

U.S. Attorney General. "Review of Passenger Name Records Data." Washington, DC: Office of the Attorney General, 2010.

U.S. Department of Justice. "Hearing on the Financial War on Terrorism and the Administration's Implementation of the Anti-Money-Laundering Provisions of the USA Patriot Act." US Senate Committee on Banking, Housing, and Urban Affairs, 2002. Washington, DC.

U.S. House of Representatives. "Helping Federal Agencies Meet their Homeland Security Missions: How Private Sector Solutions Can be Applied to Public Sector Problems." Subcommittee on Technology and Procurement, February 26, 2002. Washington, DC.

———. "Testimony of Mr William Galione of Philips Semiconductors." Subcommittee Hearing on RFID—What the Future Holds for Security, Commerce and the Consumer, July 14, 2004, Washington, DC.

U.S. Senate Committee. "Ten Years after 9/11: Is Intelligence Reform Working?" Statement of Dennis C. Blair, before the U.S. Senate Committee on Homeland Security and Governmental Affairs, 2011, Washington, DC.

Updike, John. *Terrorist*. London: Hamish Hamilton, 2006.

Valverde, Marianna, and Michael Mopas. "Insecurity and the Dream of Targeted Governance." In *Global Governmentality: Governing International Spaces*, edited by Wendy Larner and William Walters, 233–49. London: Routledge, 2004.

Van der Ploeg, Irma. "Biometrics and the Body as Information: Normative Issues of the Socio-Technical Coding of the Body." In *Surveillance as Social Sorting*, edited by David Lyon, 57–73. London: Routledge, 2003.

Van Dijk, Jose. *The Transparent Body: A Cultural Analysis of Medical Imaging*. Seattle: University of Washington Press, 2005.

Van Munster, Rens. "When the Exception Becomes the Rule." *International Journal for the Semiotics of Law* 17, no. 1 (2004): 141–53.

Walker, R. B. J. "Conclusion: Sovereignties, Exceptions, Worlds." In *Sovereign Lives: Power in Global Politics*, edited by Jenny Edkins, Veronique Pin-Fat, and Michael J. Shapiro, 239–49. New York: Routledge, 2004.

———. *Inside/Outside: International Relations as Political Theory.* Cambridge: Cambridge University Press, 1993.

———. "War, Terror, Judgement." *September 11, 2001: War, Terror and Judgement*, ed. Bulent Gokay and R. B. J. Walker, 62–83. London: Frank Cass.

Walters, William. "Border/Control." *European Journal of Social Theory* 9, no. 2 (2006): 187–204.

Weiss, Peter. "Beyond Bar Codes: Tuning Up Plastic Radio Labels." *Science News* 169, no. 6 (2006): 83.

Whitehead, Alfred North. *Science and the Modern World.* New York: Simon and Schuster, 1967.

Wigan, Duncan. "Financialisation and Derivatives: Constructing an Artifice of Indifference." *Competition and Change* 13, no. 2 (2009): 157–72.

Zarate, Juan Carlos. "Bankrupting Terrorists." *E-Journal USA, The Global War on Terrorist Finance.* September 14, 2004.

Žižek, Slavoj. *The Universal Exception.* London: Continuum, 2006.

Zweiniger-Bargielowska, Ina. *Austerity in Britain: Rationing, Controls, and Consumption, 1939–1955.* Oxford: Oxford University Press, 2000.

Index

intelligence, 24, 51, 73, 84–85, 89–90, 93, 103

Intelligence Reform and Terrorist Prevention Act (IRTPA), 85

intuition, 44, 54, 66, 69–70

Iraq, 94; Inquiry, 23, 57–59, 75

judgment, 44, 50–52, 96–97, 158, 162–65

Keenan, Thomas, 165, 169–70

law, 13–18, 34, 45–47, 84–85, 101–2, 174

life signature, 24, 79–104

lines, 92–93, 140; of beauty, 135–42; of sight, 93–101

link analysis, 73, 139, 151

location, 24, 105–26

London, 55–56, 124–26, 140–43, 153; July 7 bombings and, 72, 159, 164–65

Madrid bombings, 79–81

Massumi, Brian, 2, 52, 62, 66, 68–70, 160–61

match analysts, 24, 88, 139. See also analytics

mathematics: code and, 70; homeland security and, 42–43, 54, 59, 64

mobility, 5, 70, 72, 97–101, 107, 114, 140–44, 152

mosaic, 81, 84–93, 101, 174

Muybridge, Eadweard, 97–99, 101

National Security Strategy, 7, 130, 179n24

Netherland (O'Neill), 164, 170–71

New York, 115–16; subway bomb plot and, 90; Times Square bomb and, 90; urban life in, 172, 175

norms, 33–35, 48–50; differential, 18, 65–66, 73; law and, 45–47; mobile, 17–18, 49–51, 64–68, 75

novels, 158, 170

Obama, Barack, 3, 130

objects, 107, 109, 114, 118–24, 129–54, 166, 167

passenger name record (PNR), 3, 70–71, 86–88, 91, 93–94; EU-US agreement on, 68, 89, 93, 178n7. See also travel

passenger information unit (PIU), 88–93

person of interest, 93

photography, 49, 96, 99, 101, 160

physics, 149, 150, 153. See also quantum physics

politics, 14, 100, 103; of possibility, 8, 11, 23, 26, 52–54, 73, 112, 153, 155–57, 159, 169, 171, 173; of potentiality, 155–76

population, 33, 47, 56, 61

possibility, 5, 68, 69, 72–73, 101, 156; risk and, 8–9, 67–69. See also politics

potentiality, 26, 76, 131, 155–76, 180n58

precautionary principle, the, 9–10

prediction, 9, 11, 29, 41, 43, 51, 153, 168, 175

preemption, 9–10, 32, 41–42, 59, 62, 80, 85–86, 120

probability, 1, 12, 23–24, 43, 73–74, 81; Bayesian models of, 44–45; conditional, 44; forms of, 8, 10, 30–31, 44, 56, 61, 67, 101–2, 137; history of, 44–45, 53, 55–56

profiling, 42, 51–52, 57, 96, 100, 137–38

projection. *See* future

quantum physics, 149–54

Quetelet, Adolphe, 48–50, 137

radio frequency identification (RFID), 3, 21, 25, 105–8, 118–24, 167–69

rationing, 23, 34–39, 47–50

risk, 7–13, 55–76; assessment of, 66, 68, 93, 140; calculus of, 9, 23, 57–61, 73, 119; consulting and, 22, 43, 71; embracing of, 8–9, 11, 68–69, 71–73; flags, 68–69, 74; management, 6, 21; practices of, 53–54, 56, 72, 161; scoring, 2, 18, 60, 66–69, 71, 74, 88, 157; tail, 137, 157; technologies of, 82, 88, 90, 99. *See also* probability

scanners, 17, 84, 99, 109, 122

science: knowledge and, 8–9, 67, 87, 149, 154, 186n13; instruments of, 142–45

screen, 2, 18, 63, 69–70, 99–100, 105, 129–30

security: decisions, 59–60, 67, 72, 75, 80, 93, 101–3, 140, 163, 171; devices, 5, 17, 24–25, 73, 99, 105–6, 126, 129, 153, 159; homeland, 3, 51; state and, 44, 117, 124–26

sequencing, 69, 75, 80, 89, 91, 98, 112, 152, 172

September 11, 2001, 1, 4, 8, 11, 21, 23, 41, 56–59, 72, 86, 132–33, 159, 170

Shahzad, Faisal, 90

sieve, 67–68, 73, 80, 90, 133, 159

social network analysis, 42–43, 73, 89, 132–33, 151

Society for Worldwide Interbank Financial Telecommunications (SWIFT), 87

software, 43, 51–52, 64, 66, 67, 69, 73, 101, 129, 139, 162